Memory Machine

ADVANCE PRAISE

'Belinda Barnet has given the world a fine-grain, blow-by-blow report of how hypertext happened, how we blundered to the World Wide Web, and what other things electronic literature might still become. Congratulations!'

—*Ted Nelson, hypertext pioneer*

'This is a fine and important book, the first to capture the rich history of ideas and people that led to the World Wide Web. *Memory Machines* carefully examines what the key figures were trying to do, and judiciously explores what they accomplished and how the systems we now use daily sometimes exceed their dreams and sometimes fall embarrassingly short of their early achievements.'

—*Mark Bernstein, chief scientist at Eastgate Systems*

'This is a well-researched and entertaining story, full of personal anecdotes and memories from the people who built these important early systems.'

—*Dame Wendy Hall DBE FREng, professor and dean of physical and applied sciences, University of Southampton*

'Walter Benjamin wrote that "It is not that what is past casts its light on what is present, or what is present its light on what is past; rather […] what has been comes together in a flash with the now to form a constellation." *Memory Machines* is, even for one among its participants, such a constellation of the now.'

—*Michael Joyce, professor of English, Vassar College, New York*

'*Memory Machines* provides an invaluable close-and-personal, warts-and-all look at how Englebart, Nelson and van Dam created the foundations of hypertext, doing a particularly fine job of setting their thought within the histories of engineering.'

—*George Landow, professor of English and art history at Brown University and author of 'Hypertext: The Convergence of Contemporary Critical Theory and Technology'*

Memory Machines

The Evolution of Hypertext

Belinda Barnet

With a Foreword
by Stuart Moulthrop

ANTHEM PRESS
LONDON · NEW YORK · DELHI

Anthem Press
An imprint of Wimbledon Publishing Company
www.anthempress.com

This edition first published in UK and USA 2014
by ANTHEM PRESS
75–76 Blackfriars Road, London SE1 8HA, UK
or PO Box 9779, London SW19 7ZG, UK
and
244 Madison Ave #116, New York, NY 10016, USA

First published in hardback by Anthem Press in 2013

British Library Cataloguing-in-Publication Data
A catalogue record for this book is available from the British Library.

Library of Congress Cataloging-in-Publication Data
The Library of Congress has catalogued the hardcover edition as follows:
Barnet, Belinda.
Memory machines : the evolution of hypertext / Belinda Barnet ; with a foreword by
Stuart Moulthrop.
pages cm
Includes bibliographical references and index.
ISBN 978-0-85728-060-2 (hardcover : alkaline paper)
1. Hypertext systems–History. I. Title.
QA76.76.H94B37 2013
006.7–dc23
2013019339

ISBN-13: 978 1 78308 344 2 (Pbk)
ISBN-10: 1 78308 344 1 (Pbk)

Cover image © Melissa Slattery 2013

This title is also available as an ebook.

For Mum and Dad, because you believed in me;
For Ollie, Isabel and Laura, because I believe in you

There is a vision offered in these pages, simple unified and sweeping: it is a unified concept of interconnected ideas and data, and of how these ideas and data may be stored and published [...] this new way of handling information is to represent its true interconnections.
—Ted Nelson, *Literary Machines*

CONTENTS

Foreword

TO MANDELBROT IN HEAVEN

Stuart Moulthrop

A certain confusion may befall us when we praise pioneers, especially while they are still with us. This hazard was apparent to the troubadour and know-hit wonder Jonathan Coulton, when he wrote one of the great tunes of popular science, 'Mandelbrot Set':

> Mandelbrot's in heaven
> At least he will be when he's dead
> Right now he's still alive and teaching math at Yale

The song was released in October 2004, giving it a nice run of six years before its lyrics were compromised by Benoît Mandelbrot's passing in 2010. Even thus betrayed to history, 'Mandelbrot Set' still marks the contrast between extraordinary and ordinary lives, dividing those who change the world, in ways tiny or otherwise, from those who sing about them or merely ruminate. The life of ideas, perhaps like ontogeny, works through sudden transformations and upheavals, apparent impasses punctuated by instant, lateral shift. Understanding is catastrophic. Genius finds 'infinite complexity [...] defined by simple rules', as Coulton also sings, though any such simplicity depends crucially on the beholder. Cosmic rules may have gorgeous clarity to a mind like Mandelbrot's. For the rest of us, the complexities of the universe are more often bewildering. Nothing is more bewildering, of course, than genius.

As simple minds see it, those who light the world go to heaven before their time, and the pathos of this fate stamps the work of any chronicler with embarrassment. The singer, enraptured, invents a rapture: Mandelbrot's in heaven – well, actually not (originally not, though he is now) – you get the idea. Time is not on our side when we try to give genius its due; we get no help, likewise, from metaphysics. We say the wrong thing, then catch ourselves in nets of qualification, tangled in the paradox of transcendence, of lives that outwardly seem like ours but are actually lived on another scale, perhaps a different plane of being. Even while they breathe our ordinary air, true leaders of thought are always someplace else. We may call it heaven, and in relatively happy cases like Mandelbrot's, maybe that's the place.

But genius can arise in any field, and local conditions differ. It is one thing to revolutionize mathematics, perhaps something else to uproot the foundations of global media, or literacy itself. Not all bringers of light can be primarily solvers of problems, able to explain fluctuations of cotton prices, skitterings of heartbeats, the shapes of clouds and coastlines. Some catastrophists come among us to raise questions rather than resolve them, to instigate practices that bring on interesting times. One of these more harassing masters, by their own estimate, has not ended up in heaven, but somewhere like the other place. 'I see today's computer world, and the Web', Theodor Holm Nelson tells the author of this book, 'as resulting from my failure' (Nelson 2011).

Genius may be as genius decrees, but some claims demand comment. A word from the audience, here. Please, I want to say: isn't it enough you've given us bidirectional linking and hypermedia, and at least plausible visions of transclusion, an open-source, universal archive, and a life without files? Whatever the Web has become ('diving boards into the darkness' still fits), wasn't the dream of Xanadu® enough?* Do you also need to offer everyone who works in 'the computer world' a universal guilt pass? Sorry about your miserable user experience, but really it's all Nelson's fault. Just ask him.

More words from the audience: I have somewhere, redundantly preserved on various media, a prized possession. It is the digitized excerpt of a recording made by John McDaid during the Association for Computing Machinery's second conference on hypertext and hypermedia, in Pittsburgh, 1989. Its waveforms encode the rivetingly clear, stage-brilliant voice of Nelson, delivering a phrase I will not forget: 'You! Up there! … WRONG!' Please imagine that last word as the tolling of some numinous cathedral bell, struck in case of heresy. It may be the most amazing thing I've ever heard.

As it happened, the recording was made at the session where I delivered my first published paper; though I was on the dais and happily not the target of Nelson's correction – memory fails, but that may have been Michael Lesk, later director of the National Science Foundation, who had perceptively asked if my paper was some kind of joke (although that wasn't the point with which Nelson took issue). More than many other things, this performance introduced me to hypermedia polemics, academic theater, and the Ted Nelson experience. Two decades later, my partner and I still recite Ted's line, as if it

---

*   Xanadu is a registered trademark of Theodor H. Nelson.

were Shaw or Shakespeare, when someone in authority says something really dim. Genius is evergreen.

But now to my own embarrassment, because while I cannot imagine Nelson ever saying anything dull-witted or simply dull, I want to feed back his own protest with, and out of, a profound respect. You, up there, already in heaven, may it be many years of grace before your time. You're right about nearly everything, but in this instance... wrong!

The current state of networked, computational media may be as ugly and benighted as Nelson says (some of us remain thickly optimistic), but it is hard to see here the failure of a single vision. Many other culprits could be named. My list includes business and academic interests who imagine that intellect can be property; the financial illusionists behind collateralized debt obligations, who pervert hypertext into cryptomoney; and of course, an undiscerning, terminally amused consumer culture whose idea of a good time is a status update or a cow click (Bogost 2010).

If anyone has failed, it's surely the rest of us, who sit some distance from the edge of revelation, blinking into the light. Understanding or embracing this peripherality may be the one feat of wisdom no genius can manage, the necessary blindness that accompanies insight. Failure never belongs to one alone; it takes a nation, or perhaps these days a species.

The computer world we live in is indeed broken far away from any higher vision. Too much is still governed by maladaptive models like page, document and file, which, as Nelson always said, distract from true electronic literacy. We think we are cutting and pasting when we are in fact making copies, which as Lawrence Lessig echoes, really is the fundamental operation in computational media (Lessig 2008, 98). We seize on objects and overlook transformations and flows. Because of these blinkered notions, we tend to approach problems of intellectual property in backward, unproductive ways, as in the recent US crusade against 'online piracy', which on first presentation, at least, seems as ill-considered as our War on Terror. We think to defend content, a concept inexorably tied to materialized media, when our true concern lies with data or information, a radically trans-material concern and one whose nature most of us do not begin to grasp.

Working across categories of matter and sign requires techniques such as abstraction and algorithm, as we learn from the likes of Mandelbrot. But geometry is one thing; architecture and engineering, something else. Visionary procedures must be deployed or instantiated in appropriate tools: protocols, data frameworks, programming languages and development interfaces. Along with these instruments, we need adequate cultures of learning and teaching, imitation and sharing, to make the tools broadly useful. In these respects the computer world, or our engagement with it, falls very short. For all our progress in what Alexander Galloway calls 'protocological' media (Galloway 2004) (for example Hypertext Transport Protocol, or the Document Object Model), digital communication remains tied to arcane, often impenetrable infrastructures, a thousand testimonies to the lasting unwisdom of entrepreneurial engineering.

Nor have theory and reflection been much help. Absent any unified expectation of technical expertise, scholars invent each day some new add-modifier – e-literacy, or numeracy, or videocy – to further fragment any nascent understanding of media. Awash in possibilities for signification, we produce still more of this still and silent writing: 'scribble, scribble, scribble, Mr. Gibbon', as Marshall McLuhan liked to quote. Somehow we conceive writing-out (rhetoric) and writing-forward (programming) as distinct subjects, not as they should be: sign and countersign of a single practice. For all the broad adoption of smartphones, tablets, and the heavenly Cloud, our intellectual cultures seem as far apart today as they appeared to C. P. Snow a lifetime earlier; literature vs. science reprised in content vs. data.

The worst of it is that many or even most seated on the academic dais, or in editorial offices, or the reclining accommodations of business class, do not see a problem. We are all sunk in the grinding ice of incremental adaptation, or what I call misremediation: not true reinvention of old media practices in new technical contexts, but reassertion or encapsulation of ancient practices within the new. As if there is any possibility of substitution or remedy. As if the e-book is identical to the book. As if Farmville is the same thing as Monopoly. As if we should still be concerned simply with computation. As if the time had not come, as early perhaps as 1968, to look beyond writing.

Speaking of 1968, and of writing, I am reminded of another of my heroes who appears in this book, the great demonstrator, Douglas C. Engelbart. If Nelson has taught me (among more important things) how to sell a line, I have learnt from Engelbart the crucial importance of showing, not telling: how the letter gives information, but the active application changes lives. So, writes Belinda Barnet in this text, when sceptics doubted whether augmentation tools for human intellect could truly alter our experience,

> Engelbart provided a counter-example: he strapped a brick to a pencil and requested that people write with the assemblage. It didn't take long to discover that 'our academic work, our books – a great deal would change in our world if that's how hard it had been to write'. (52)

Or as if it isn't hard enough to practise, or even conceive of, anything more than writing, Engelbart's deaugmented chirographic device was perhaps his first great demo; today it might be better understood as living parable, a mirror of our present state. It is not so much that we write today with bricks attached, but rather that writing in the most general sense, our textual systems and institutions, has become distinctly hard, massy, and gritty to the touch. We think with the benefit of masonry. Writing has become the brick. As the experiment suggests, it is no wonder we do not succeed at our assigned tasks, let alone find the way to Engelbart's or Nelson's augmented realities. Our failure is inevitable, or as my friends from Generation M like to say, it's epic.

As anyone whose mind has been warped by videogames knows, computational sign-systems (sometimes called 'cybertexts') radically revise the function, and perhaps the core meaning, of failure. When a story unfolds according to contingencies determined equally by logic, chance, and player action, there is no simple way to move from start to finish, no single streambed of discourse. To paraphrase a US philosopher, stuff happens, often with considerable complexity, though driven by deceptively simple rules. Under such sensitively dependent conditions, what constitutes failure, or indeed success?

Compositions incorporating multiple pathworks, such as games and simulations, create experiences that are inherently repetitive, reiterative or recursive. Our various avatars live to die, and often die to live again. We lose countless battles in the prosecution of pointless wars. This may make Generation M likely to suspect, as some Iraq and Afghanistan veterans have begun to suggest, that most wars are pointless. The battle hymn of this paradoxical condition has been written, unsurprisingly, by the indispensable Mr Coulton, in a song that backs the final credits of a remarkable videogame, Valve Software's *Portal* (2007). The song is called 'Still Alive', the final soliloquy of a murderous artificial intelligence who has seized control of a military-industrial lab. The system sings,

Aperture Science
We do what we must
Because we can.
For the good of all of us.
Except the ones who are dead.
But there's no sense crying over every mistake.
You just keep on trying till you run out of cake.
And the Science gets done.
And you make a neat gun.
For the people who are still alive.

There would be much to say here, if space allowed, about cake and companion cubes, government labs, test subjects, videogames and their players, people and nonpeople (see another US philosopher, W. R. Romney, on the ontological status of corporations). For the moment it is enough to note that Coulton's title applies both to the arch-villain of the game (GLaDOS, or Genetic Lifeform and Disk Operating System), as well as everyone who beats the final level, becoming perhaps the most important 'people who are still alive', if you are a game designer. Such at least was the song's first rhetorical situation, before it went viral on YouTube: if you are hearing this message, congratulations, your long history of failure has paid off. You have traversed or configured the game logic to reach this not entirely meaningless outcome. Okay, you win; the game, of course, goes on.

Welcome to the cultural logic of software or cybertext, that larger domain to which hypertext, the subject of this book, inevitably articulates, either as first revelation or arcane orthodoxy.

Seeing a world composed of paths and networks makes a difference. In the regime of play and simulation we do what we can because we must, or must because we can; you get the idea. Play's the thing. Iteration is all. Failure is a given, but we fail forward, converging in our own ways toward ultimate solution – and bonus levels, and sequels, each its own absurdly delightful reward. To play is to remain in the loop, always alive to possibilities of puzzle, travail and further trial-by-error.

To further explain this situation, an old postmodernist may perhaps be forgiven a certain worn-out word: deconstruction. I invoke not the current, degraded sense of simple disassembling, but the original meaning of radical scepticism, or resistance to our own dissembling. The iterative logic of cybertext deconstructs failure, stripping out the metaphysic of providence or necessity in which the idea was originally dressed – failure as singular fatality – and directing our understanding instead to pragmatics, process, possibility and play – failure as permutation.

This crucial shift may offer some answer to Nelson's gloom, and perhaps even to the generally negative affect of our broken-down times. If our failure has become epically ludic, then perhaps it is no longer the dire outcome our forebears fretted over: that failure to survive, as civilization or species, that seemed to hang over the latter half of the twentieth century. It's worth remembering, as this book reminds us, that this particular fear of ending was the spectre that haunted Douglas Engelbart, sitting in his radio shack somewhere in the South Pacific in 1945. Reading news of the bomb, he came (after any GI's understandable euphoria) to the recognition that the world must fundamentally change if it wanted to escape burning. The science of industrial destruction would have to yield (and yield to) augmentations of communication and cognition. Engelbart thus passed early on through a turning point of human history, the great course correction that has allowed our species to reach later, scarier levels of the Darwin game. In making this passage, however, Engelbart also fell into a kind of failure, at least by the common understanding of an engineer's calling in the national security state. As Engelbart told the author of this book in 1999, he was often told to mind his own business and keep off well-defined turf:

> After I'd given a talk at Stanford, [three angry guys] got me later outside at a table. They said, 'All you're talking about is information retrieval.' I said no. They said, 'YES, it is, we're professionals and we know, so we're telling you don't know enough so stay out of it, 'cause goddamit, you're bollocksing it all up. You're in engineering, not information retrieval.' (Engelbart 1999)

My hero; the man who never knew too much about disciplinary confines, professional flocking rules and the mere retrieval of information; the man who straps bricks to pencils, who annoys the specialists, who insists on bollocksing up the computer world in all kinds of fascinating ways. An epic failure, indeed: the wily Odysseus of so-called failure.

Undeterred by all those angry guys, Engelbart hacked together a few modest solutions – time-shared CPU, word processor, windowing system, wireless network, mouse – and showed the ACM and the Johnson administration a very plausible future. No doubt, the IR crowd failed (less than epically) to grasp the message of the new medium, and their spiritual descendants rule the increasingly ramshackle kingdom of content even now; but there is yet some evidence of progress, some sense that by following outriders like Engelbart and Nelson, we may manage to fail forward.

History (or historiography) is always essential, even though it must struggle against the gravitic pull of narrative. Narrative can be a problem, not only for all the usual problems of subjectivity and imperfect understanding, but because history is perhaps more valuable considered not as recitation but as cybertext – not teleologic, necessitarian telling, but improvisation or computation; an iterative exploration of possibilities in which the way forward often looks, in local terms, quite different from success. In this respect, it is important to note that not all writing is necessarily dry, massy and bricklike. This book is an exception, with its keen sense of person and place, and through its account of the peculiar, inorganic logic of technical evolution, its sensitivity to the essentially fractal nature of history. In all these respects, the book you are now reading resembled another very good non-brick, James Gleick's *Information: A History, a Theory, a Flood* (2011).

Two of the actors in Gleick's complex and populous account seem particularly relevant here. The first is Charles Babbage, creator of the Difference Engine and projector of the Analytical Engine, celebrated by

Lev Manovich (2001, 20–23) as a precursor of new media, and by William Gibson and Bruce Sterling (1991, 21) as the first ancestor of hackers. That eminence is, of course, an afterthought. Gleick quotes a rather different assessment of Babbage from an early twentieth-century edition of the *Dictionary of National Biography*:

> Mathematician and scientific mechanician [...] obtained government grant for making a calculating machine [...] but the work of construction ceased, owing to disagreements with the engineer; offered the government an improved design, which was refused on grounds of expense [...] Lucasian professor of mathematics, Cambridge, but delivered no lectures. (Cited in Gleick 2011, 121)

In the words of the information retrievers, Babbage seems a resounding failure, no matter if he did (undeservedly, according to the insinuation) have Newton's chair. Perhaps biography does not belong in dictionaries. Among other blessings that came to Babbage was one of the great friendships in intellectual history, with Augusta Ada King, Countess Lovelace. She also fell into obscurity for nearly a century after her death, but is now remembered as prodigy and prophet, the first lady of computing. Ada's story is full of pathos; she died far too young, never managing to convey to the greater world her astonishingly clear understanding of the Analytical Engine and its applications. In intellect and imagination she was well ahead of her century, and in some ways ours as well. Comparing herself to her father, Lord Byron, she wrote to Babbage, 'I do not believe that my father was (or ever could have been) such a Poet as I shall be an Analyst (& Metaphysician); for with me the two go together indissolubly' (cited in Gleick 2011, 119).

Babbage never completed the Analytical Engine, so Lady Lovelace could not show the world what it would mean to be analyst and metaphysician. A hundred years later we came to high-speed digital computing, and Mandelbrot, and a new geometry of nature (hold the metaphysics) – and the penny finally began to drop. But even as those pennies from heaven become Gleick's eponymous flood, we still have much to gain in wisdom. According to Lev Manovich, innovation in media operates in three dimensions: ontology, epistemology and pragmatics (Manovich 2001, 46). The last is the easiest to assimilate, and so it is the axis along which the most rapid and unreflecting changes occur; see, for example, the World Wide Web. When we try to work in those other two dimensions (ontology and epistemology) we encounter historical strandings like Babbage's and Ada's. As noted earlier, work of serious innovation stands at some remove from the ordinary world. It falls far from the tree diagram of influence and inheritance. With direct, cladistic lines cut off or unextended, it is hard to tell a story of progress. The history of technology is rife with castaways, isolatoes, unredeemed Prosperos stuck forever on uncharted desert isles, unaware of brave new worlds arising elsewhere.

A certain oversimplified parallelism suggests itself at this point. If Engelbart and Nelson are the Babbage and Lovelace of our times, and Xanadu our answer to the Analytical Engine, then we might expect these mighty names to be wistfully celebrated, in about a century's time, for their sadly clear grasp of what was not immediately to be. Following this line, we would have to wonder what unimaginable paradigm shift is waiting somewhere, destined to render digital machines as quaint as steam engines. Neo-analog, quantum computing? Faster-than-light neutrino processors? Gravitonics? We drift into science fiction, which is an honorable branch of literature, but more or less tangential to history.

History is the story of change, and our history itself, or at least our understanding of its patterns, may also undergo mutation. Given a cultural logic of deconstructed failure, a history not of lineages but of networks and pathways, progress may no longer depend on tectonic shift. Engelbart and Nelson were, in fact, never left alone on the beach, but have always had company, however complicated, broken and sometimes bitter these associations have occasionally been. Andries van Dam kept the hypertext idea alive at Brown (and, for a while, at Apple), so that it could be picked up by a second wave of experimenters, including Jay Bolter, Michael Joyce and Mark Bernstein. The same ACM conference that heard Nelson cry 'Wrong!' also featured a poster session by one Tim Berners-Lee on something called the World Wide Web, downgraded from full paper status (so legend goes) because of doubts about the system's scalability. Wrong indeed, and to a classical historian this might look like the kind of misjudgment that separates was from might have been.

Yet in a cultural network, as in a game, we are perhaps better equipped to survive our errors. Difference is no longer tied to fatality. Babbage exhausted his political support and ready money. Lady Lovelace ran out of time, energy and health, and could not bring her opus on the Analytical Engine to the wider audience it deserved. Yet today, even in our globally straitened circumstances, informational resources (at least) are considerably more abundant. The world of the Web, and weblogs, zines, wikis and social networks supports a massively composite culture threaded with many millions of subcultures. At least some of these cultures take part in open-source software development, including some for whom Xanadu is not just a vision in a dream.

There are some grounds for hope. However poorly conceived the general infrastructure, however corrupt and benighted the superstructure, the society of networks does support, somewhat obscurely, a plurality of ideas. Even on what ostensibly counts as the ascendant side, there is room for Berners-Lee to envision a Semantic Web that aims to cast some light below our diving boards – and for great institutional innovators such as Wendy Hall of Southampton to extend the affordances of the Web through artful exploitations on the server side.

Hypertext takes no single line. The concept itself arises from the idea of extension or complication – writing in a higher-dimensional space – so how could it be confined to one chain of transmission? Hypertext belongs to cybertext not just as an idea but as a matter of social practice. It's a multiplying, ramifying business. For every Google and Facebook tycoon, there are millions of names less recognisable, but just as important within the active, imaginative spheres they inhabit. Some are paracelebrities like Coulton; some are more secret masters like Katherine Phelps and Andrew Pam, the sages of Melbourne, who have been making digital culture since the days of acoustic connectors and BBS. One of this company is Belinda Barnet, who has had the patience and wisdom to see how our moments of failure and folly articulate to some yet grander set of stories.

These stories embrace all of us, strange and awkward children of Ada, Queen Mother of Geeks, who joked that her true portrait should show MATHEMATICS lettered across 'the capacious space of my jawbone' (cited in Gleick 2011, 108). Though we've probably all been known to talk in numbers, the legends that cross our images may be different these days. They probably start and end with angle brackets, and may have computable consequences, signifying that we live in complicated space and time, a domain of deadly games and serious play where we fail forward toward what we cannot know. Who could blame Nelson for the state of this casually marvelous, endlessly disappointing computer world? Any blame must be shared generally, be it for epic disaster or fortunate fall. The times move not straight ahead but crosswise, following endless turns and runnings of the net. Whether we are making our way to hell or heaven remains in doubt, though you can be reasonably sure that wherever we think we're going, we'll get there before our time.

PREFACE

This book would not have been possible without the cooperation of its subjects. Like technology historian Steve Shapin and sociologist Thierry Bardini, I write in the 'confident conviction that I am less interesting than the subjects I write about' (Shapin cited in Bardini 2000, xiv). I have had the great privilege of meeting many of the people you will read about in these pages – except for Vannevar Bush, who died in 1974 – the colourful anecdotes, magical visions and prescient ideas you will find here have come directly from them or from their work. At times I felt like a media studies bowerbird, procuring brightly coloured memories, sticky notes and cryptic computer manuals from various computing science professors, writers and visionaries across the globe. In that sense, this book may be read as a simple history book. There is no need to be self-reflexive or clever when presented with such a treasure trove; it is intrinsically interesting and needs no posthistorical garnish (I'll confine that to the preface). That said, I do not claim to present you with the final word on hypertext history; this is an edited selection, a woven structure of deeply interconnected stories contributed in large part by the people who lived them.

I have spent months, years in fact, arranging this collection; it was first assembled as a PhD thesis in 1999, before I had children and consequently when I had the luxury of time. Time to do things like roam around Brown University gathering documents and stories from Andries van Dam and the Hypertext Editing System (HES) team; time to rummage through the Vannevar Bush archives at the Library of Congress looking for interesting correspondence; time to interview Doug Engelbart and feel embarrassingly starstruck; and time to travel to Keio University in Japan to meet Ted Nelson. I also had time to ponder how it all might fit together, and more deeply, if it is even possible to say that a technical system 'evolves'. What, exactly, am I tracing the path of here? In one of those delightful recursive feedback loops that punctuates any history, I discovered that Doug Engelbart is also concerned with how technology evolves over time – so concerned, in fact, that he constructed his own 'framework' to explain it. Inspired, I went off and interviewed one of the world's most eminent palaeontologists, Niles Eldredge, and asked him what he thought about technical evolution. His response forms the basis of Chapter 1.

This hodgepodge of oral histories and technical visions worked quite well, so in the following decade I added a few extra twigs and blue plastic bottle caps and published it as a series of articles. Now, with the encouragement of my editor at Anthem Press, Paul Arthur and Stuart Moulthrop, I have chased down some of my original interviewees and coaxed more stories from them. I've also added a new chapter on Storyspace and the birth of a literary hypertext culture. In the interim, the subjects I am writing about have also published important work of their own, which I have duly read and woven into the story (though not soon enough, as Ted crankily pointed out). So I've arranged a new cross-tangle of stories for you to walk around in and inspect. These stories are not at all linear; many of them overlap in time, and most of them transfer ideas and innovations from earlier systems and designs.

According to Eldredge (2006), this is actually how technologies evolve over time – by transfer and by borrowing (he calls this the 'lateral spread of information'). Ideally the chapters would be viewed and read in parallel, side-by-side strips, with visible interconnections between them: you would be able to see where all the different ideas have come from and trace them back to their original source. If that comes across all Xanadu, well, that's because it is.

The metaphor of a bower, a matted thicket, is an appropriate one. A leitmotif recurs throughout this history, a melody that plays through each chapter, slightly modified in each incarnation but nonetheless identifiable; it is the overwhelming desire to represent complexity, to 'represent the true interconnections' that crisscross and interpenetrate human knowledge, as Ted puts it (1993). This riff does not come from me; it is as old as information science. How can we best organize the tangle of human thought, yet preserve its structure? It is not just the ideas that are important when we read or write or conduct historical research, but the connections between them. We should be able to see and follow those connections, and we should be able to write with them. This was playing in the background of every interview I conducted, and it was explicitly stated in many of the dusty old manuals, project proposals, letters and articles from the '40s,'50s and'60s through which I sneezed and highlighted my way. It is the theme song of hypertext.

Now for the important bit: this story stops before the Web. More accurately, it stops before hypertext became synonymous with the Web. As Ted put it to me in 1999, 'people saw the Web and they thought, "Oh, that's hypertext, that's how it's meant to look"'. But hypertext is not the Web; the Web is one particular implementation of hypertext, one particular model of how it might work. It is without a doubt the most successful and prevalent model, but it is also an arguably limited one. The goal of this book is to explore the visions of the early hypertext pioneers, and in the process, to broaden our conception of what hypertext could or should be. I will define precisely what I mean by the word hypertext in the next chapter, but for now we will use Ted Nelson's popular definition, branching and responding text, best read at a computer screen (Nelson 1993).

The first hypertext systems were deep and richly connected, and in some respects more powerful than the Web. For example, the earliest built system we will look at here – the oN-Line System (NLS) – had fine-grained linking and addressing capabilities by 1968. On the Web, the finest level of 'intrinsic' addressability is the URL, and if that page is moved, your link breaks. In NLS, the address was attached to the object itself, so if the document you were linking to moved, the link followed it. No broken links, no 404 errors, and the 'granularity' was as fine as sifted flour. Try doing that with HTML. As Stuart Moulthrop writes in *Hegirascope* (1997), HTML stands for many things ('Here True Meaning Lies'), one of which is 'How to Minimise Linking'.

These early systems were not, however, connected to hundreds of millions of other users. You could not reach out through FRESS and read a page hosted in Thailand or Libya. The early systems worked on their own set of documents in their own unique environments. Although Ted certainly envisioned that Xanadu would have the domestic penetration of the Web, and NLS had nifty collaborative tools and chalk-passing protocols, none of the early 'built' systems we look at either briefly or in depth in this book – NLS, HES, FRESS, WE, EDS, Intermedia or Storyspace – were designed to accommodate literally billions of users.[1] That's something only the Web can do.

As Jay Bolter put it in our interview:

> What the World Wide Web did was two things. One is that it compromised, as it were, on the 'vision' of hypertext. It said 'this is the kind of linkage it's always going to be, it's always going to work in this way', [but] more importantly it said that the really interesting things happen when your links can cross from one computer to another [...] So global hypertext – which is what the Web is – turned out to be the way that you could really engage, well, ultimately hundreds of millions of users. (Bolter 2011)

This story stops before the birth of mass 'domesticated' hypertext – before hypertext escaped its confines in university labs and wrapped itself around the globe like electronic kudzu to become the Web. It stops before we made up our mind about what hypertext is meant to look like. In that sense, the book is also a call to action. Hypertext could be different; it doesn't have to be the way it is today. Imagine if we could read history in side-by-side parallel strips with visible interconnections, such as Xanadu would provide. Imagine a hypertext system with no broken links, with no 404 errors, with 'frozen state' addressability like NLS. Imagine if the link structure were separable from the content. Imagine if there were no artificial distinctions between readers and writers, such as HES would provide. As Ted has been saying for over 50 years, the computing world could be completely different.

This book is about an era when people had grand visions for their hypertext systems, when they believed that the solution to the world's problems might lie in finding a way to organize the mess of human knowledge, to create powerful tools for reading and writing: the 'first generation' of hypertext systems. These systems were prescient and visionary, but they were also useful. Most of it took place well before I was born and it terminates in the late '80s. With the exception of Memex, which existed entirely on paper, the first generation of hypertext systems were mainframe-based; they were built on large, clunky machines that cost a small fortune and had to be kept in special air-conditioned rooms.

The story changes in the mid-1980s with the emergence of several smaller workstation-based, 'research-oriented' systems (Hall et al. 1996, 14). I have included only two of these here, arguably the two that had the least commercial or financial success: Storyspace and Intermedia. I could have included several others from that period – most obviously NoteCards, Office Workstations Limited's Guide, KMS, Microcosm, or Apple's very popular HyperCard program released in 1987. The latter systems were all commercialized in some form, but HyperCard was the most successful, largely because it was bundled free with every Macintosh sold after 1987 (Nielsen 1995).

HyperCard is the elephant in the pre-Web hypertext room; it popularized hypermedia before the Web and introduced the concept of linking to the general public. In some media accounts, one could be forgiven for thinking there was no hypertext before HyperCard (as *New Scientist*'s Helen Knight implies in her piece on pre-Web hypertext, 'The Missing Link' (2012, 45)). Actually computer-based hypertext had been around for twenty years before HyperCard, and the systems we will explore in this book were all built (or imagined) well before its release in 1987.

If I had another ten thousand words to play with, I would include a chapter on Microcosm and Professor Dame Wendy Hall. Microcosm was a commercial application, but it deserves a mention here because it was also the harbinger of a new era: network culture. Microcosm was a pioneering open-linking service designed to deal with large-scale distributed hypertexts and (unlike Intermedia or Storyspace, for that matter, which still arguably belongs to an earlier era) it was quickly incorporated into the Web. It was built by Wendy Hall, Gary Hill and Hugh Davis at the University of Southampton, and influenced by the ideas of Ted Nelson. As Wendy Hall put it to me:

> Microcosm started out as a research system. But we did commercialise it. We launched the company – then called Multicosm Ltd and later Active Navigation – in 1994 just as the Web was taking off. The company did well for a while but in the end was overtaken by events. (Hall 2012)

Hall started her career in hypermedia and hypertext at Southampton in 1984, and is now one of the world's foremost computer scientists. She is founding director, along with Professor Sir Tim Berners-Lee, Professor Nigel Shadbolt and Daniel J. Weitzner, of the Web Science Research Initiative. She became a Dame Commander of the British Empire in 2009, due in no small part to her contributions to computing science.

These systems were all pioneering in their own right, but they are (to my mind, at least) part of a different story: the commercialization of hypertext and the birth of network culture. That is a different book for a different time, and perhaps a different scholar. As Stuart Moulthrop pointed out to me one day as we were rattling along a freeway in Melbourne, this story traces the paired antiparticle that disappeared in a puff of subatomic debris before the Web. The other antiparticle, the one that survived, smashed into the bright links and baubles of HTML. The systems I look at here were exciting and revolutionary in their era, but like mermaid gold from children's storybooks, they turned to ashes when brought to the surface.

This is not my story; it is the story of the hypertext pioneers who designed and built the first systems and wrote the first hypertexts – and I need to thank them now. First and foremost, I would like to thank Stuart Moulthrop. Stuart has been a mentor and an inspiration to me for over fifteen years, and he first set me on the forking path to hypertext theory by hosting me as a visiting researcher at the University of Baltimore in 1999. His work has been deeply influential, both on my own writing and on hypertext as a critical discourse. I won't risk crediting him with inspiring this book, however; Ted once told me that the problem with inspiring people is that they then try to credit you with things you don't like. So just in case, I take full credit and full responsibility. I should also point out that he wouldn't consider himself a pioneer in the league of Ted Nelson or Andy van Dam or Wendy Hall – more a 'Storyspace groupie', as he put it to me. I disagree. But we'll get to that in the final chapter, a chapter he argued quite convincingly for me to include.

I would also like to thank Ted Nelson, who first set aside a chunk of time to speak to me in Japan in 1999, and then came to stay with us in Melbourne in 2011. He provided me with his time, books, memories and a wad of yellow sticky notes he left in the spare room. He also provided extensive feedback on the Xanadu chapter, much of which has been incorporated. I am quite certain that he will disagree with parts of this book, but I hope that I have given his vision of Xanadu, and the importance of this vision to the history of computing, the prominence it deserves. This idea of a guiding vision, or a 'technical image of potentiality' (Paisley and Butler cited in Smith 1991, 262), has always been the focus of my work – as Michael Joyce pointed out to me in our interview (though I think this was intended as more of a warning than a compliment at the time).

I do not claim to be Ted's biographer, and he has no need of one anyway: he published his own autobiography, *Possiplex*, in 2010. Ted is a master documenter and has been documenting his own life in astonishing detail since the early '60s, largely for the benefit of future researchers. Unlike Stuart Moulthrop or Michael Joyce, he is not a modest man. As he put it in *Possiplex*, 'modesty is for those who are after the Nobel, and that chance (if any) is long past' (2010c, 9). He feels he should be front and centre in any history of hypertext, and he is absolutely right. His work, his vision and the memories he has shared are woven throughout every chapter of this book. Marlene Mallicoat has also been supportive; Marlene is Ted's partner, but she is also an accomplished software engineer in her own right.

Andries van Dam at Brown University gave over his time for two interviews a decade apart and provided extensive comments on the HES/FRESS chapter (a task that took multiple days and was 'no Sunday afternoon in the park' as he put it in an email to me (van Dam 2012)). Throughout this time he has been knowledgeable, approachable and encouraging. The HES/FRESS chapter would not have been possible without Andy's time and assistance. This is not to say I have incorporated all of his suggestions, or that he is happy with every aspect of it; this interpretation of the HES/FRESS history, and any errors in it, are my own. Rosemary Michelle Simpson from Brown University sat through two interviews and provided useful comments; she suggested the original article title for the HES/FRESS chapter, among other things. Her input and comments have been invaluable.

In the end neither Ted nor Andy was happy with the HES/FRESS chapter. There are also parts of the Xanadu chapter that Ted disagrees with, and parts of this book he finds plain offensive. He provided me with some very insightful and at times emphatic comments, many of which have been relegated to the endnotes in the Xanadu chapter (follow them at your peril). At times I received conflicting versions of the same story from my subjects, and in that instance I have tried to put both sides of the argument forward and let the reader decide. It is not my place to adjudicate. That said, the history of hypertext is filled with colourful, opinionated and at times fractious personalities; to suggest that

it all unfolded neatly and without radical disagreements would be false. So
the reader will find this text is peppered with comments and retorts from the
pioneers themselves. Most of these will be in the form of a quote from an
interview or personal communication. This is not the way traditional history is
done, but this is not a traditional history. Hypertext is still evolving, and some
of my subjects are still alive and have their own opinions.

For the chapter on Storyspace, Mark Bernstein of Eastgate Systems
donated his time for an interview. He also read the entire manuscript and
provided extensive comments and suggestions. Again, I have not incorporated
all of these suggestions, but all were useful. Michael Joyce volunteered his
time for an interview, and also read the book and provided some comments
on the Storyspace chapter. John B. Smith and Jay David Bolter also gave
their time for interviews in 2011. Stuart Moulthrop read the whole book and
provided comments, as well as a beautiful foreword. I'd like to thank Michael
for permission to use his personal photos from the late '80s and for a copy of
his unpublished manuscript *Re:mindings*, which I cite in this chapter.

Doug Engelbart sat for an interview in 1999. Bill Duvall, a member of
Engelbart's original team at SRI, also donated his time for an interview in
2011, and provided feedback on the NLS chapter. Thierry Bardini, author
of the seminal work on Engelbart, *Bootstrapping* (2000), provided important
corrections to this chapter in 2011. On occasion Bardini disagrees with my
interpretation, and I have tried to incorporate this dialogue where possible.
Bill English, co-inventor of the mouse and the chief engineer in Engelbart's
original team, sat for an interview in 2011. Again, this chapter would not have
been possible without their support and comments.

Professor Niles Eldredge spent much time responding to my convoluted
questions in 2004. This turned into an interview, which was published later
that year (Eldredge and Barnet 2004). He also read – and, much to my surprise,
found no fault with – Chapter 1 (I am still sceptical about this; any errors are
my own). He gave me permission to use the diagram in Chapter 1.

Paul Kahn kindly read the Memex chapter and provided important
corrections and comments. I am also indebted to Greg Lloyd for his memories
of HES and FRESS, permission to use some early photographs he took of HES
and the EDS, his 'HES Questions' document (courtesy Traction Software)
and for his conference notes. SRI International gave me permission to use
the photographs of NLS and Doug Engelbart. Adrian Miles, Noah Wardrip-
Fruin and Chris Chesher also provided interviews or comments on a chapter.

Paul Arthur approached me with the idea for a book in 2010, having read
an article of mine in *Digital Humanities Quarterly* (*DHQ*). He also taught me
how to write a book proposal and helped me navigate the various stages in
its production. My colleagues in the Faculty of Life and Social Sciences at

Swinburne University, Hawthorn, have been supportive and encouraging – in particular, Dr Karen Farquharson, Dr Darren Tofts, Lisa Gye and Dr Esther Milne. Professor Julian Thomas from the Institute for Social Research (ISR) at Swinburne was instrumental in bringing Ted Nelson to Australia.

Many of these chapters first appeared as articles in academic journals. Chapter 2, on Vannevar Bush and Memex, and Chapter 5, on HES and FRESS, were adapted from articles that first appeared in the *DHQ.* Chapter 3, on Xanadu, was adapted from an article in *Screening the Past* in 2001. Parts of the chapter on Engelbart and NLS first appeared in an article in *Continuum Journal* in 2003. Parts of Chapter 1, on technical evolution, first appeared in *CTHEORY.* I'd like to thank the various journals for permission to republish. The whole project began as a thesis supervised by Dr Andrew Murphie and Dr Chris Chesher at the University of New South Wales (UNSW), and I'd also like to thank UNSW for permission to republish.

Now for the personal bit. Dr Kieron Thomson has been my intellectual sparring partner for over twenty years, and Melissa Slattery designed the cover of this book (and refused payment for it). Marina and Rose have been there for me through thick and thin. They are also my dear friends, and I'd like to thank them for that. Last but not least, I'd like to thank my husband, Mark Baldwin, and my three beautiful children, Oliver, Isabel and Laura. Every page of this book was checked by a small boy who wants to be a ninja one day. You have my heart and you always will. In memory of my precious teacher, Traleg Kyabgon Rinpoche IX.

Chapter 1

TECHNICAL EVOLUTION

How does one write the story of a computer system? To trace a technical history, one must first assume that there is a technical 'object' to trace – a system or an artefact that has changed over time. This technical artefact will constitute a series of artefacts, a lineage or a line. At a cursory level, technical 'evolution' seems obvious in the world around us; we can see it in the fact that such lineages exist, that technologies come in generations. Computers, for example, adapt and adopt characteristics over time, 'one suppressing the other as it becomes obsolete' (Guattari 1995, 40). But are we to understand this lineage from a sociological, an archaeological or a zoological perspective? And what is a technical artefact?

I need to address these questions here for two reasons. First, because it is impossible to write a technical history without defining how that history will be constructed, and second, because these questions also concerned Douglas Engelbart, one of the early pioneers whose work we investigate in this book. The relationship between human beings and their tools, and how those tools extend, augment or 'boost' our capacity as a species, is integral to the history of hypertext and the NLS system in particular.

Traditionally, history has ignored the material dimension of technical artefacts. Historians are interested in tracing cultural formations, personalities and institutions, and especially the social 'constructions' they erect around themselves. Technical artefacts don't have their own history; they are perceived as the products of culture. I have always found it strikingly odd, even offensive, that viruses or star formations are allowed to have their own history, but technologies are not. It's as though silicon (or calculus, or mathematics) has no existence outside of its function for human beings. As philosopher Daniel Little writes in a blog post:

> History is the sum total of human actions, thoughts, and institutions, arranged in temporal order. Call this 'substantive history'. History is social action in time, performed by a specific population at a time. Individuals act, contribute to social institutions, and contribute to change. People had beliefs and modes of behavior

in the past. They did various things. Their activities were embedded within, and in turn constituted, social institutions at a variety of levels. (Little 2011)

I do not have the space to unpack this in more detail here (that is another book for another time, but interested readers may find my article on the topic).[1] Suffice it to say that I think the material dimension of technical artefacts is important, and I pay attention to that here. Technologies like microfilm or digital computing have their own materiality, their own limits and resistances, and these limits affect the process of invention. Technical prototypes in particular are more than just the product of one person's genius; they are physical artefacts, and they generate new devices and new systems by *demonstrating* what is possible with steel wheel-and-disc integrators or with FORTRAN. Computer languages like Pascal also have their own control structures, procedures and functions that influence the shape of the software. There is actually a historical approach that is interested in how objects change over time, but it does not come from the humanities. It comes from evolutionary biology.

Since the early days of Darwinism, analogies have been drawn between biological evolution and the evolution of technical artefacts. In the background, there has been a long and bloody Hundred Years War among cultural anthropologists as to whether human culture as a whole can be said to evolve (Fracchia and Lewontin 2002, 52).[2] From the middle of the nineteenth century on, and arguably before this, scholars started remarking on the alarming *rate* at which technological change was accelerating. This sense of 'urgency', that technological change is accelerating and that we need to understand how it occurs, comes through most strongly in Engelbart's work. As he put it in an interview with the author, 'technologies are going to make our world accelerate faster and faster and get more and more complex, and we're not equipped to cope with that complexity [...] [We] need to establish a balanced co-evolution' (Engelbart 1999). This would be the most important project mankind could undertake.

The analogy of technical 'evolution' can only go so far, however. Technological systems are not like biological systems in a number of important ways – most obviously the fact that they are the products of conscious design. Unlike biological organisms, technical artefacts are *invented*. Silicon does not rise up and make itself into a computer; Pascal or C++ does not coalesce on the screen to form a hypertext system. Consequently, the mode of transfer of 'ensconced information' – designs, techniques and processes – is different from biological organisms.

We must also be clear about what we mean by 'evolution'. 'Change over time' is a good place to start, but it is far too vague to be useful; political parties, ice cream and conversations also change over time, but cannot be said to 'evolve'. On the other hand, it is dangerous (and conceptually vacuous) to import the language of genetics into historiography. As palaeontologist Niles Eldredge puts it:

> It is not *ipso facto* wrong to seek parallels between biological and material cultural evolution in an attempt to clarify the underlying ontological structure and causalities within each system [...] [But] before such comparisons can be made, however, it is important to start with a definition of 'evolution' that is both suitable and appropriate to both systems. (Eldredge 2011, 298)

For our purposes here, Eldredge's definition is perfect: 'the long-term fate of transmissible information' (Eldredge 2011, 298). By 'transmissible information', we mean not just designs and innovations (for example hyperlinks or the mouse), but also the techniques and processes that might be said to make hypertext unique as an information system (I will be arguing that is the organizational technique of association). To explain this more clearly, I spoke to Eldredge about trumpets, trilobites and historiography.

Tracing a Technical Artefact

> In both biology and material cultural systems, history is indeed staring you in the face when you look at a wombat or a [technical object]. But there is no way to divine that history unless you compare a series of objects that you assume *a priori* are related. (Eldredge and Barnet, 2004)

Professor Niles Eldredge collects things for a living, and there are two great collections in his life. The public one is on display at New York's Museum of Natural History; its 1,000 individual specimens stretch floor to ceiling for 30 metres across the Hall of Biodiversity. There are beetles, molluscs, rotifers and fungi, spiders, fish and birds, all arranged into genealogical groups. The other collection is private; it spans an entire wall in his home in rural New Jersey. This collection contains over 500 specimens, but of the 'musical rather than the biological variety' (Walker 2003, 41). He collects cornets, a type of musical instrument. There are silver and gold ones, polished and matte, large and small, modern and primitive. Ever the biologist, Eldredge has them arranged in taxonomic relationships of shape, style and date of manufacture. Much of the variety in cornet design is based on the way the pipe is wound.

Late in 2002, Eldredge's curiosity got the better of him. He decided to feed these specimens through the phylogenetic computer program he uses for his trilobites, to apply the 'scientific method' to technical evolution for the first time. As usual, he asked the computer to come up with all the possible evolutionary trees and then make a 'best guess' based on the existing specimens. The results were astounding. Compared to the phylogenetic diagram for trilobites, the diagram for a technical artefact seemed much more 'retroactive': new designs could borrow ideas from the distant past. Eldredge's musical instruments could step outside time.

In the world of living things, there are basically only two ways creatures can obtain a characteristic: by inheriting it from a previous generation or by evolving it in the present one. This last form of evolution is itself the subject of debate; an organism can't change its DNA in one lifetime. The only proven exception is found in the world of viruses. Biological organisms evolve gradually over thousands of generations, subject to natural selection. If a species dies out – biological 'decimation' – its lineage dies with it. But technical artefacts are different. With technical evolution comes the capacity to co-opt innovations at a whim. Time after time, when one of Eldredge's cornets acquired a useful innovation, other designers quickly copied the idea.

Technical artefacts are not dependent on the previous generation; they can borrow designs and innovations from decades or even centuries ago (retroactivate), or they can borrow from entirely different 'branches' of the evolutionary tree (horizontal transfer). As Eldredge put it:

> The key difference [between technical evolution and biological evolution] is that biological systems predominantly have 'vertical' transmission of genetically ensconced information, meaning parents to offspring [...] Not so in material cultural systems, where horizontal transfer is rife – and arguably the more important dynamic. (Eldredge and Barnet, 2004)

The lines in the cornet evolutionary tree were thoroughly confused. Instead of a neat set of diagonal V-shaped branches, a cone of increasing diversity, you would see flat lines from which multiple instruments appeared. When this happens in biology, it implies explosive radiation – the appearance of multiple new species in a geologically short period. In the biological world it is vanishingly rare (though as Eldredge argued with Stephen Jay Gould in their 1972 theory of 'Punctuated Equilibria' (Eldredge and Gould 1972), it is not impossible). The striking thing is that it appears to characterize the evolution of technical artefacts. In the cornet diagram, the gradual passage of time and generations does not precede the development of characteristics. Innovations appear spontaneously, often with no physical precursor.

Most striking of all, and most relevant to the history we are about to trace, outdated or superseded models could reappear with new designs, as if they

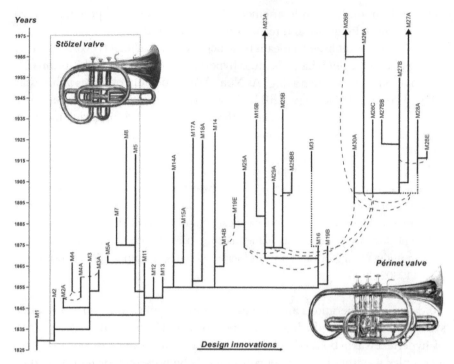

Photo courtesy Niles Eldredge © 2011.

were held in memory and only needed a certain innovation to burst into activity again. Technical *visions* from the past can be resurrected. This is what we mean by 'retroactivity'; technical designs can reappear, incorporate new bits and pieces from whatever is around at the time (microfilm, for example, was the newfangled thing in Vannevar Bush's era, and digital computing in Doug Engelbart's era) and then rapidly evolve in a single generation.

> [Virtually] all permutations and combinations were possible – including 'retrofitting' older designs with new ideas. Bottom line: information can easily spread back across separate branches (lineages) after they are already established as phylogenetically distinct. (Eldredge 2011, 301)

In biological evolution, when branches diverge, they diverge irrevocably; similarly, when branches die out, they cannot reappear. Technical artefacts are different. There is no extinction; nothing is irrevocable. That is why technical visions, or 'images of potentiality' as we call them in this book, can be influential over decades. In tracing the history of hypertext, then, we will be paying attention to instances of transfer and retroactivity – to innovations jumping from one system to another – but also to images of potentiality that appear to have longevity and recur over time. To abiding dreams.

So we have established a means by which technical artefacts evolve: transfer and retroactivity. But what, exactly, is hypertext, and what is the 'transmissible information' that we are tracing? As Noah Wardrip-Fruin observes in his essay 'Digital Media Archeology' (2011), in approaching any media artefact it is important to understand the systems that support it, and for digital media in particular, the specific 'operations and processes' that make it unique:

> Digital media are not simply representations but machines for generating representations. Like model solar systems (which might embody a Copernican or geocentric perspective while still placing the sun and planets in similar locations), the operational and ideological commitments of digital media works and platforms are visible more in the structures that determine their movements than in the tracing of any particular series of states or outputs. (Wardrip-Fruin 2011, 302)

To define the 'operations and processes' behind hypertext as an information system, Ted Nelson is the logical first port of call. His original 1965 definition of hypertext was 'a body of written or pictorial material interconnected in such a complex way that it could not conveniently be presented or represented on paper' (Nelson 1965, 85). This is a useful definition because it emphasizes the most obvious aspect of hypertext: *interconnectivity*. But it also defines hypertext by what it is not: paper.[3] This does not tell us very much about the underlying processes that might define hypertext as an historical artefact, however.

Nelson's next definition of hypertext is more useful for our purposes. In his 1974 book, *Computer Lib/Dream Machines* (the copy I refer to here is the 1987 reprint), Nelson proposed a definition of hypertext that emphasized branching or responding text – text that automatically extends itself upon request. 'Hypertext means forms of writing which branch or perform on request; they are best presented on computer display screens' (Nelson 1987, 134). This definition is useful in that it emphasizes that the 'interconnections' identified in the first definition should be *automated upon request*; they should go somewhere, do something, 'perform' or expand. They are also best read at a screen. This distinguishes hypertext from, say, proto-hypertexts like Cortazar's *Hopscotch* (a common example in the literature); although these works demonstrate deep interconnectivity, the interconnections are not automated. What Nelson meant by the word 'perform', however, also included some computer-based writing systems that haven't gained mass adoption.

One of those systems was stretch-text, a term Nelson coined in 1967 to mean text that automatically 'extends' itself when required – more like zooming in on a sentence than following a link. In the manner of a link, it still needs to be activated or automated, but it is not based on passing through to another node. The important point about stretch-text is that it doesn't fragment the text; it doesn't take you from one place to another. As George Landow observes, instead of following a link in the text, a stretch-text document 'retains the text on the screen that gives context to an anchor formed by a word or phrase even after it has been activated' (Landow 2006, 95). Although numerous systems have attempted to realize Nelson's conception of stretch-text, it has not gained mass adoption like the 'chunk-style' hypertext Nelson also identified in *Computer Lib/Dream Machines*; chunk-style hypertext consists of modular units of text or media connected by links (like most websites).

As Wardrip-Fruin wrote in a 2004 paper, although there have been excursions into the other forms of hypertext posited by Nelson (for example, the attempts to build stretch-text), chunk-style hypertext is now the dominant form. The most obvious reason is the Web, the largest chunk-style hypertext system in existence. Another reason might be that all the early hypertext systems (for example, NLS, HES and FRESS) were chunk-style – with the exception of Peter J. Brown's Guide, which was, as Mark Bernstein points out, 'the first commercial hypertext system, and which was deeply stretch-text' (Bernstein 2012).

> [In] the literary community, the definition of hypertext shifted so that it applied almost exclusively to chunk-style media. It could be speculated that this took place because most authors who called their work hypertext fiction or poetry worked in link-oriented forms (though exceptions such as the work of Jim Rosenberg were well known) […] With the rise of the Web (a chunk-style hypertext media system) the term's popular understanding shifted. (Wardrip-Fruin 2004, 126)

In this book, we trace visions and designs that have recurred over time, that have obtained 'stability' in that recurrence and hence constitute a lineage. For that reason, we trace the path of node-link or chunk-style hypertext; the lineage of stretch-text, for example, might be entirely different.[4] Based on Nelson's own suggestions, and having explained that we are focusing on chunk-style hypertext not stretch-text, I now offer a definition of what we are tracing here:

> Written or pictorial material *interconnected* in an *associative* fashion, consisting of units of information retrieved by *automated* links, best read at a screen.

There is a word here that I'm fairly sure raises a little red flag for some readers: 'association'. In the last century this word has come to acquire a meaning quite different from its original formulation by Aristotle in 400 BC; it currently implies a personalized, rhizomic (or for the 'first wave' hypertext theorists, even liberatory) technique opposed to a strict sequence or cognitive control. In contemporary critical theory, 'association' is often counterposed to 'hierarchical' structures as though these were distinct entities – *nomos* versus *logos*.

This is misleading. In its original formulation, association was a cognitive technology designed to fit ideas into determined sequences for easy recall. It has a long and venerable history as a technique for imposing order on seemingly disconnected elements. It is certainly not about making whimsical, haphazard connections.[5] Amazon, for example, is organized associatively, and this is about as 'hierarchical' as it gets. It is possible to be hierarchical and associative at the same time, something that hypertext theory has never really acknowledged (with the exception of Steven J. DeRose's important 1989 paper, 'Expanding the Notion of Links'). The hypertext systems we will look at, however, have acknowledged this in their structure; NLS was both deeply hierarchical and associative, and Storyspace is both associative and 'obviously interested in hierarchy' (Bernstein 2012). I explain this in more detail in Chapters 2 and 3. For now I simply wish to note that association is one of the organizational techniques I trace here.

As I explained in the Introduction, there is also a recurrent 'vision' in hypertext history that has found many different incarnations: the desire to *represent complexity*, to 'represent the true interconnections' that interpenetrate literature and human knowledge. Each of the hypertext systems we investigate here has a different interpretation of what that means. As Ted Nelson has said in numerous places (first in *Computer Lib*, and also to me in 2011), 'Everyone who builds software is projecting the back of their mind into that software' (Nelson 2011). Everyone's conception of interconnectivity is different, so each system will behave differently.

There is also an important difference between technical *vision* and technical *prototype*. As I argue in the next chapter, on Bush and Memex, we can dream of time machines and of warp speed, but the reason an engineering prototype has a rapid and often 'brutal' productive effect on its milieu is that it displaces technical and financial limits and demonstrates what is possible. A good working prototype sends a shock wave through the engineering culture it is associated with; inventors see the device or system in action and transfer aspects of that prototype into their own designs. Bush's prototype computing machines – the Analyzer and also the Selector – did exactly this, and as a result, they influenced the design of his own proto-hypertext device, Memex. As technical vision, Memex also incorporated the innovations that were current at the time – for example, microfilm.

The most influential demonstration in computing history is, of course, Doug Engelbart's 1968 demo of NLS. But as one of the original members of Engelbart's Augmentation Research Centre (ARC) at the Stanford Research Institute, Bill Duvall, put it in an interview with the author:

> The one thing I would say – and this isn't just true about NLS, this is true about innovation in general – is that [...] sometimes just *showing* somebody a concept is all that you have to do to start an evolutionary path. And once people get the idea of 'hey we can do that', then somebody does something, somebody does something better, that just keeps developing. (Duvall 2011)

This book investigates both technical vision and technical prototypes, but more important, it investigates the relationship between them.

Technical visions are not simply 'translated' into artefacts. The process of development is much more tangled than that, and presents its own material and technical limits. We investigate this in more detail in Chapter 3, when discussing Douglas Engelbart's NLS system. NLS was the computing world's most influential prototype, yet it was inspired by Vannevar Bush's *vision* of Memex. Engelbart updated this design with digital computing technologies. Chapter 4 is on Nelson's Xanadu, which has never been built in its entirety, yet it has inspired dozens of prototypes. Andries van Dam's first hypertext system, HES, was inspired by Nelson's technical vision of Xanadu, and was in turn an important prototype. His second system, FRESS, was inspired by Engelbart's prototype, and directly transferred over some of those technologies. Each system differently translated the systems and processes behind hypertext, and incorporated different technologies. Yet all of these visions and prototypes, as I demonstrate, have had an influence over the evolution of hypertext qua material artefact.

We begin where Doug Engelbart began, with Vannevar Bush's memory extender or Memex. As the reader will discover, this has become the oldest image of potentiality for hypertext.

Chapter 2

MEMEX AS AN IMAGE OF POTENTIALITY

It was the ultimate memory machine: a device that would store information associatively, keeping a record of all the interconnections between ideas – but never forget things. In this chapter I tell the story of a technical 'vision' that has survived for over seventy years: Vannever Bush's memory extender, or Memex. Memex was an electro-optical device designed in the 1930s to provide easy access to information stored associatively on microfilm, an 'enlarged intimate supplement' to human memory (Bush [1945] 1991, 102). Literary and historical works routinely trace the history of hypertext through Memex, and so much has been written about it that it is easy to forget the most remarkable thing about this device: it has never been built. Memex exists entirely on paper. As any software engineer will tell you, technical white papers are not known for their shelf life, but Memex has survived for generations. What, then, can we say about a dream that has never been fulfilled, but nonetheless recurs? Memex has become an *inherited vision* within hypertext literature.

In 1991 Linda C. Smith undertook a comprehensive citation-context analysis of literary and scientific articles produced after the 1945 publication of Bush's article on Memex, 'As We May Think', in the *Atlantic Monthly*. She found that there is a conviction, without dissent, that modern hypertext is traceable to this article (Smith 1991, 265). In each decade since the Memex design was published, commentators have not only lauded it as vision, but also asserted that 'technology [has] finally caught up with this vision' (ibid., 278). Noah Wardrip-Fruin makes similar assertions for Bush's article in 2003, but claims a special distinction in the new media literature:

> The field of information retrieval has been inspired by Bush's vision of simple, elegant information access. New media, however, has been inspired by a different aspect of Bush's vision: the scholar creating links and pathways through this information – associative connections that attempt to partially reflect the 'intricate web of trails carried by the cells of the brain' [...] This remains one of the defining dreams of new media. (Wardrip-Fruin 2003, 35)

To represent the 'true interconnections' that interpenetrate and crisscross human knowledge, as Nelson puts it (1993), is without doubt the defining dream of hypertext, if not new media. Paisley and Butler (cited in Smith 1991, 262) have noted that 'scientists and technologists are guided by "images of potentiality" – the untested theories, unanswered questions and unbuilt devices that they view as their agenda for five years, ten years, and longer.' Memex has never been built, but like Ted Nelson's Xanadu, it has become an image of potentiality for hypertext. It has also had a formative role in information science.

The social and cultural influence of Bush's inventions is well known, and his political role in the development of the atomic bomb is also well known. Bush was a very successful engineer who registered hundreds of patents and managed the development of weapons systems during World War II.[1] What is not so well known is the way that Memex came about as a result of both Bush's earlier work with analogue computing machines and his understanding of the mechanism of associative memory. I would like to show that Memex was the product of a particular engineering culture, and that the machines that preceded Memex – the Differential Analyzer and the Selector in particular – helped engender this culture and the discourse of analogue computing in the first place.

The artefacts of engineering, particularly in the context of a school such as MIT, are themselves productive of new techniques and new engineering paradigms. Prototype technologies create cultures of use around themselves; they create new techniques and new methods that were unthinkable prior to the technology. This was especially the case for the Analyzer. 'In the context of the early 20th-century engineering school, the analyzers were not only tools but paradigms, and they taught mathematics and method and modeled the character of engineering' (Owens 1991, 6). Bush transferred technologies directly from the Analyzer and also the Selector into the design of Memex. I trace this transfer in the first section below. He also transferred into Memex from the science of cybernetics an electromechanical model of human associative memory that he was exposed to at MIT.

The associative model of human memory was deeply influential on cybernetics and the nascent field of artificial intelligence, which in turn directly influenced Doug Engelbart and Andries van Dam, as we explore in Chapters 3 and 5. Many of the pioneers we will meet later in this book cut their teeth on computing systems that modelled human associative memory or neural networks, right up into the 1980s. There is a strange continuity in metaphor between early associationist models of mind and memory and hypertext. In writing this story I pay particular attention to the migration path of this model into technical artefacts, and the material structure and architecture of the machines concerned.

I want to emphasize from the outset, however, that the only piece of Bush's work that had any influence over the evolution of hypertext was his successful 1945 article, 'As We May Think'.[2] It would be wrong to suggest that his early writing, or any other published work I refer to here (for example, his autobiography, *Pieces of the Action*, published in 1970) had historical influence. Inventors like Doug Engelbart, Andy van Dam and Ted Nelson did not read the other pieces I cite here until James Nyce and Paul Kahn published their landmark 1991 book, *From Memex to Hypertext*, which included some of Bush's earlier and later essays – many years after the first and second generation of hypertext systems had been designed and shipped (or decommissioned). This book is still the seminal text on Memex. 'As We May Think' was a runaway success, a success that Bush did not achieve again with any other piece of writing in his lifetime, including his later essays.[3]

We begin the Memex story with Bush's first analogue computer, the Differential Analyzer.

The Analyzer and the Selector

The Differential Analyzer was a giant electromechanical gear-and-shaft machine that was put to work during the war calculating artillery ranging tables. In the late 1930s and early 1940s it was 'the most important computer in existence in the US' (Owens 1991, 3). Before this time, the word 'computer' had meant a large group of mostly female humans performing equations by hand or on limited mechanical calculators. As Doug Engelbart told Henry Lowood in a 1986 interview:

> I'll tell you what a computer was in [the 1940s]. It was an underpaid woman sitting there with a hand calculator, and they'd have rooms full of them, that's how they got their computing done. So you'd say, 'What's your job?' 'I'm a computer.' (Engelbart 1986)

The Analyzer evaluated and solved these equations by mechanical integration. It automated a task that was previously done by human beings and created a small revolution at MIT. Many of the people who worked on the machine (for example Harold Hazen, Gordon Brown and Claude Shannon) later made contributions to feedback control, information theory and computing (Mindell 2000). The machine was a huge success that brought prestige and a flood of federal money to MIT and Bush.

However, by the spring of 1950 the Analyzer was gathering dust in a storeroom; the project had died. Why did it fail? Why did the world's most important analogue computer end up obsolescing in a backroom? It is not uncommon for a successful engineering prototype to become obsolescent within twenty years. Technical evolution often moves in rapid steps. The reason in this case also relates to why Engelbart was able to build the NLS system; research into analogue computing technology, the Analyzer in particular, contributed to the rise of digital computing. It demonstrated that machines could automate the calculus, that machines could automate human cognitive techniques.

The decade between the Great War and the Great Depression was a bull market for engineering (Owens 1991, 29). Enrolment in the MIT Electrical Engineering Department almost doubled in this period, and the decade witnessed the rapid expansion of graduate programmes. The interwar years found corporate and philanthropic donors more willing to fund research and development within engineering departments, and communications failures during the Great War revealed serious problems to be addressed. In particular, engineers were trying to predict the operating characteristics of power-transmission lines, long-distance telephone lines, commercial radio and other communications technologies (Beniger 1986 (19) calls this the 'early' period of the control revolution). MIT's Engineering Department undertook a major assault on the mathematical study of long-distance lines.

Of particular interest to the engineers was the Carson equation for transmission lines. Although it was a simple equation, it required intensive mathematical integration to solve.

> Early in 1925 Bush suggested to his graduate student Herbert Stewart that he devise a machine to facilitate the recording of the areas needed for the Carson equation [...] [and a colleague] suggested that Stewart interpret the equation electrically rather than mechanically. (Owens 1991, 7)

This equation was transferred to an electromechanical device: the Product Intergraph. Many of the early analogue computers that followed Bush's machines were designed to automate existing mathematical equations. This particular machine physically mirrored the equation itself. It incorporated the use of a mechanical 'integrator' to record the areas under the curves (and thus the integrals), which was 'in essence a variable-speed gear, and took the form of a rotating horizontal disk on which a small knife-edged wheel rested. The wheel was driven by friction, and the gear ratio was altered by varying the distance of the wheel from the axis of rotation of the disk' (Hartree 2000).

A second version of this machine incorporated two wheel-and-disc integrators, and was a great success. Bush observed the success of the machine, and particularly the later incorporation of the two wheel-and-disc integrators, and decided to make a larger one, with more integrators and a more general application than the Carson equation. By the fall of 1928 Bush had secured funds from MIT to build a new machine. He called it the Differential Analyzer, after an earlier device proposed by Lord Kelvin, which might externalize the calculus and 'mechanically integrate' its solution (Hartree 2000).

As we saw in Chapter 1, a large part of technical invention occurs by transfer, whereby the functioning of a structure is analogically transposed onto another structure. This is what happened with the Analyzer; Bush saw the outline of such a machine in the Product Intergraph. The Differential Analyzer was rapidly assembled in 1930, and part of the reason it was so quickly done was that it incorporated a number of existing engineering developments, particularly a device called a torque amplifier, designed by Henry Niemann (Shurkin 1996, 97). But the disk integrator, a technology borrowed from the Product Intergraph, was the heart of the Analyzer and the means by which it performed its calculations. When combined with the torque amplifier, the Analyzer was 'essentially an elegant, dynamical, mechanical model of the differential equation' (Owens 1991, 14). Although Lord Kelvin had suggested such a machine previously, Bush was the first to build it on such a large scale, and it happened at a time when there was a general and urgent need for such precision. It created a small revolution at MIT.

In engineering science, there is an emphasis on working prototypes or 'deliverables'. As computer science professor Andries van Dam put it in an interview with the author, when engineers talk about work, they mean 'work in the sense of machines, software, algorithms, things that are *concrete*' (van Dam 1999). This emphasis on concrete work was the same in Bush's time. Bush had delivered something that was the stuff of dreams; others could come to the laboratory and learn by observing the machine, by watching it integrate, by imagining other applications. A working prototype is different from a vision or a white paper. It creates its own milieu; it teaches those who use it about the possibilities it contains and its material technical limits. It gets under their skin.

Bush, himself, recognized this, and believed that those who used the Analyzer acquired what he called a 'mechanical calculus', an internalized knowledge of the machine. This is like a combination of motor memory and mathematical skill, learned directly from the machine. When the army wanted to build their own machine at the Aberdeen Proving Ground, he sent them a mechanic who had helped construct the Analyzer. The army wanted to pay the man machinist's wages; Bush insisted he be hired as a consultant:

> I never consciously taught this man any part of the subject of differential equations; but in building that machine, managing it, he learned what differential

Vannevar Bush seated at a desk. This portrait is credited to 'OEM Defense', the Office for Emergency Management during World War II. It was probably taken some time between 1940 and 1944. Licensed under a Creative Commons License.

equations were himself [...] [It] was interesting to discuss the subject with him because he had learned the calculus in mechanical terms – a strange approach, and yet he understood it. That is, he did not understand it in any formal sense, he understood the fundamentals; he had it under his skin. (Bush cited in Owens 1991, 24)

Watching the Analyzer work did more than just teach people about the calculus. It also taught people about what might be possible for mechanical calculation – for analogue computers. Several laboratories asked for plans, and duplicates were set up at the US Army's Ballistic Research Laboratory in Maryland, and at the Moore School of Electrical Engineering at the University of Pennsylvania (Shurkin 1996). The machine assembled at the Moore School was much larger than the MIT machine, and the engineers had the advantage of being able to learn from the MIT machine's mistakes and limits (ibid.). Bush also created several more Analyzers, and in 1936 the Rockefeller Foundation awarded MIT $85,000 to build the Rockefeller Differential Analyzer (Owens 1991).

This provided more opportunities for graduate research, and brought prestige and funding to MIT.

> But what is interesting about the Rockefeller Differential Analyzer is what remained the same. Electrically or not, automatically or not, the newest edition of Bush's analyzer still interpreted mathematics in terms of mechanical rotations, still depended on expertly machined wheel-and-disc integrators, and still drew its answers as curves. (Owens 1991, 32)

Its technical processes remained the same. It was an analogue device, and it turned around a central analogy: the rotation of the wheel shall be the area under the graph (and thus the integrals). The Analyzer directly mirrored the task at hand; there was a mathematical transparency to it that at once held observers captive and promoted, in its very workings, the 'language of early 20th-century engineering' (Owens 1991, 32). There were visitors to the lab, and US military and corporate representatives who would watch the machine turn its motions. It seemed the adumbration of future technology.

Harold Hazen, head of the MIT Electrical Engineering Department in 1940 predicted the Analyzer would 'mark the start of a new era in mechanized calculus' (Hazen cited in Owens 1991, 4). Analogue technology held much promise, especially for military computation, and the Analyzer had created a new era. The entire direction and culture of the MIT lab changed around this machine to woo sponsors, as Nyce and Kahn observe (1991). In the late 1930s the department became the Center of Analysis for Calculating Machines.

Many of the Analyzers constructed in the 1930s were built using US military funds. The creation of the first Analyzer, and Bush's promotion of it as a calculation device for ballistic analysis, had created a link between the military and engineering science at MIT that endured for more than 30 years. Manuel De Landa (1994) puts great emphasis on this connection, particularly as it was further developed during WWII. As he puts it, Bush created a 'bridge' between research engineers and the US military, he 'connected scientists to the blueprints of generals and admirals' (De Landa 1994, 119), and this relationship would grow infinitely stronger during and after WWII. It would result in the formation of the Advanced Research Projects Agency (ARPA) in 1958 – an agency that funded many of the early computing science projects conducted at universities around the United States (including Doug Engelbart's lab at SRI). Bush started this relationship.

This chapter has been arguing that the Analyzer prototype accomplished something dreams or white papers can't do: it demonstrated the potential of analogue computing technology for analysis, and it engendered an engineering culture around itself that took the machine to be a teacher. This is why, even after its obsolescence, the Analyzer was kept around at MIT for its educational value (Owens 1991). It demonstrated that machines could automate the calculus, and that machines could automate human cognitive techniques: something that required proof in steel and brass. The aura that the Analyzer generated as a prototype was not lost on the US military.

In 1935 the US Navy came to Bush for advice on machines to crack coding devices like the new Japanese cipher machines (Burke 1991). They wanted a long-term project that would give the United States the most technically advanced cryptanalytic capabilities in the world, a superfast machine to count the coincidences of letters in two messages or copies of a single message. Bush assembled a research team for this project that included Claude Shannon, one of the early information theorists and a significant part of the emerging cybernetics community (Nyce and Kahn 1991).

Three new technologies were emerging at the time that handled information: photoelectricity, microfilm and digital electronics.

> All three were just emerging, but, unlike the fragile magnetic recording [Bush's] students were exploring, they appeared to be ready to use in calculation machines. Microfilm would provide ultra-fast input and inexpensive mass-memory, photoelectricity would allow high-speed sensing and reproduction, and digital electronics would allow astonishingly fast and inexpensive control and calculation. (Burke 1991, 147)

Bush transferred these three technologies to the new design. This decision was not pure genius on his part; they were perfect analogues for a popular conception of how the brain worked at the time. The scientific community at MIT were developing a pronounced interest in man-machine analogues, and although Claude Shannon had not yet published his information theory (Dutta 1995), it was already being formulated. Much discussion also took place around MIT about how the brain might process information in the manner of an analogue machine.

Bush thought and designed in terms of analogies between brain and machine, electricity and information. He shared this central research agenda with Norbert Weiner and Warren McCulloch, both at MIT, who were at the time 'working on parallels they saw between neural structure and process and computation' (Nyce and Kahn 1991, 63; see also Hayles 1999). To Bush and Shannon, microfilm and photoelectricity seemed perfect analogues to the electrical relay circuits and neural substrates of the human brain and their capacities for managing information.

Bush called his new machine the Comparator. It was to do the hard work of comparing text and letters for the humble, error-prone human mind.

Like the analytic machines before it and all other technical machines being built at the time, this device was analogue; it directly mirrored the task at hand on a mechanical level. In this case, it mirrored the operations of 'searching' and then 'associating' on a mechanical level. Bush began the project in mid-1937, while he was working on the Rockefeller Analyzer, and agreed to deliver a code-cracking device based on these technologies by the next summer (Burke 1991, 147).

Immediately there were problems. Technical prototypes often depart from their fabricating intention; sometimes because they are used differently from their intended use when invented, and sometimes because the technology itself breaks down. Microfilm did not behave the way Bush wanted it to. As a material it was very fragile, sensitive to light and heat and it tore easily. The switch was made to paper tape with minute holes, although paper was only one-twentieth as effective as microfilm (Burke 1991). There were subsequent problems with this technology: paper is flimsy, and it refused to work well for long periods intact. There were also problems shifting the optical reader between the two message tapes. Bush was working on the Analyzer at the time, and he didn't have the resources to fix these components effectively. By the time the Comparator was turned over to the navy, it was very unreliable, and didn't even start up when it was unpacked in Washington (Burke 1991, 148).[4] The Comparator prototype ended up gathering dust in a navy storeroom, but much of the architecture was transferred to subsequent designs.

By this time, Bush had also started work on the Memex design. He transferred much of the architecture from the Comparator to the Memex, including photoelectrical components, an optical reader and microfilm. In tune with the times, Bush had developed a fascination for microfilm in particular as an information storage technology, and although it had failed to work properly in the Comparator, he wanted to try it again. It would appear as the central technology in the Rapid Selector and also in the Memex design.

In the 1930s many believed that microfilm would make information universally accessible and thus spark an intellectual revolution (Farkas-Conn cited in Nyce and Kahn 1991). As we explored in Chapter 1, inventors often cherry-pick from the newfangled technologies around them. Bush had been exploring the potential of microfilm in his writing (Bush [1933] 1991, 1939) as well as the Comparator; the *Encyclopaedia Britannica* 'could be reduced to the volume of a matchbox. A library of a million volumes could be compressed into one end of a desk' he wrote (Bush [1945] 1991, 93). In 1938 H. G. Wells even wrote about a 'Permanent World Encyclopaedia' or planetary memory that would carry all the world's knowledge. It was based on microfilm.

By means of microfilm, the rarest and most intricate documents and articles can be studied now at first hand, simultaneously in a score of projection rooms.

> There is no practical obstacle whatever now to the creation of an efficient index to
> all human knowledge, ideas, achievements, to the creation, that is, of a complete
> planetary memory for all mankind. (Wells cited in Nyce and Kahn 1991, 50)

Microfilm promised faithful reproduction as well as miniaturization. It was
state-of-the-art technology, and not only did it seem the perfect analogy for
material stored in the neural substrate of the human brain but it also seemed
to have a certain permanence that the brain lacked. Bush put together a
proposal for a new microfilm selection device, based on the architecture of the
Comparator, in 1937.

Corporate funding was secured for the Selector by pitching it as a microfilm
machine to modernize the library (Nyce and Kahn 1991). Abstracts of
documents were to be captured by this new technology and reduced in size by
a factor of 25. As with the Comparator, long rolls of this film were to be spun
past a photoelectric sensing station. If a match occurred between the code
submitted by a researcher and the abstract codes attached to this film (Burke
1991), the researcher was presented with the article itself and any articles
previously associated with it. This was to be used in a public library, and unlike
his nascent idea concerning Memex, Burke wanted to tailor it to commercial
and government record-keeping markets.

Bush considered the Selector as a step towards the mechanized control of
scientific information, which was of immediate concern to him as a scientist.
He felt that the fate of the nation depended on the effective management of
these ideas lest they be lost in a brewing data storm. Progress in information
management was not only inevitable but 'essential if the nation is to be strong'
Bush writes in his autobiography (Bush 1970, 149). This was his fabricating
intention. He had been looking for support for a Memex-like device for years,
but after the failure of the Comparator, finding funds for this 'library of the
future' was very hard (Burke 1991, 149). Then in 1938 Bush received funding
from the National Cash Register Company and the Eastman Kodak Company
for the development of an apparatus for rapid selection, and he began to
transfer the architecture from the Comparator across to the new design.

But as Burke writes, the technology of microfilm and the tape scanners
began to impose their material limitations:

> Almost as soon as it was begun, the Selector project drifted away from its original
> purpose and began to show some telling weaknesses [...] Bush planned to spin
> long rolls of 35mm film containing the codes and abstracts past a photoelectric
> sensing station so fast, at speeds of six feet per second, that 60,000 items could
> be tested in one minute. This was at least one hundred-fifty times faster than the
> mechanical tabulator. (Burke 1991, 150)

The Selector's scanning station was similar to that used in the Comparator. But in the Selector, the card containing the code of interest to the researcher would be stationary. Bush and others associated with the project 'were so entranced with the speed of microfilm tape that little attention was paid to coding schemes' (Burke 1991, 151), and when Bush handed the project over to three of his researchers – John Howard, Lawrence Steinhardt and John Coombs – it was floundering. After three more years of intensive research and experimentation with microfilm, Howard had to inform the navy that the machine would not work because microfilm warps under heat and would deform at great speed (Burke 1991, 149).

Solutions were suggested (among them: slowing down the machine and checking abstracts before they were used (Burke 1991, 154)), but none of these were particularly effective, and a working prototype wasn't ready until the autumn of 1943. At one stage, because of an emergency problem with Japanese codes, it was rushed to Washington – but because it was so unreliable, it went straight back into storage. In 1998 the Selector made Bruce Sterling's Dead Media List, consigned forever to a lineage of dead or failed technologies. Microfilm did not behave the way Bush and his team wanted it to. It had its own material limits that didn't support the speed of access he so desired. The thing about visions is that they encounter material limits when they are translated into artefacts.

Technical limits are not always roadblocks; in engineering practice, these failures can teach inventors about the material potentials of the technology as well. Engelbart's mouse would never have been invented if he hadn't earlier mucked around with an obsolete device called the planimeter, as we discover in the next chapter. Technical limits shape the way a vision comes into being, but not in the sense of a rude awakening – more like a mutual dance. Science historian Andrew Pickering calls this process the 'mangle of practice' (Pickering 1995). Invention is not simply, or not only, about the translation of vision into artefact; it is about discovering and working with the limits of technologies, and playing around with those limits.

The Memex design changed significantly through the 1950s; Bush had learned from the failures he was encountering. But most noticeable of all, Bush stopped talking about microfilm and about hardware. 'By the 1960s the project and machine failures associated with the Selector, it seems, made it difficult for Bush to think about Memex in concrete terms' (Burke 1991, 161).

The Analyzer, meanwhile, had being used extensively during WWII for ballistic analysis and calculation, but wartime security prevented its public announcement until 1945, when it was hailed by the press as a great 'electromechanical brain' ready to advance science by freeing it from the pick-and-shovel work of mathematics (*Life* magazine cited by Owens 1991, 3). It had created an entire culture around itself. But by the mid-1940s the enthusiasm had died down; the machine seemed to pale beside the new generation of digital machines. The war had also released an unprecedented sum of money into MIT and spawned numerous other new laboratories. It 'ushered in a variety of new computation tasks, in the field of large-volume data analysis and real-time operation, which were beyond the capacity of the Rockefeller instrument' (Owens 1991, 5).

What happened? The reasons the Analyzer fell into disuse were quite different from the Selector: its limits were *external* to the device itself. They were related to a fundamental paradigm shift within computing, from analogue to digital. The birth of a new technical paradigm can be rapid and unforeseeable; for digital computing, the change was fast and brutal. It rendered a whole suite of technologies obsolete. We will explore this in more detail at the end of the chapter.

Human Associative Memory and Biological-Mechanical Analogues

> There is another revolution under way, and it is far more important and significant than [the industrial revolution]. It might be called the mental revolution. (Bush [1959] 1991, 165)

We now turn to Bush's fascination with, and exposure to, new models of human associative memory gaining currency in his time. Bush thought of and designed his machines in terms of biological-mechanical analogues; he sought a symbiosis between 'natural' human thought and his thinking machines. This issue is also important because the analogy between human thought and associative retrieval systems recurs in every chapter of this book.

As Nyce and Kahn observe, in all versions of Bush's Memex essay (1939, [1945] 1991, [1967] 1991), Bush begins his thesis by explaining the dire problem we face in confronting the great mass of the human record, criticizing the way information was then organized (Nyce and Kahn 1991, 56). He then goes on to explain the reason why this form of organization doesn't work: it is artificial. Information should be organized by association, which is how the mind works. If we fashion our information systems after this mechanism, they will be truly revolutionary:

> Our ineptitude at getting at the record is largely caused by the artificiality of systems of indexing. When data of any sort are placed in storage, they are filed alphabetically or numerically, and information is found (when it is) by tracing it down from subclass to subclass. It can only be found in one place, unless

duplicates are used; one has to have rules as to which path will locate it, and the rules are cumbersome. Having found one item, moreover, one has to emerge from the system and re-enter on a new path.

The human mind does not work that way. It operates by association. With one item in grasp, it snaps instantly to the next that is suggested by the association of thoughts, in accordance with some intricate web of trails carried by the cells of the brain. (Bush 1939, [1945] 1991, [1967] 1991)

These paragraphs were important enough that they appeared verbatim in all versions of the Memex essay: 1939, 1945 and 1967 (Nyce and Kahn 1991). No other block of text remained unchanged in this essay; the technologies used to implement the mechanism changed, Memex grew 'intelligent', the other machines (the cyclops camera, the vocoder) disappeared. These paragraphs, however, remain a constant. Given this fact, Nelson's assertion that the major concern of the essay was to point out the artificiality of systems of indexing, and to propose the associative mechanism as a solution for this, seems reasonable (Nelson 1991, 248). Nelson also maintains that these precepts of the design have been 'ignored' by commentators (Nelson 1991, 245).

With due respect to Nelson, I would contend that they have not been ignored; these two paragraphs are often cited, particularly the one relating to association (it usually appears verbatim in hypertext and internet history papers). What is ignored is the relationship between the paragraphs – the central contrast he makes between conventional methods of indexing and the associative indexing Memex was designed to support (Nyce and Kahn 1991). It makes sense that Nelson would pick up on this; he believes that conventional methods of indexing are hopeless, and that association is a far more logical way to structure information. Alphabetical indexing, for example, is next to useless for Nelson: not one of his books contains an alphabetical index.[5] It might also be said that when he incorporates numerical indexing, he does so reluctantly – and mischievously (in *Literary Machines* there is a chapter 0, several chapter 1s, one chapter 2 and several chapter 3s). For many of the hypertext pioneers, but most obviously Bush and Nelson, conventional methods of indexing are disastrous, and association is more 'natural', more human.

Which is interesting, because Bush's model of mental association was itself technological; the mind 'snapped' between allied items, an unconscious movement directed by the trails themselves, trails 'of brain or of machine' he writes in his autobiography (Bush 1970, 191). Association was a technique that worked independently of its substrate, and there was no spirit attached to this machine: 'my brain runs rapidly – so rapidly I do not fully recognize that the process is going on' (Bush 1970, 191). The 'speed of action' in the retrieval process from neuron to neuron (Bush 1970, 102) resulted from a 'mechanical switching'[6] (Bush 1970, 100), and the items that this mechanical process resurrected were also stored in the manner of magnetic or drum memory: the brain is like a substrate for 'memories, sheets of data' (Bush 1970, 191). The line between natural and mechanical was blurred in Memex, probably due to its origins in cybernetics.

Bush's model of human associative memory was an electromechanical one – a model that was being keenly developed by Claude Shannon, Warren McCulloch and Walter Pitts at MIT, and would result in the McCulloch-Pitts neuron (Hayles 1999, 65). The MIT model of the human neuronal circuit constructed the human in terms of the machine, and later articulated it more thoroughly in terms of computer switching. In a 6th November 1944 letter to Weeks, for example, Bush argued that 'a great deal of our brain cell activity is closely parallel to the operation of relay circuits', and that 'one can explore this parallelism [...] almost indefinitely' (cited in Nyce and Kahn 1991, 62).

In the 1930s and 1940s the popular scientific conception of mind and memory was a mechanical one. An object or experience was perceived, transferred to the memory library's receiving station and then 'installed in the memory-library for all future reference' (Dennett 1993, 121). It had been known since the early 1900s that the brain comprised of a tangle of neuronal groups that were interconnected in the manner of a network, and recent research had shown that these communicated and 'stored' information across the neural substrate, in some instances creating further connections, via minute electrical 'vibrations'. According to Bush, memories that were not accessed regularly suffered from this neglect by the conscious mind and were prone to fade. The pathways of the brain, its indexing system, needed constant electrical stimulation to remain strong. This was the problem with the neural network: 'items are not fully permanent, memory is transitory' (Bush [1945] 1991, 102). The major technical problem with human memory was its tendency to fade.

At the same time, there was a widespread faith in biological-mechanical analogues as techniques to boost human functions. The US military had been attempting for many years to develop technologies that mimicked and subsequently replaced human faculties (De Landa 1994, 127), especially in the years before, during and immediately following World War II. At MIT in particular, there was a tendency to take 'the image of the machine as the basis for the understanding of man' and vice versa, writes Harold Hatt in his seminal book on cybernetics (Hatt 1968, 28). The idea that humans and their environment are mechanical systems that can be studied, improved, mimicked and controlled was growing, and later gave way to disciplines such as cognitive science and artificial intelligence. Wiener and McCulloch 'looked for and worked from parallels they saw between neural structure and process and computation' (Nyce and Kahn 1991, 63), a model that changed with the onset of digital computing to include on/off states. The motor should first of all model itself on man, and eventually augment or replace him.

Bush explicitly worked with such methodologies – in fact, 'he not only thought with and in these terms, he built technological projects with them' (Nyce and Kahn 1991, 62). The first step was to understand the mechanical 'process' or nature of thought itself; the second step was transferring this process to a machine. Thus, a double movement is present within Bush's work, the location of a 'natural' human process within thought, a process that is already machinelike, and the subsequent refinement and modelling of a technology on that process. Technology should depart from nature or from an extant human process: this saves us so much work. If this approach is taken, writes Bush in his autobiography, '[it] should be possible to beat the mind decisively in the permanence and clarity of the items resurrected from storage' (Bush 1970, 191).

So Memex was first and foremost an extension of human memory and the associative movements that the mind makes through information. Bush transferred this idea into information management; Memex was distinct from traditional forms of indexing not so much in its mechanism or content, but in the way it organized information based on association.

The design did not spring from the aether, however; the first Memex design incorporates the technical architecture of the Rapid Selector and the methodology of the Analyzer – the machines Bush was actually building at the time. He learned from the technologies he was using, and incorporated pieces of them: the mangle in practice.

The Design of Memex

Bush's autobiography, *Pieces of the Action*, and also his essay, 'Memex Revisited', tell us that he started work on the design in the early 1930s (Bush [1967] 1991, 1970). Nyce and Kahn also note that he sent a letter to Warren Weaver describing a Memex-like device in 1937 (Nyce and Kahn 1991). The first extensive description of it in print, however, is found in the 1939 essay 'Mechanization and the Record' (Bush 1939). The description in this essay employs the same methodology Bush had used to design the Analyzer: combine existing lower-level technologies into a single machine with a higher function that automates the 'pick-and-shovel' work of the human mind (Owens 1991, 3).

In their important book *From Memex to Hypertext* (1991), Nyce and Kahn maintain that Bush took this methodology from the Rapid Selector; I have been arguing that it was first deployed in the Analyzer (and that transfer and retroactivity in fact characterize technical evolution). The Analyzer was the first working analogue computer at MIT, and it was also the first large-scale engineering project to combine lower-level, extant technologies and automate what was previously a human cognitive technique: the integral calculus. It incorporated two lower-level analogue technologies to accomplish this task: the wheel-and-disk integrator and the torque amplifier, as we have explored.

The idea of creating a machine to aid the mind did not belong to Bush, nor did the technique of integral calculus (or association for that matter); he was, however, arguably the first person to externalize this technology on a grand scale. Observing the success of the Analyzer qua technical artefact, the method proved successful. Design on the first microfilm selection device, the Comparator, started in 1935. This, too, was a machine to aid the mind; it was essentially a counting machine, to tally the coincidence of letters in two messages or copies of a single message. It externalized the 'drudge' work of cryptography, and Bush 'rightly saw it as the first electronic data-processing machine' (Burke 1991, 147). The Rapid Selector that followed it incorporated much of the same architecture, as we have explored, and this architecture was in turn transferred to Memex:

> The Memex-like machine proposed in Bush's 1937 memo to Weaver shows just how much [the Selector] and the Memex have in common. In the rapid selector, low-level mechanisms for transporting 35mm film, photo-sensors to detect dot patterns, and precise timing mechanisms combined to support the high-order task of information selection. In Memex, photo-optic selection devices, keyboard controls, and dry photography would be combined [...] to support the process of the human mind. (Nyce and Kahn 1991, 44)

Bush was very good at assembling old innovations into new machines. As professor of engineering at MIT (and after 1939, president of the Carnegie Institute in Washington), he was in a unique position: he had access to a pool of ideas, powerful connections, techniques and technologies to which the general public, and engineers at smaller schools, did not. Bush had a 'global' view of the combinatory possibilities and the technological lineage. He admitted this; in fact, he believed that engineers and scientists were the only people who could or *should* predict the future of technology; anyone else had no idea.

In 'The Inscrutable Thirties', an essay he published in 1933, Bush tells us that politicians and the general public simply can't understand technology as they have 'so little true discrimination' (Bush [1933] 1991, 77) and are 'wont to visualize scientific triumphs as *faits accomplis*' before they are even ready (ibid., 75). Bush believed that prediction should be left to engineers; only they can

MEMEX in the form of a desk would instantly bring files and material on any subject to the operator's fingertips. Slanting translucent viewing screens magnify supermicro-film filed by code numbers. At left is a mechanism which automatically photographs longhand notes, pictures and letters, then files them in the desk for future reference.

© Alfred D. Crimi, The Memex desk, from *Life* magazine 19 (11), p. 123.

'distinguish the *possible* from the virtually *impossible*' (Nyce and Kahn 1991, 49), and only they can read the future from technical objects.

Memex was a future technology. It was originally proposed as a desk at which the user could sit, equipped with two 'slanting translucent screens' upon which material would be projected for 'convenient reading' (Bush [1945] 1991, 102). There was a keyboard to the right of these screens, and a 'set of buttons and levers' which the user could depress to search the information using an electrically powered optical recognition system. If the user wished to consult a certain piece of information, 'he [tapped] its code on the keyboard, and the title page of the book promptly appear[ed]' (103). The images were stored on microfilm inside the desk, 'and the matter of bulk [was] well taken care of' by this technology – 'only a small part of the interior is devoted to storage, the rest to mechanism' (102). It looked like an 'ordinary' desk, except it had screens and a keyboard attached to it. To add new information to the microfilm file, a photographic copying plate was also provided on the desk, but most of the Memex contents would be 'purchased on microfilm ready for insertion' (ibid.). The user could classify material as it came in front of him using a teleautograph stylus, and register links between different pieces of information using this

stylus. This was a piece of furniture from the future, to live in the home of a
scientist or an engineer, to be used for research and information management.

The 1945 Memex design also introduced the concept of 'trails', a concept
derived from work in neuronal storage-retrieval networks at the time, which was
a method of connecting information by linking units together in a networked
manner, similar to hypertext paths. The process of making trails was called
'trailblazing', and was based on a mechanical provision 'whereby any item
may be caused at will to select immediately and automatically another' (Bush
[1945] 1991, 107), just as though these items were being 'gathered together
from widely separated sources and bound together to form a new book' (104).
Ted Nelson noted in response to this chapter that items could be put on more
than one trail – they could be reused (Nelson calls this 'tranclusion', a concept
we will explore in more depth in the Xanadu chapter).

Electro-optical devices borrowed from the Rapid Selector used spinning
rolls of microfilm, abstract codes and a mechanical selection head inside the
desk to find and create links between items. 'This is the essential feature of
the Memex. The process of tying two items together is the important thing'
(ibid., 103). Bush went so far as to suggest that, in the future, there would be
professional trailblazers who took pleasure in creating useful paths through the
common record in such a fashion.

The Memex described in 'As We May Think' was to have permanent
trails, and public encyclopaedias, colleagues' trails and other information
could all be joined and then permanently archived for later use. Unlike the
trails of memory, they would never fade. In 'Memex Revisited' (Bush [1967]
1991), however, an adaptive theme emerged whereby the trails were mutable
and open to growth and change by Memex itself as it observed the owner's
habits of association and extended upon these (ibid., 213). After a period of
observation, Memex would be given instructions to search and build a new trail
of thought, which it could do later 'even when the owner was not there' (ibid.).
This technique was in turn derived from Claude Shannon's experiments with
feedback and machine learning, embodied in the 'mechanical mouse':

> A striking form of self adaptable machine is Shannon's mechanical mouse.
> Placed in a maze it runs along, butts its head into a wall, turns and tries again, and
> eventually muddles its way through. But, placed again at the entrance, it proceeds
> through without error making all the right turns. (Bush [1959] 1991, 171)

In modern terminology, such a machine is called an intelligent 'agent', a concept
we discuss later in this work. In 'Memex II', Bush not only proposed that the
machine might learn from the human via what was effectively a cybernetic
feedback loop, but proposed that the human might learn from the machine.

© Alfred D. Crimi, Bush's Memex screens, from *Life* magazine 19 (11), p. 124.

As the human mind moulds the machine, so the machine also 'remoulds' the human mind, '[remoulding] the trails of the user's brain, as one lives and works in close interconnection with a machine' (Bush [1959] 1991, 178).

> For the trails of the machine become duplicated in the brain of the user, vaguely as all human memory is vague, but with a concomitant emphasis by repetition, creation and discard [...] as the cells of the brain become realigned and reconnected, better to utilize the massive explicit memory which is its servant. (Ibid.)

Bush was theorizing the posthuman long before Donna Haraway wheeled out the figure of the cyborg. In this paragraph he is imagining the human brain as an analogue machine, and not only that, but a machine that shapes thought itself, forming a prosthesis of the inside. Derrida couldn't have done it better. This aspect of Bush's work has been surprisingly ignored in contemporary readings of the design; Nyce and Kahn pay it a full page of attention, and Diane Greco (1996, 86) explores how both Bush and Engelbart sought to 'effect a symbiosis of person and machine' in a 1996 ACM paper. But aside from that, the full development of this concept from Bush's work has been left to Doug Engelbart.[7]

Engelbart would be quite explicit about the symbiosis between humans and technology: he didn't just set out to create a computer program – he set out to create a new model of the human system. This connection to Bush's work is also neglected in the literature; Engelbart certainly took the idea of associative trails and 'interactivity' from Bush and Memex, but he also took the underlying idea of an active symbiosis between human and device.

In our interview, Engelbart claimed it was Bush's concept of a 'co-evolution' between humans and machines, and also his conception of our human 'augmentation system', that inspired him (Engelbart 1999). Both Bush and Engelbart believe that our social structures, our discourses and even our language can and should 'adapt to mechanization' (to cite Bush [1967] 1991, 210); all of these things are learned. This process is not only unavoidable but is desirable. Bush also believed machines to have their own logic, their own language, which 'can touch those subtle processes of mind, its logical and rational processes' and alter them (Bush [1959] 1991, 177). And the 'logical and rational processes' that the machine connected with were our own memories – every last cell and neuron. This vision of actual human neurons changing to be more like the machine, however, would not find its way into the 1967 essay (Nyce and Kahn 1991, 122).

Paradoxically, Bush retreats on this close alignment of memory and machine in his later essays. In 'Memex II' he felt the need to demarcate a purely 'human' realm of thought from technology, a realm uncontaminated by machines. One of the major themes in 'Memex II' is defining exactly what machines can and cannot do:

> Two mental processes the machine can do well: first, memory storage and recollection, and this is the primary function of the Memex; and second, logical reasoning, which is the function of the computing and analytical machines. (Bush [1959] 1991, 178)

Machines can remember better than human beings can; machines' trails do not fade, and their logic is never flawed. Both of the 'mental processes' Bush locates above take place within human thought; they are forms of internal 'repetitive' thought (Bush [1967] 1991, 189), perfectly suited to being externalized and improved upon by technology. But exactly what is it that machines can't do? Is there anything inside thought that is purely human? Bush demarcates 'creativity' as the realm of thought that exists beyond technology:

> How far can the machine accompany and aid its master along this path? Certainly to the point at which the master becomes an artist, reaching into the unknown with beauty and versatility, erecting on the mundane thought processes a thing of beauty [...] This region will always be barred to the machine. (Bush [1959] 1991, 183)

Bush had always been obsessed with mechanizing human thought, as we have explored. But near the end of his career, when 'Memex II' and 'Memex Revisited' were written, he became concerned with the boundary between them, between what is personal and belongs to the human alone, and what can be automated.

In all versions of the Memex essay, the machine was to serve as a personal memory support. It was not a public database in the sense of the modern Internet; it was first and foremost a private device. It provided for each person to add their own marginal notes and comments, recording reactions to and trails from others' texts, and adding selected information and the trails of others by 'dropping' them into their archive via an electro-optical scanning device. In the later adaptive Memex, these trails fade out if not used, and 'if much in use, the trails become emphasized' (Bush 1970, 191) as the network adjusts its shape mechanically to the thoughts of the individual who uses it.

The idea of a 'personal' machine to amplify the mind flew in the face of the emerging paradigm of human–computer interaction that reached its peak in the late 1950s and early 1960s, which held computers to be rarefied calculating machines used only by qualified technicians in white lab coats in air-conditioned rooms at many degrees of separation from the 'user'. 'After the summer of 1946', writes Ceruzzi, 'computing's path, in theory at least, was clear' (Ceruzzi 1998, 23). Computers were, for the moment, impersonal, institutionally aligned and out of the reach of the ignorant masses who did not understand their workings. They lived only in university computer labs, wealthy corporations and government departments. 'Memex II' was published at a time when the dominant paradigm of human–computer interaction was sanctified and imposed by corporations like IBM, and 'it was so entrenched that the very idea of a free interaction between users and machines as envisioned by Bush was viewed with hostility by the academic community' (De Landa 1994, 219).

In all versions of the essay, Memex remained profoundly uninfluenced by the paradigm of digital computing. As we have explored, Bush transferred the concept of machine learning from Shannon, but not information theory. Bush transferred neural and memory models from the cybernetic community, but not digital computation (this paradigm was far more influential for Engelbart, as we shall explore). The analogue computing discourse Bush and Memex created never 'mixed' with digital computing (Bush 1970, 208). In 1945 Memex was a direct analogy to Bush's conception of human memory; in 1967, after digital computing had swept engineering departments across the country into its paradigm and the first hypertext systems had been created, Memex was still a direct analogy to human memory. It mirrored the technique of association in its mechanical workings.

Consequently, the Memex redesigns responded to the advances of the day quite differently from how others were responding at the time. As far back as 1951 the Eckert-Mauchly division of Remington Rand had turned over the first 'digital' computer with a stored-program architecture, the UNIVAC, to the US Census Bureau (Ceruzzi 1998, 27). 'Delay Lines' stored 1,000 words as acoustic pulses in tubes of mercury, and reels of magnetic tapes that stored invisible bits were used for bulk memory. This was electronic digital technology, and did not mirror, or seek to mirror, 'natural' processes in any way (although Claude Shannon, and parts of the cybernetic community, were using naturalistic metaphors in their work). It steadily replaced the most popular form of electromechanical memory from the late 1940s and early 1950s: drum memory. This was a large metal cylinder that rotated rapidly beneath a mechanical head, where information was written across the surface magnetically (Ceruzzi 1998).

In 1950 Warren Weaver and Samuel Caldwell met to discuss the Analyzer and the analogue computing programme it had inspired at MIT, a large programme that had become out of date more swiftly than anyone could have imagined. They noted that, in 1936, no one could have expected that within ten years the whole field of digital 'computer science' would so quickly overtake Bush's project (Weaver and Caldwell cited in Owens 1991, 4). Bush, and the department at MIT that had formed itself around the Analyzer and analogue computing, had been left behind.

I do not have the space here to trace the evolution of digital computing at this time in the United States and the United Kingdom; excellent accounts have already been written by Beniger (1986), Ceruzzi (1998, and an excellent update in 2003), Shurkin (1996) and Edwards (1997), to name but a few. All we need to realize at this point is that the period between 1945 and 1967 – the years between the publication of the first and the final versions of the Memex essays, respectively – had witnessed enormous change. The period saw not only the rise of digital computing, beginning with the construction of a few machines in the postwar period and developing into widespread mainframe processing for US business, but also the explosive growth of commercial television and the beginnings of satellite broadcasting (Spar 2001, 197). By 1967 Engelbart was already hard at work on NLS at SRI, and the Hypertext Editing System (HES) was built at Brown University. Digital computing had arrived.

Bush, however, was not a part of this revolution. He had not been trained in digital computation or information theory, and knew little about the emerging field of digital computing. He was immersed in a different technical system: analogue machines interpreted mathematics in terms of mechanical rotations, storage and memory as a physical 'holding' of information, and drew their answers as curves. They directly mirrored the operations of the calculus. Warren Weaver expressed his regret over the passing of analogue machines and the Analyzer in a letter to the director of MIT's Center of Analysis:

It seems rather a pity not to have around such a place as MIT a really impressive Analogue computer; for there is a vividness and directness of meaning of the electrical and mechanical processes involved [...] which can hardly fail, I would think, to have a very considerable educational value. (Weaver cited in Owens 1991, 5)

The passing away of analogue computing was the passing away of an ethos: machines as mirrors of mathematical tasks. But Bush and Memex remained in the analogue era, even when this era of direct reflection and analogy in mechanical workings had passed.

Technological evolution moves faster than our ability to adjust to its changes. More precisely, it moves faster than the *techniques* that it engenders and the culture it forms around itself. Bush expressed some regret over this speed of passage near the end of his life, or, perhaps, sadness over the obsolescence of his own engineering techniques.

As he writes in his autobiography: 'The trend [in the '50s] had turned in the direction of digital machines, a whole new generation had taken hold. If I mixed with it, I could not possibly catch up with new techniques, and I did not intend to look foolish' (Bush 1970, 208). He remained enamoured of physical recording and inscription. His 1959 essay proposes using organic crystals to record data by means of phase changes in molecular alignment. '[I]n Memex II, when a code on one item points to a second, the first part of the code will pick out a crystal, the next part the level in this, and the remainder the individual item' (Bush [1959] 1991, 169). This was new technology at the time, but certainly not the direction that commercial computing was taking via Digital Equipment Corporation (DEC) or IBM.

Bush was fundamentally uncomfortable with digital electronics as a means to store material. In 1965 he wrote, 'The brain does not operate by reducing everything to indices and computation' ([1965] 1991, 190). He was aware of how out of touch he was with emerging digital computing techniques, and this essay bears no trace of engineering details whatsoever, details that were steadily disappearing from all his published work. He devoted the latter part of his career to frank prophecy, reading from the technologies he saw around him and taking 'a long look ahead' (Bush [1959] 1991, 166). Of particular concern to him was promoting Memex as the technology of the future, and encouraging the public that 'the time has come to try it again' (ibid.).

In 1968, Bush received a phone call from a young man called Ted Nelson, who was visiting the area for a conference. Nelson told Bush he had started work on a computer-based system that had a lot in common with Memex. Bush was interested and 'wanted very much to discuss it' recalls Nelson, but Nelson decided he didn't like the sound of Bush's voice on the phone and didn't pursue it. 'He sounded like a sport coach,' Nelson said.

Memex, Inheritance and Transmission

> No memex could have been built when that article appeared. In the quarter-century since then, the idea has been with me almost constantly, and I have watched new developments in electronics, physics, chemistry and logic to see how they might help bring it to reality. (Bush 1970, 190)

Memex became an image of potentiality for Bush himself near the end of his life. In the later essays, and particularly in his autobiography, he writes in a different tone entirely: Memex was an image he would bequeath to the future, a gift to the human race. For most of his professional life he had been concerned with augmenting human memory, and preserving information that might be lost to human beings. He had occasionally written about this project as a larger idea that would boost 'the entire process by which man profits by his inheritance of acquired knowledge' (Bush [1945] 1991, 99). But in 'Memex II', this project became grander, more urgent – the idea itself far more important than the technical details. He was nearing the end of his life, and Memex was still unbuilt. Would someone eventually build this machine? He hoped so, and he urged the public that it would soon be possible to do this, or at least, the 'day has come far closer' (Bush 1970, 190): 'in the interval since that paper ["As We May Think"] was published, there have been many developments [...] Steps that were merely dreams are coming into the realm of practicality' (Bush [1959] 1991, 166). Could this image be externalized now, and live beyond him? It would not only carry the wealth of his own knowledge beyond his death but would be like a gift to all mankind.

In fact, Memex would be the centrepiece of mankind's true revolution: transcending death.

> Can a son inherit the Memex of his father, refined and polished over the years, and go on from there? In this way can we avoid some of the loss which comes when oxygen is no longer furnished to the brain of the great thinker, when all the patterns of neurons so painstakingly refined become merely a mass of protein and nucleic acid? Can the race thus develop leaders, of such power and intellect, and such forces of conviction, that the world can be saved from its follies? This is an objective of far greater importance than the conquest of disease, even than the conquest of mental aberrations. (Bush [1959] 1991, 183)

Near the end of his life, Bush thought of Memex as more than just an individual's machine: the 'ultimate [machine] is far more subtle than this' (ibid., 182). Memex would be the centrepiece of a structure of inheritance and transmission, a structure that would accumulate with each successive generation. In 'Science Pauses', Bush titled one of the sections 'Immortality in a Machine' (Bush [1965] 1991, 189): it contained a description of Memex, but this time there was an emphasis on its 'longevity' over the individual human mind (190). This is the crux of the matter; the trails in Memex would not grow old; they would be a gift from father to son, from one generation to the next.

Bush died on the 30th of June 1974. The image of Memex has been passed on beyond his death, and 'As We May Think' continues to be read and cited. It also continues to inspire a host of new machines and new systems. Had Bush attempted to assemble this machine in his own lifetime, it would undoubtedly have changed in its technical workings; the material limits of microfilm, of photoelectric components, and later of crystalline memory storage, would have imposed their limits; the possible uses of the machine would itself have changed as it demonstrated its own potential. If Memex had been built, the object would have invented itself differently from the outlines Bush cast on paper. This never happened. Memex has entered into the intellectual capital of new media as an image of potentiality.

Chapter 3

AUGMENTING THE INTELLECT: NLS

Dr Douglas Engelbart is a softly spoken man. His voice is low yet persuasive, as though 'his words have been attenuated by layers of meditation', his friend Nilo Lindgren wrote in 1971 (cited in Rheingold 2000, 178). I struggled to hear him, being partially deaf myself, but that didn't matter; he has been describing the same vision in great detail to journalists, historians and engineers for over 60 years. The words change slightly in each interview, but the vision remains clear and sweeping, like a horizon line on a bright summer's day. Engelbart wants to improve the model of the human, to 'boost our capacity to deal with complexity' as a species (Engelbart 1999).

To get what he means by 'boost our capacity' as a species, we must first understand his philosophical framework. This is important for two reasons. Firstly, this framework profoundly influenced his own approach to invention in the '60s and '70s. Secondly, it represents a fascinating (and novel) theory of technical evolution, a topic we have already started to explore in this book.

Engelbart believes that human beings live within an existing technical and cultural system, an 'augmentation' system. We are born with a particular set of genetic capabilities, and then we build on these innate capabilities using tools, techniques, skills, language and technology. There is no 'naked ape'; from the moment we are born we are always already augmented by language, tools and technologies. This augmentation system defines the limits of what is possible for us as a species.

> Here's a human [...] He's got all these capabilities within his skin we can make use of, a lot of mental capabilities we know of, and some of it he's even conscious of. Those are marvellous machines there – motor machinery to actuate the outside world, and sensor and perceptual machinery to get the idea of what's going on [...] Then we've got a whole 'culture-full' of things we are indoctrinated and trained into, both conscious things and unconscious things. (Engelbart 1988, 213)

Our 'augmentation system' is more than just technology; it includes the whole subset of learned behaviours and physiological capabilities that allow humans to modulate and interact with the environment. It includes pens and toothbrushes and computers and hypertext systems – but it also includes the social structures we live within, the techniques and discourses we acquire, the 'training, knowledge and skills that have to be installed as well as language, an extremely important invention' (Engelbart 1988, 216). This is a giant, complicated structure that has evolved over generations, and it 'gives us the benefit of what others before us have learned' (Engelbart cited in Rheingold 1985, 181). Most importantly, the elements within this augmentation system are acquired. We are not born with them; we are born into them and take them on as our own – he uses a software metaphor for this process; they are 'installed' (Engelbart 1988, 216).

Engelbart divides this system into two parts. One part has the material artefacts in it, and the other has all the 'cognitive, sensory motor machinery' (Engelbart 1999). 'I called these the "tool system" and the "human system"' (Engelbart 1988, 216). Together the tool system and the human system are called the 'capability infrastructure'. One lot of technologies is inside thought (and also the body – as motor memory), and the other has been externalized as technical artefact. The 'human system' is not, however, just a subsidiary of the material world: it *equips* us to use material artefacts in a recursive feedback loop. This is the basis of bootstrapping – the technique he would later use to invent parts of the tool system.

For Engelbart, the most important element of the 'human system' is language. As Thierry Bardini details in his seminal book on Engelbart, *Bootstrapping* (2000), he was heavily influenced early in his career by the work of language theorist Benjamin Lee Whorf.[1] Whorf's central thesis is that the world view of a culture is limited by the structure of the language this culture uses. Engelbart would eventually build a computer system that externalized the 'networked' structure of language. Language is a deeply interconnected network of relationships that mark the limit of what is possible.

> With the view that the symbols one works with [...] represent a mapping of one's associated concepts, and further that one's concepts exist in a network of relationships as opposed to the essentially linear form of actual printed records, it was decided that the concept-manipulation aids derivable from real-time computer support could be appreciably enhanced by structuring conventions that would make explicit the various types of network relationships among concepts. (Engelbart and English 1968, 398)

Underneath this networked 'concept structure' are what Engelbart considers our basic human capabilities: perceptual and motor machinery. But these are not pure or natural either. Humans invent themselves within a particular technical system, and 'what we consider to be natural is just what we have grown to accept' (Engelbart 1988, 217) from within a historically specific structure. Consequently, when it comes to the tool system, there is no truly natural technology or way of doing things for human beings. 'Whenever you hear somebody say it has to be "easy to learn and natural to use", put up a little flag and go question it. What's "natural"? Is there a natural way to guide a vehicle, as with reins? Well that didn't last long' (ibid.). Any new technology requires a period of learning, and we must learn new skills if we are to evolve.

Importantly, the elements within the 'human system' were developed as techniques and as skills in order that we might better utilize technical objects. The human system invents itself to better utilize the tool system in a symbiotic relationship. This is the reverse of the liberal human perspective, where human culture exists prior to and separate from technology. For liberal humanism, the tool is envisioned 'as an object that is apart from the body, an object that can be picked up and put down at will' (Hayles 1999, 34), an object that exists outside of a 'natural' human being. What Engelbart is suggesting is that man's unique nature is defined by tool use; all human action is, after a fashion, technical. Hayles (1999) calls this perspective posthumanism; Engelbart calls it an 'integrated man-machine relationship' (1962b, 237).

Like Bush before him, Engelbart modelled the human psyche as a technical system, and proposed a fundamentally technical solution to the problem of human knowledge. As Bardini points out, his tool and human systems 'communicate' via a process of 'feedback' (Bardini 2000, 34), a fundamentally systemic process. Humans and technical machines are also articulated together as different kinds of systems – one of the hallmarks of cybernetics (Hayles 1999). This is not surprising; cybernetics influenced most engineers working in the 1950s (Bardini 2000). Like Norbert Wiener, Engelbart also has a systemic explanation for social structures and for life itself, a theory for the co-evolution of humans and technics.

But for Engelbart, this is an unbalanced evolution; until now, it has been the tool system that has been driving human beings. The tool system moves faster than the human system, and it takes a lot of time (sometimes generations) before we can develop the appropriate human infrastructure to deal with changes. Engelbart believes that technology moves in large, rapid steps, which can cause distress amongst human beings as old paradigms and techniques are outdated. Further, he believes that this is accelerating; the world is far more complex now than it was 100 years ago. But there is hope. Engelbart thinks that we might be able to change this, to create a more 'balanced' evolution. But first, we have to understand how it works.

It takes a long time (generations) to discover and implement all of the changes in the human system made possible by a given, radical improvement in technology.

Where, as is the situation now, technology moves in large, rapid steps [...] the human system will become critically stressed in trying to adapt rapidly in ways that formerly took hundreds of years [...] The technology side, the tool system, has inappropriately been driving the whole. What has to be established is a balanced co-evolution between both parts. How do we establish an environment that yields this co-evolution? (Engelbart 1988, 217)

Engelbart's framework fundamentally influenced his own approach to invention. Not only did he explicitly seek out our 'basic cognitive machinery' in the '60s via empirical experiments to 'augment' them with tools, but he explicitly refused to take on board the dominant mantra of the engineering community.[2] 'Easy to learn, natural to use' is the mantra of usability (Engelbart 1988, 201), and it implies that humans should not have to learn from technology. Engelbart believed otherwise, and designed technical systems accordingly. Nothing is just natural; everything is acquired. Humans learn from technology; they acquire new techniques and new skills from material artefacts, and this process is not only desirable but is unavoidable. So the only way we can direct this evolutionary dynamic is to become conscious of the process itself; we have to become 'conscious of the candidates for change – in both the tool system and the human system' (Engelbart 1988, 217). Technical evolution doesn't have to be unbalanced.

Some changes, Engelbart believes, will greatly benefit mankind. To locate the changes that will benefit mankind, one must focus on the human system – what our current social structures and methods are for doing things, and more important, how these might be *boosted* using elements from the tool system. Engineers should reflect on their own basic cognitive machinery first, specifically on where its limits reside. Language is the most important cognitive machinery. If we can effectively map this 'pattern system' and externalize it, we can begin to change the limits of what is possible.

This reflexive technique is what he calls 'bootstrapping', and it was the methodological basis of the lab he set up at the Stanford Research Institute (SRI) in the early 1960s. The philosophy is also a return to liberal humanism, and sits in contrast to the rest of Engelbart's thinking on technical evolution; he believes that humans can and should learn to direct the tool system, to control the direction technology takes. At the moment it is an unbalanced evolution, but it doesn't have to be this way. Changing the relationship in favour of human beings is possible. More deeply, this implies that Doug's revolution requires a reversal of the current relationship between humans and technology; we need to be back in the driver's seat.[3] Hayles (1999) locates a similar contradiction in Norbert Wiener's work.

In particular, Engelbart feels we need to create tool systems that help us deal with knowledge work in a more effective way. This objective is something he claims he inherited from Bush's 1945 paper, 'As We May Think' (Engelbart 1962), and it formed the basis of the 'Conceptual Framework for Augmenting Man's Intellect' he would later erect to explain and support the development of the oN-Line System (NLS), a prototype hypertext system. As he told me:

> We need to think about how to boost our collective IQ, and how important it would be to society because all of the technologies are just going to make our world accelerate faster and faster and get more and more complex and we're not equipped to cope with that complexity. We need a way to harness it. (Engelbart 1999)

This sense of urgency – this feeling that the world is getting more complex and moving faster, that we need a way to 'harness' the inherited mess and that this would be the most important project mankind could undertake – has obvious parallels to Bush's project:

> The summation of human experience is being expanded at a prodigious rate, and the means we use for threading through the consequent maze is the same as was used in the days of square-rigged ships. (Bush [1945] 1991, 89)

Boosting our capacity to deal with the complexity of human knowledge is the grand challenge; it is the grand challenge we also find in Nelson's work. Engelbart shared this basic understanding of the problem with Nelson and Bush.

For Engelbart, there is also a structure to this acquired knowledge, a *networked structure* we should seek to preserve. All our ideas have basic interconnections and this structure is what enables the creation of new concepts as well as recall. Bush explicitly theorized this structure in terms of association, and considered association the best technique and model for organizing information. Engelbart theorizes it in terms of 'basic mental structures' and, in particular, 'basic concept structures' (Engelbart 1962b, 35; see also Bardini 2000). Unlike Bush, however, Engelbart considers this basic structure derivative of language (Bardini 2000). For Engelbart, language is a vast system of interconnections that defines the limits of what we know and of what is possible. As a technology, it also engenders our basic mental structure and enables or enframes our basic concept structures. This is a systemic process.

> A natural language provides its user with a ready-made structure of concepts that establishes a basic mental structure, and that allows a flexible, general-purpose concept structuring. (Engelbart 1962a, 35)

This general-purpose concept structure is common to all who use a particular language. Consequently, it can be refined and elaborated into a shared network: we can *improve* on it. Engelbart sought to externalize this networked concept structure so that recording could be refined and boosted, which would improve the capacity of the individual human minds who tap into it. Bardini (2000) argues that Engelbart's philosophy is consequently opposed to association; association relies on personal, haphazard connections that do not translate into abstract general principles. The connections Engelbart saw in language are more general, and the structure they carry is public property, not based purely on personal experience.

> [Bush's] philosophy revolved around the 'association' of ideas on the model of how the individual mind is supposed to work. [Engelbart's] revolved around the intersubjective 'connection' of words in the systems of natural languages. (Bardini 2000, 40)

According to Bardini, the idiosyncratic thinking implied by the technique of association 'and assumed by most authors dealing with hypertext or hypermedia systems' to be the organizational principle behind hypertext (2000, 38) is consequently inadequate to describe Engelbart's system.

Bardini is right in one important sense: as we shall presently discover, Engelbart's system imposed a general hierarchical structure on all content. Every item had a section header, and underneath that would be some text, and underneath that some subtext; in layman's terms, the system imposed a treelike structure on all content. Though it may seem rigid and modularized at first blush, this structure provided many benefits.[4]

Bill Duvall, one of the original members of Engelbart's team at SRI, remembers the hierarchy in our interview: 'What you would call a paragraph, a "statement", was sort of the bottom node in the hierarchy. And any time a statement was changed, I think there was a change history kept on that' (2011). Not only did Engelbart want to sort and refine ideas into this shared structure; he wanted to be able to track the changes and operate upon the data. One of the most important aspects of NLS is that it allowed multiple different 'views' and ways of operating on these pieces of information:

> You could express documents as a hierarchy, and then you could, using various commands, do operations on different parts of the hierarchy. You could see, for example, all of the top-level nodes, and [with] the next level nodes you could move entire sections from one place to another. So it was basically a paradigm that enabled you to do a lot of macro-level editing. (Duvall 2011)

Although they saw the brilliance in Engelbart's system, both Nelson and van Dam saw this organizational structure as restrictive. They visited Engelbart's lab on separate occasions, but had a similar response: *That's amazing, but not how I want to do it.* As Nelson told me, when he first saw NLS he 'thought, no, that's hierarchical, I just – I don't want to do that' (Nelson 2011). Although Nelson and van Dam admired Engelbart's work, the hierarchy did not allow for the 'freewheeling' personal experience they were both after (Carmody et al. 1969, 8).

According to Nelson, the most important reason for Engelbart's imposed structure was that it facilitated collaboration. Everyone knew the order of things and worked within that structure. This was a crucial difference between NLS and Xanadu: 'The difference between Doug Engelbart and me is that he sees the world in terms of harmony, and I see it in terms of disagreement. My systems were built with the express anticipation that we would be dealing with disagreement at every level' (Nelson 2011). Engelbart's model, derived as it was from his conception of language, assumed a common stock of conceptions, a common structure radically opposed to personalized side trails. There were many reasons for this, as Bill Duvall remembered in our interview,

'not the least of which was that a lot of the work was done under government financing, and if you looked at it the structure of NLS pretty closely mapped the structure of government documents. (Duvall 2011)

An important point to remember about NLS (a point, I feel, Bardini misses) is that the linking structure was separate from the system structure. Although information was carefully articulated into headers, subheaders and statements, you could link from anywhere to anywhere. Unlike in contemporary hypertext systems (those built with HTML, for example), the links were not part of the architecture; they were a mode of transport.

According to Bill Duvall, who designed the software, the linking structure was also separable from the content: it was not embedded in the text like in HTML. 'The linking structure must have been stored separately, since the text could be processed as pure text without regard to links' (Duvall 2011). Nelson also recalls Engelbart telling him this.[5] Regardless, in NLS you could link from the bottom of the hierarchy straight to the top if you felt like doing so. The system structure was hierarchical; the linking structure, which was separate from this hierarchical system structure, was associative.[6]

As Simpson, Renear, Mylonas and van Dam (1998) put it at the 1998 Bush Symposium, 'Engelbart's theories on the nature of the human mind are a logical extension and expansion of Bush's dual vision of cognitive and associative processing.' Part of Bush's philosophy was that people should be able to tie two items together from any point in the system.

Engelbart added an extra element, however: a generalized organizational structure designed to facilitate powerful macro-editing. Perhaps, as Duvall suggests, this organizational structure was inspired by the structure of government documents. Bill English disagreed with this in our interview: 'I don't think there's anything unique about the structure of government documents' (English 2011). Engelbart suggests in his writing that it was also (at least in part) inspired by the structure of language. Wherever it came from and whatever it was inspired by, it was imposed on all content.

This structure also needed to be learned. Unlike Nelson, Bush and van Dam, Engelbart was not opposed to hierarchy and control, and he was not opposed to engineering what others might consider best left alone; this would be a controversial aspect of his system and his philosophy. NLS was a refinement of a human process: knowledge work.

> [To] externalize your thoughts in the concept structures that are meaningful outside; moving around flexibly, manipulating them and viewing them. It's a new way to operate on a new kind of externalized medium. (Engelbart 1998)

The greatest challenge an engineer can undertake is to augment or extend our capacity to externalize language like this. Engineers are also in a privileged position to be able to do it, with access to specialized techniques and discourses (Engelbart 1988, 189). But unlike Bush, Engelbart was not elitist about the discipline of engineering; he believed that other disciplines had something to contribute as well – psychology, in particular, as this discipline has deep knowledge of the human system. He would employ a psychologist at the SRI labs.

Engelbart still remembers reading about Memex (Engelbart 1999), as well as the moment when he became 'infected' with the idea of building a means to extend and navigate this great pool of human knowledge. This story is legendary now. He was a military radar technician out in the Philippines when he first picked up a reprint of Bush's article, 'As We May Think', in the summer of 1945, and wandered into a Red Cross library that was built up on stilts to read it.[7] News of Hiroshima was devastatingly fresh; Engelbart was 20 years old and deep in thought. He was wondering how he could 'maximize [his] contribution to humankind' as an engineer (Engelbart 1999). He had specialized access to a tool system and a discipline that might enable him to do this. He was thinking about whether the same set of skills that produced nuclear bombs might be used to prevent such destruction in the future.

As we have explored, in this article Bush looked towards the postwar world as an engineer and predicted an exponential increase in human knowledge, especially scientific and technological knowledge. How are we to keep track of it all?

How are we to prevent great ideas from being lost? Bush urged men of science to turn their efforts to making this great body of human knowledge more accessible. We cannot progress if we cannot keep track of where we have been.

Some ideas are like seeds. 'Or viruses. If they are in the air at the right time, they will infect exactly those people who are most susceptible to putting their lives in the idea's service' (Rheingold 1985, 176). Although he didn't think about the article again for many years, the ideas in it infected Engelbart. Shortly thereafter, he made up his mind to use his skills as an engineer to make knowledge more accessible to human individuals. It was a long trail before he actually went back to look at Bush's article – somewhere around 1961 (Engelbart 1999). Then in 1962, as this constellation of ideas was beginning to translate into a series of technical designs, Engelbart wrote a letter to Bush to thank him for the article. In it he reflected:

> I was startled to realize how much I had aligned my sights along the vector you [Bush] had described. I wouldn't be surprised at all if the reading of this article sixteen and a half years ago hadn't had a real influence upon the course of my thoughts and actions. (Engelbart 1962a, 236)

Radar Screens, Transfer and Retroactivity

But five years after he had read 'As We May Think' in the Philippines, Engelbart claims, 'I formulated [my] goal on [...] human intellectual effectiveness' (Engelbart 1962a, 236). These three 'flashes' were to become the framework he worked from for the rest of his career:

FLASH-1: The difficulty of mankind's problems was increasing at a greater rate than our ability to cope.

FLASH-2: Boosting mankind's ability to cope with complex, urgent problems would be an attractive candidate as an arena in which a young person might 'make the most difference'.

FLASH-3: Ahah-graphic vision surges forth of me sitting at a large CRT console, working in ways that are rapidly evolving in front of my eyes (beginning from memories of the radar-screen consoles I used to service). (Engelbart 1988, 189)

This vision of a radar-screen console attached to a computer is important. Engelbart transferred this technology from the radars he was servicing in the Philippines to computers as he had learnt about them in engineering school (Cathode ray tube phosphors came into common use around WWII). This image of a human sitting at a screen is the image from which all future work would depart. By the time Engelbart started work on NLS ten years later, progress had been made on 'presenting computer-stored information to the human [...] by which a cathode-ray-tube (of which the television picture tube is a familiar example) can be made to present symbols on their screens of quite good brightness, clarity, and with considerable freedom as to the form of the symbol' (Engelbart 1962b). The technology had been developed sufficiently for him to use it. In 1951, however, computers didn't have screens, so Engelbart had to mentally extrapolate from radar screens. As he told me in 1999: 'I put together what I knew about computers and what I knew about radar circuitry, etc. to picture working interactively, and it just grew from there' (Engelbart 1999).

This was a radical idea in the 1950s. At that time, computers were large electronic devices stored in air-conditioned rooms, at many degrees of separation from the 'user'. They were attended to by technicians and fed their information out to these technicians on punch cards and printouts. The results were then collected and given to the people who had requested them. The idea that a screen might be attached to a computer, and that humans might interact directly via this surface, was quite radical at the time. It would provoke lots of resistance from the engineering community.

To Engelbart, however, the idea was obvious. In fact, it was *implied* in both radar technology and in computing technology as they existed at the time. As he sees it, he was in the peculiar position of being schooled in both. He understood the way information was drawn from the innards of a computer and represented on a punched card and, similarly, how information was drawn from the innards of a radar and represented graphically in real time. The principles were the same; they just needed to be joined together. He already had an image of screen-based interactivity that outlined what such a union might look like: Memex.

Memex was the product of a different era. It was drawn from within the paradigm of analogue computing – but as we explored in Chapter 1, such images can be retroactivated: they can be taken from the past, from a different technical lineage, and 'updated' with new technology.

> Was Engelbart in fact proposing something new, or was he harking back to a technology that had already been discarded? The answer to both questions is 'Yes'. Innovation sometimes depends on revisiting previous [technologies] and employing them in new contexts. (Bardini 2000, 62)

In this book I have been arguing that innovation always depends on revisiting previous technologies and visions. For Engelbart, the benefit of a screen was that it harnessed our ability to decipher graphical symbols, an ability already finely tuned by the technology of writing. Putting a screen onto a computer was obvious. It was also closer to the image of potentiality that Memex had bequeathed him; in Memex, users sat at a screen. They didn't translate things into cryptic rows of holes on punched tape or cards:

> When I saw the connection between a cathode-ray screen, an information processor, and a medium for representing symbols to a person, it all tumbled together in about half an hour. I started sketching a system in which computers draw symbols on the screen for you, and you can steer it through different information domains [...] I was designing all kinds of things you might want to do if you had a system like the one Vannevar Bush had suggested. (Engelbart cited in Rheingold 1985, 177)

Another technology that Engelbart transferred to the design was a device based on the planimeter. The planimeter was a basic position-indicating technology used in electrical engineering the operating principle of which was based on the mechanical integrator – the wheel-and-disc technology Bush had integrated into the Analyzer. Engelbart had used them when he was at college; the Planimeter translated motion into an x-y position by drawing a curve. This technology, and the integrator behind it, would become the mouse.

> I remember sitting at some graphics conference [in 1963] and thinking 'Oh, how would you control a cursor in different ways?' I remember how my head went back to a device called the Planimeter that engineering uses. It's a little simple mechanical thing [...] I saw that used when I was a senior and I was fascinated. (Engelbart cited in Bardini 2000, 95)

The computer, screen and mouse would become Engelbart's parallel to Memex's microfilm storage desk, tablet display and stylus. With these technologies, Engelbart would 'update' an image of potentiality from a different era and bring it to digital computing.

Licklider, Engelbart and NLS

Although Engelbart felt the transition to screen-based computing was obvious, the idea that computers might be transformed from million-dollar numerical devices into workstations was far from obvious to the engineering community in the 1950s. It was also difficult for Berkeley to swallow as a doctoral thesis. 'In those days the thought of doing a Ph.D. on this, even talking about how you could manipulate symbolic logic with a computer, was just too far out to be acceptable as a thesis' (Engelbart 1999). Computer science was a subsidiary of electrical engineering, and as we have explored, this discipline emphasized practical skills; in the 1950s electrical engineering was about building machines, not speculating about human effectiveness. So he settled for 'something else' as a PhD topic and then went to SRI to pursue his original designs.

It was 1957, the year of *Sputnik*. SRI was conducting military, commercial and scientific research into computers. In our interview he told me that:

> I did a study [there] on dimensional scaling of electronic components [...] how to make things smaller and smaller. Suddenly you realize the rate at which things happen, like with a mousetrap, if you made one thousands of times smaller it would snap shut in a millionth of a second [...] What I came out of it with is an understanding that digital components would get smaller and faster and cheaper, and eventually we would have all the computing power we could want, so it's best to work out what to do with it now. (Engelbart 1999)

Working with the dimensional scaling of electronic components taught Engelbart that the power of digital computers would escalate. This drove home the urgency of creating a way for humans to harness this power. 'If we don't get proactive, the human side of [the equation] is going to always get pushed by just the technology' (Engelbart 1999). He wanted to build a laboratory at SRI filled with psychologists and computer scientists to research the new 'field' of intellectual augmentation. Initially, though, SRI was skeptical, and Engelbart was put to work in magnetics.

If the project was to have the kind of impact on the engineering community he wanted, he needed the support of his peers. Engelbart decided to write a conceptual framework for it, an agenda that the computing (and engineering) community could understand.

It was 'remarkably slow and sweaty work' (Engelbart 1988, 190), but he wrote the paper in 1962 and published it in 1963. It is interesting to note here that both Engelbart and Ted Nelson found writing difficult; they were far from prolific, and would draft and redraft multiple times. In Nelson's case this frustration was largely with the paradigm of paper, and it led him to design an alternative.[8] For Engelbart, it appears to be a frustration at expressing his ideas in a form that the computing community would understand.

He sent a version of this paper to Bush to ask for his comments and to invite him to participate, but Bush never replied personally. Titled 'A Conceptual Framework for the Augmentation of Man's Intellect' (Engelbart 1963), the paper met with much misunderstanding in the academic community and, even worse, angry silence from the computing community. It did not garner the peer support Engelbart was seeking.

At the time, he had no working prototypes, no demonstrable or working system, no work in the sense that engineers talk about work. This may have contributed to the resistance he encountered. Engelbart, however, believes that his paper failed not for lack of prototypes but because the institution of computing science at the time 'kept trying to fit [his] ideas into the existing paradigm', claiming that he should just 'join their forefront problem pursuits' and stop setting himself apart with far-flung augmentation babble (Engelbart 1988, 190). He protested that he was doing neither 'information retrieval' nor 'electrical engineering', but a new thing somewhere in between, and that it should be recognized as a new field of research. In our interview he remembered that:

> After I'd given a talk at Stanford, [three angry guys] got me later outside at a table. They said, 'All you're talking about is information retrieval.' I said no. They said, 'YES, it is, we're professionals and we know, so we're telling you don't know enough so stay out of it, 'cause goddamit, you're bollocksing it all up. You're in engineering, not information retrieval.' (Engelbart 1999)

Computers, in large part, were still seen as number crunchers, and computer engineers had no business talking about psychology and the human beings who used these machines. 'A Conceptual Framework' was a cultural as well as a technological watershed. It suggested that the inherited system of concepts, language, skills, knowledge and methods on the human side of the computer needed to be taken into account in the design. It also proposed a theory of technical evolution that put human beings in a symbiotic relationship with technology.

> By 'augmenting human intellect' we mean increasing the capability of a man to approach a complex problem situation, to gain comprehension to suit his particular needs, and to derive solutions to problems [...] [The means] to do this can include many things – all of which appear to be but extensions of means developed and used in the past to help man apply his native sensory, mental and motor capabilities, and we consider the whole system of a human and his augmentation means as a proper field of research. (Engelbart 1962b, 1–2)

This is precisely what confused the computing community: thinking about thinking was something psychologists did, not engineers.

Fortunately, one of the few people who had the disciplinary background to be able to understand the new conceptual framework was moving through the ranks at the Advanced Research Projects Agency (ARPA). This man was

J. C. R. Licklider, a psychologist from MIT. 'The hope is that, in not too many years, human brains and computing machines will be coupled together very tightly, and the resulting partnership will think as no human brain has ever thought', wrote Licklider in a 1960 paper called 'Man-Computer Symbiosis' (Licklider 1988, 131).

When Licklider came from MIT to take over ARPA's new Information Processing Techniques Office (IPTO) in 1962, he brought with him an entirely different set of skills, goals and disciplinary techniques; he was heavily involved in the field of cybernetics. In particular, he was interested in simulating the activities of the human brain in electronic machines, especially human 'perceptual mechanisms' like sight or hearing. His research specialty during WWII was psychoacoustics – working out how electronics could be used to boost an existing human faculty. Licklider was no ordinary psychologist.

In tune with cybernetic theory he envisioned the human being as a kind of complex system that processed information based on feedback from the environment (Licklider 1988, 132), and also had a theory of technical evolution that put the human in a 'symbiotic' relationship with technology, as the title of his 1960 paper indicates. One of the fundamental tenets of cybernetics as a discipline and a science was that it articulated humans and machines together, as different kinds of systems; thought was a form of information processing, and consequently it could be transferred to, or amplified by, technical artefacts.

Licklider began financing projects that developed thought-amplifying technologies. ARPA funds fostered the development in the early 1960s of timesharing computers, a concept that was distinct from the earlier batch-processing machines of the 1940s and 1950s in that processing time was divided into minute quantities and distributed among several users at once. If someone had a problem to be solved, they need not have lined up outside the lab with a box of cards to be handed to a technician and retrieved at a later date. As Andries van Dam (1997, 63) remembers it, this was 'the second period in the evolution of interfaces', and it engendered a new set of techniques and processes for working with computers. Timesharing enabled multiaccess computing, where several people in different parts of the lab or department could have access to the machine at once instead of waiting in line for the technician to perform each person's task sequentially.

ARPA support began in 1963, 'at varying levels – during 1965, about eighty thousand dollars' (Bardini 2000, 23). Engelbart's project was not heavily funded by ARPA-IPTO until 1967, after Bob Taylor had taken over direction of IPTO. At this point, the timesharing system (an SDS 940) was delivered, which changed the direction at the Augmentation Research Center (ARC) considerably.

But as Bardini points out (in his book and in a personal communication), it was Bob Taylor, initially working as a psychologist at NASA, who mustered the strongest support for the project. Initially he invested $85,000 from NASA from mid-1964 to mid-1965 (Bardini 2000, 23). Then, when he moved from NASA to ARPA in 1964, he told Engelbart that IPTO 'was prepared to contribute a million dollars initially to provide one of the new time-sharing systems, and about half a million dollars a year to support the augmentation research' (Rheingold 1985, 86). That was a lot of money in 1964.

Around this time Engelbart asked a bright young SRI engineer named Bill English if he'd present a paper for him. English accepted and joined Engelbart's project shortly thereafter. As English told me in 2011, 'I saw what he was doing and I was interested in it. So I joined him and that's how it all began' (English 2011). He became Engelbart's chief engineer in 1964, and began work on some of the basic ideas we'll explore in the next section.

Initially, Engelbart and English had rudimentary equipment. 'We had one display and a simple computer, [but] even on that simple computer you had links, you could jump to another place, it was very crude but that's where we demonstrated links' (English 2011). That was in 1965. SRI, meanwhile, began to take notice of their new million-dollar man.

Bill Duvall joined SRI in 1966, but didn't start work on the NLS project until 1968. He remembers reading about Andries van Dam's HES project at Brown around 1968 and becoming interested in hypertext as a result. He asked to be moved onto Engelbart's team, but first he had to meet with the head of engineering at SRI.

> [He] was a very traditional engineer. I was a 24-year-old kid, or 23 years old, and he had this big corner office that had bookshelves to the ceiling and the little ladder that goes around, and a big desk. He sat on the other side of his desk and I sat in a chair, and he looked at me, and he said, 'You don't really think what they're doing up there is science, do you?' I think that reflected a lot of the official attitude towards what Doug was doing. (Duvall 2011)

It would be years, 20 years in fact, before the engineering community in general would get behind Engelbart's ideas. To say that what he was doing was not viewed as 'science' may be overstating the case though; Engelbart did, after all, have some big grants under his belt and he was running a lab at a prestigious organization, so he wasn't shut out in the cold. For the moment, there was a ready supply of funds, if not peer support. There was also a technical vision that seemed *feasible* based on this setup and a group of people willing to work within Engelbart's 'conceptual framework'.

Assembling the Hardware for the NLS

The freshly outfitted laboratory, the ARC, began its work in 1965. It started with a series of experiments focused on the way people select and connect objects together across a computer screen. A section of the lab was given over to 'screen selection device' experiments, and different technologies were tested for speed and flexibility (Engelbart 1988, 195). Light pens, which were analogous to the Memex stylus, knee- or head-mounted selection devices, joysticks and the mouse were all tested (Engelbart 1988, 197). Participants selected small units of text displayed on a cathode-ray screen, and the error rate and time for each different device was recorded.

The motivation behind these experiments was Engelbart's conviction that the speed and flexibility of tools affect symbol manipulation. To all people who denied this, Engelbart provided a counterexample: he strapped a brick to a pencil and requested that people write with the assemblage. It didn't take long to discover that 'our academic work, our books – a great deal would change in our world if that's how hard it had been to write' (Engelbart 1988, 200). The technologies we interact with aren't just tools to 'express' our thought; they actively mark the limits of such thought. Each technical artefact has its own material limits and resistances, and these dictate what humans can achieve when they are connected to such artefacts. Some technical objects allow for more speed and efficiency than others, however. The material limits will be different for each technology.

Importantly, these devices did not seem 'natural' or easy to use. Technical knowledge is never natural; it only seems that way if we have already acquired the principles behind it. 'Someone can just get on a tricycle and move around, or they can learn to ride a bicycle and have more options' (Engelbart 1999; also Engelbart 1988, 200). This is Engelbart's favourite analogy. Augmentation systems must be learnt, which can be difficult; there is resistance to learning new techniques, especially if they require changes to the human system. But the extra mobility we could gain from particular technical objects and techniques makes it worthwhile.

NLS was difficult to learn. But it offered more intellectual mobility than punched cards. Engelbart found himself using the tricycle-bicycle analogy frequently because the technologies developed for NLS were new and caused a lot of argument within and outside the team, especially the concept of a hand-held screen selection device like the mouse.

> There was a lot of argument about light pens and tracking balls [...] but none of those arguments served our needs directly. I wanted to find the thing that would serve us in the context in which we wanted to work – text and structured items and interactive commands. (Engelbart 1988, 195)

Doug Engelbart circa 1967 © SRI International.

In the context of screen-based interactivity, Engelbart and English's 'mouse' consistently beat other devices for fast, accurate selection in a series of controlled tests. Yet it took over 20 years to enter the commercial market, a time period that Engelbart considers strikingly long (Engelbart 1988, 196). Given the theories of technical evolution we have been exploring here, however, this is understandable; there was neither a computing culture nor a market to support it before the Macintosh commercialized the windows-menu-mouse interface in 1984. It was not just social resistance that stalled the uptake of the mouse. The flows of capital and market conditions presented a limit to the evolution of the technology.

The first timesharing system that the lab received, in 1968, was an SDS 940. After several attempts to find a fast, well-resolved display system, they produced their own (Engelbart 1988, 197). The system shared its time among multiple 5-inch CRTs, to each of which was added a high-quality video camera. The resulting images, amplified and fed through to the lab, drove the video monitors (Engelbart 1988, 197). According to Engelbart,

Image of the mouse © SRI International.

ARC computer and screen display system 1964–1966 © SRI International.

the body of research that went into the development of this setup was as much about behavioural science as computing. The 'limits' of the system were designed to run with the limits of a human's sensory, motor and mental 'augmentation means', as Engelbart (1962b, 2) describes them. So by late 1968, the lab had a multiuser computer display system, with a keyboard and mouse for each terminal, designed to facilitate human–computer interactivity.

This constellation of machines allowed for the design and development of the system software.

Assembling the Software for the NLS

At the heart of NLS was a basic philosophy that you should be able to link to anything, anywhere ('unless there was a specific reason not to do so' (Duvall 2011)). This approach to information was entirely new – an approach that assumed from the outset that connectivity is important, that the relationship between and among ideas was just as important as the unit of information (or 'statement') itself. As Duvall remembers:

> The thing that I would say distinguished NLS from a lot of other development projects was that it was sort of the first – I'm not sure what the right word is; 'holistic' is almost a word that comes to mind – project that tried to use computers to deal with documents in a two-dimensional fashion rather than in a one-dimensional fashion. Up until that time computers had been primarily viewed as being useful for numerical analysis, limited databases and things like that. The real step forward in NLS was putting forth a contextual framework whereby you could interact with text in a two-dimensional way. (Duvall 2011)

Content insertion and navigation involved four basic commands: insert, delete, move and copy. The mouse served as a pointer to indicate where content was to be inserted or deleted in existing text. Most important, however, the link function allowed cross-referencing to another statement – and the user could define cross-references at any level in the hierarchy. Links were character strings within a statement 'indicating a relationship' (Engelbart 1999) to another statement, and they could be made in the same file or between different files. Effectively, the linking structure skipped across and between Engelbart's hierarchical system structure.

The NLS design changed as it was created, evolving around the technical activities of the project team itself as they documented their efforts. In the process of designing the software, the team generated a number of technical reports, source code versions, communications, release notes, problems and associated solutions. These were linked together and tracked by date and version.

Consequently, between 1969 and 1971 NLS was changed to include an electronic filing arrangement that served as a linked archive of the development team's efforts (Bardini 2000). This eventually cross-referenced over 100,000 items (Engelbart 1988). It was called the software Journal, the most explicit model of a hypertextual environment with embedded associative links to surface in the digital environment in the 1960s.

The software Journal emphasized interoperability between ideas generated by individual professionals, and access to a shared communication and 'thought space' on the working subject. Because it evolved around the techniques and processes of the humans who used it, it was also a primary instance of 'bootstrapping'. All pieces of information; publications written or cited in the field; and questions, diagrams and notes by participants during the project were catalogued into the Journal, and they could be retrieved and discussed on the fly.

> We had linkages and internal addressability, so an embedded link in one document could directly cite an arbitrary passage in any other. Successive documents could be entered in the system and easily be cross-referenced back to each other [...] We originally designed our Journal system to give the user a choice as to whether to make an entry unrecorded (as in current mail systems), or to be recorded in the Journal [...] I eventually ordained that all entries would be recorded – no option. (Engelbart 1988, 213)

It was the evolving memory of the development team. But, as with Engelbart's imposed filing structure, the decree that all fragments and all communications be stored within the linked file-and-directory structure of the Journal proved controversial. Some participants did not want their notes stored, their speculative jottings immortalized or their mistakes remembered; this technology had real social effects. As a result, suggests Bardini, ARC lost one of its members (who was 'violently opposed' to some of the 'basic concepts' behind the project, and believed 'Doug was way off base on some of his social ideas' (Bardini 2000, 193)).

But the Journal was not the only feature that seemed omniscient. As mentioned previously, the entire NLS system was set up for perfect storage and recall. Everything was tracked and identifiable. 'The concept is of making a permanent record [...] which then is always available' (Engelbart, in Bardini 2000, 190). In NLS, every object in the document was intrinsically addressable, and most important, these addresses never disappeared (Engelbart 1999). They were permanent, attached to the object itself, which meant that they followed the object wherever it was stored, so links could be made at any stage to any object in the system. As Duvall remembers:

> Then [in NLS] we had it that every object in the document was intrinsically addressable, right from the word 'go'. It didn't matter what date a document's development was, you could give somebody a link right into anything, so you could actually have things that point right to a character or a word or something. All that addressability in the links could also be used to pick the objects you're going to operate on when you're editing. (Duvall 2011)

The NLS team called this a 'frozen state' addressing scheme (Engelbart 1997), which is in contrast to the World Wide Web, where the finest level of intrinsic addressability is the URL (Universal Resource Locator, a character string that identifies an Internet resource, invented by Tim Berners-Lee in 1994).[9] Unlike the NLS object-specific address, the URL is simply a location on a server; it is not attached to the object itself. When the object moves, the address is outdated. You can never be sure an old link will work; on the Web, links are outdated, and information is replaced or removed daily. NLS was far more permanent. That said, it was working in its own little environment, on its own documents. As English puts it, although this addressability was powerful,

> NLS had a fairly well-defined environment in which to work, whereas the Web has to work [around the] world. In NLS you could clearly link to another document because you knew that document, you knew where it was. (English 2011)

Not only did NLS create a new form of storage and a new way of working with computers, but it created a new technical paradigm: software engineering. Programming and software engineering were not rigorous disciplines in the mid-1960s – 'talking about how symbolic logic could be manipulated on a computer' was still considered slightly wacky (Engelbart 1999). Like the technical paradigm that formed around the Analyzer, NLS created new engineering techniques. The team found that when working with software, you need version control, and especially ways of integrating different versions together. You need to 'attend' to change requests, design reports, specifications and other descriptive documents (Irby 1974, 247), and, on top of that, to compile, fix, track and problem-solve the code itself. As van Dam points out:

> [Something] most people don't know at all, even if they know something about Doug's efforts towards the augmentation of the intellect, is that he is the father of software engineering in the modern sense. Long before scientists such as Dijkstra

and Bauer started writing about formal software engineering, Doug and his crew had been living it. This really was a bootstrap community of tool builders and tool users. So on that little timesharing system they had meta-assemblers and compiler-compilers and ways of generating special-purpose problem-oriented languages. (van Dam 1988)

In a modern-day environment, software engineering is an established discipline. There are formal processes for building, breaking and testing things, and entire content management systems devoted to tracking versions, fixes and change requests. The NLS team had to learn this from the development process itself, and from the enormous quantity of code produced. NLS came in at 'about one hundred thousand instructions' and 'required the development of good software engineering practices' (Irby 1974, 247).

By 1968 NLS had matured into a massive database and set of paths through this database, the first digital hypertext system. It had successfully joined together the research and related notes from a team of researchers and made them readily accessible. It had implemented the Memex vision of associative links and trails, and fostered an entirely new way of working with this vision in the digital environment. But there was little interest in the project from outside the military; people had heard of NLS but never seen it in action. 'A few people would come and visit us, but we didn't seem to be getting the kind of general interest I was expecting', writes Engelbart (Engelbart 1988, 202).

Throughout this book I have been emphasizing the importance of working prototypes, and of people actually seeing technical solutions in action. This witnessing is fundamental to the evolution of technology. When people see a machine in action, they can visualize the future of the object and connect it with what they are doing, as well as with other machines or families of machines, which applies to engineering discourse as well. The 'main criteria applied to engineered technological solutions is that they work' (Childress 1998), or more precisely, that they are seen to work. This feature is necessary for what Simondon calls the 'inventive function of anticipation' (Simondon cited in Stiegler 1998, 81): the future of the object. The inventor is a 'combinatory' genius; selecting the best technical forms among limited combinatory possibilities – and what has been shown to work constitutes the material for transfer.

This emphasis on demos is not just historically specific to mid-twentieth-century engineering discourse, either; contemporary new media has inherited it also:

Demonstrations have had an important, perhaps even central, place in new media innovation. In some centers of new media, the traditional knowledge-work dictum of 'publish or perish' is replaced by 'demo or die'. (Wardrip-Fruin and Montfort 2003, 231)

Engelbart recognized this emphasis on working prototypes. In particular, he recognized how engineering paradigms work, and how they are moved or limited by demos and prototypes. It was time to take NLS out of the Petri dish and set it to work in front of the engineering community. Engelbart took an immense risk and applied for a special session at the ACM/IEEE-CS Fall Joint Computer Conference in San Francisco in December 1968. 'The nice people at ARPA and NASA, who were funding us, effectively had to say "Don't tell me!", because if this had flopped, we would have gotten in trouble' (Engelbart 1988, 203).

Engelbart downplays the risk. The engineering community were sceptical enough as it was: if the presentation had flopped, it would have damaged Engelbart's career (though not destroyed it – he did have a prestigious doctorate and experience running a military lab, so he would have found work somewhere). But more important, NLS would not have inspired the host of new technologies that followed directly from this conference.

Demonstration of the NLS Prototype

The conference was set up using a video projector pointing at a huge, twenty-foot screen that was linked to a host computer and piped back to the group at SRI via a temporary microwave antenna. The setup was very expensive, and although no special system capabilities were employed (NLS was run just as it was used back at the lab), the organizational and presentational machinery used almost all the remaining research funds for the year. The team was 'banking on the hope that the world would be talking about everybody starting to augment' (Engelbart 1988, 206) after the presentation. They had certainly chosen the right conference, for between 2,000 and 3,000 engineering professionals were in the audience (Bardini 2000, 142), many of them high-ranking industry representatives and academics. At the time, this was the largest computer science conference in the world.

Engelbart sat up on the stage beneath the projection screen, a mouse in one hand and his other hand playing a special one-handed keyset. He manipulated the audience's attention by controlling their view of the information being explored; he drilled down through the data structure and presented it in multiple different views, each piece connected to the last by a link. The screen was divided into neat windows containing explanatory text or graphics about NLS, and also about the presentation

San Francisco's Brooks Hall all set for the 1968 Fall Joint Computer Conference © SRI International.

itself in the hypertext Journal. A video of this demo is now available on the Web.

> One of the example tasks he demonstrated involved the creation of the presentation he was giving at the moment, from the outline of the talk to the logistics of moving their setup to the Civic Auditorium. The content of the information displayed on the screen referred to the lecture he was giving at the moment, and the lecture referred to the information on the screen – an example of the kind of self-referential procedure that programmers call 'recursion'. (Rheingold 2000, 190)

This was the first public appearance of the mouse and the first public appearance of screen splitting, computer-supported associative linking, computer conferencing and a mixed text/graphics interface. It proceeded without a hitch and received a standing ovation (Engelbart 2002).[10]

The NLS demo has subsequently entered into legend. It is remembered as computing history's 'foundational tribal tale' (Bardini 2000, 139), 'the mother of all demonstrations' (this term is attributed to Andy van Dam, who used it in a speech at the 1998 *Engelbart's Unfinished Revolution* Symposium, Session 3B), the 'demo that got everyone fired up about interactive computing' (Nielsen 1995, 37), and a 'landmark [...] in the annals of interactive computing' (Ceruzzi 1998, 260). 'If a computing Hall of Fame is ever built, Engelbart will be among the first half-dozen honorees [...] [he] demonstrated the future of interactive computing' (Segaller 1998, 125).

Many writers claim the demo actually created the paradigm of human-computer interactivity: 'the idea that the computer could become a medium to amplify man's intellect became a tangible reality for the people in Engelbart's audience' (de Landa 1994, 221). Engelbart was a 'test pilot for a new kind of vehicle that doesn't fly over geographical territory but through what was heretofore an abstraction that computer scientists called "information space"' (Rheingold 2000, 190). Engelbart's 1968 demo influenced more than just the engineers in the audience: it influenced the next generation of machines.

In the audience, Andries van Dam was 'totally bowled over' (2011) by the presentation. He had been thinking about a new version of HES for a while during 1968 because he'd 'seen its limitations and "first pancake" mistakes' (ibid.). It was immediately clear to him that NLS was a technical leap forward. In particular, van Dam saw in this demo the benefits of multiaccess computing, device independence and outline editing (van Dam 1999). These were later transferred to FRESS. One of the things he has always been 'pissed' about is that Nelson didn't tell him about Engelbart's work, even though he claimed he knew about it (van Dam 1999).

Van Dam felt an intense curiosity during the demo and went straight up to Engelbart afterwards. According to Alan Kay, van Dam proceeded to 'drill' into him; 'van Dam was as intense as Engelbart was mild mannered' (Kay cited in Markoff 2005, 158). Engelbart invited van Dam to his lab 'where I spent at least one wonderfully intense day learning about the insides of the system' (van Dam 2011). The excitement would translate into a very important technical prototype at Brown, a story we explore in Chapter 4.

As a result of this demo, many of the user interface technologies from NLS also migrated into computing over the next few years, the mouse in particular. NLS also allowed consideration of the modern windows-icon-menu-pointing-device (WIMP) interface, another major lineage extending from the demo.

Another reason that the mouse, hypertext and the WIMP interface went on to become the dominant paradigm is that some members of Engelbart's original NLS team jumped across to Xerox PARC[11] – among them Bill English, and shortly thereafter, Bill Duvall. According to Nelson, Engelbart still gets upset when he recalls the departure of English in particular: 'at a dinner a couple of years ago, Doug came to tears about how first Bill English was hired away and then the others' (Nelson 2011). The reasons for their leaving, however, were not at all straightforward.

In his book on Engelbart and the origins of personal computing, Thierry Bardini concludes that 'internal disillusionment and external disregard sealed the fate of Engelbart's vision and led to his relative failure' (Bardini 2000, 213). Bardini argues that Engelbart's staff felt frustrated that the philosophical 'crusade' had failed, and that Xerox PARC represented a new beginning with new and exciting technologies to play with – the opportunity to start afresh.

Duvall does not think, in his own case, that the decision was simple. He was reluctant to put anything on the record about the subject during our interview, but would say this:

> I think […] it wasn't just a case of people going en masse to another place, but rather it was a case of people responding to the changing focus of the group. When you the change the focus of something you want different personnel. The same people that were there last year may not be the people that will be happy there this year. (Duvall 2011)

English also felt it was time to do something different. There was not a lot going on at ARC from a technical perspective; development had finished. English felt it was 'sort of coasting'. He said in our 2011 interview:

> I think Doug wanted to move on based on his vision, based on the NLS system, on the idea of co-evolution and so forth. I felt it was time to break out of that and build independent tools.

Either way, Engelbart lost some key members of his group to Xerox PARC between 1969 and 1971, and they transferred some ideas from NLS to PARC.

NASA support ended by 1969, and although ARPA continued their support until 1977, lack of funds crippled the project. At this stage, however, commercial interest was beginning to develop, and although the team was keen to draw the project out of research and into the commercial market, the business of developing supporting applications and following 'targets organized by others' was far from Engelbart's original vector, he reflects with some regret (Engelbart 1988, 193). NLS, although designed for use by a cross-section of professional workers, needed to be maintained as a networked system by a kind of 'knowledge elite who learned complex and difficult languages' to operate it (Rheingold 2000, 201). Corporations who were interested in 'augmenting' did not wish to hire a small army of system operators, and were interested in but a few of NLS's functions.

ARPA support continued to dwindle, and SRI sold the entire augmentation system to Tymshare Corporation in 1977. The system, named 'Augment', was marketed as a package by Tymshare and adapted to the business environment through the early 1980s. Tymshare was acquired by McDonnell-Douglas in 1984, and the Augment project took a back seat to their larger office automation project – a project that in turn languished along with the company's focus on office software. NLS faded 'like the images on the surface of a stream into which a stone had been cast' (Coleridge cited in Nelson 1987, 142). Like Bush's Memex, NLS was consigned to the annals of computing history.

What We Have Inherited: NLS, Vision and Loss

Fifty years later, Engelbart soldiers on, trying to rally us to the highest cause, trying to boost our collective IQ. He imagines that we will one day have a 'global augmentation system', that we will learn to harness this structure that makes us human, and that this is just a matter of pursuing the right tool system (Engelbart 1999). With his daughters he now runs the Doug Engelbart Institute in Fremont, California, an organization he founded to continue evolving the relationship between humans and computers. Ever the visionary, 'Doug […] slog[s] on, ideals held high above the mud' (Nelson 1999a).

> We're trying to tell the world that an improvement infrastructure is something every organism has, every society has. So people need to start thinking about this on a national scale. Every nation needs to […] augment it as much as possible, and then, since countries have to do things together, we need to have a global sense of that. That's the challenge, it always has been, boosting our collective IQ. (Engelbart 1999)

Why has this grand challenge, this grand vision, translated differently qua technical artefact? Or perhaps more deeply, why did Engelbart's project fizzle out? He has not yet realized his vision. In his book, Bardini argues that, for NLS at least, Engelbart thought he had done his work with the tool system after the late 1960s and moved on to work with the 'human system' (2000). His team, however, became disillusioned with the vision and the new direction, and some of them migrated to PARC. However you slice it, NLS was no longer in serious use by the mid-1970s. The ideas, however, migrated to PARC and influenced all future hypertext systems.

The premature death of a technical project like this is not uncommon. We will see it again in Ted Nelson's legendary project, Xanadu, and we saw it in Memex's failure to translate into technical vision. These visionary systems failed at different times and for different reasons, and we have inherited different aspects of their techniques, ideas and designs. But the charge of failure qua realization of technical vision, however partial or incomplete, recurs as a motif in the evolution of hypertext, as does the dream of a perfect archive for human knowledge. A certain circularity seems to be at play.

> Perhaps the problem lies not in our technologies or the things we want to do with them, but our misunderstanding of technological history. [We] keep saying [...] that we need a revolution; an apocalyptic rupture or 'blessed break' as Robert Lowell once put it. And yet that is not what we have received, at least so far. Maybe we suffer this disappointment because we do not know what we are asking for. (Moulthrop 1991, 693)

Perhaps we are asking for something that cannot be attained. Technical visions have no essence; there is no transcendent design, no Platonic form we are striving towards. There is, however, a recurrent dream – an elusive 'blessed break' – and this dream is an ancient one. It comes from long-standing cultural desires and anxieties about the ephemerality of human knowledge. The dream is to create the perfect archive, a machine that might 'extend, through replication, human mental experience' (Nyce and Kahn 1991, 124) and capture the interconnected structure of knowledge itself. Most important, this would be a machine that we can control, whose workings are transparent to us and whose trails do not fade. Which brings us to the next chapter – my favorite chapter and the heart of this book: the Magical Place of Literary Memory, Xanadu.

Chapter 4

THE MAGICAL PLACE OF LITERARY
MEMORY: XANADU

*What I thought would be called Xanadu is called the World Wide Web and works differently,
but has the same penetration.*

—Ted Nelson, 1999

It was a vision in a dream. A computer filing system that would store and deliver the great body of human literature, in all its historical versions and with all its messy interconnections, acknowledging authorship, ownership, quotation and linkage. Like the Web, but much better: no links would ever be broken, no documents would ever be lost, and copyright and ownership would be scrupulously preserved. The Magical Place of Literary Memory: Xanadu. In this place, users would be able to mark and annotate any document, see and intercompare versions of documents side by side, follow visible hyperlinks from both ends ('two-way links') and reuse content pieces that stay connected to their original source document. There would be multiple ways to view all this on a computer screen, but the canonical view would be side-by-side parallel strips with visible connections ('visible beams'). Just imagine. This vision – which is actually older than the Web, and aspects of it are older than personal computing – belongs to hypertext pioneer Theodor Holm Nelson, who dubbed the project Xanadu in October 1966.[1]

The name comes from the famous poem by Samuel Taylor Coleridge, 'Kubla Khan'. In his tale of the poem's origin, Coleridge claimed to have woken from a laudanum-laced reverie with 'two or three hundred' lines of poetry in his head. He had noted down but a few lines when he was interrupted by a visitor, and when he returned to his work later he found that the memories had blurred irretrievably. His mythical landscape, this vision of Xanadu, had passed away 'like the images on the surface of a stream into which a stone had been cast' (Coleridge cited in Nelson 1987, 142). Like Nelson, Coleridge feared the despotism of the senses and the confusion of senseless memory;

he feared memory loss. In an introduction to the poem cited by Nelson, Coleridge writes of his muddled visions:

> Then all the charm
> Is broken – all that phantom world so fair,
> Vanishes and a thousand circlets spread,
> And each mis-shape the other.
> (Coleridge cited in Nelson 1987, 142)

One of Nelson's most cherished memories is also based on a vision of gently moving water. When he was about four or five he trailed his hand in the water as his grandfather rowed a boat. He studied the different 'places' in the water as they passed through his fingers, the 'places that at one instant were next to each other, then separated as my finger passed. They rejoined, but no longer in the same way' (Nelson 2010c, 35). These connections were infinite in number and in complexity, and they changed as the water moved. It was a religious experience, a vision that has stayed with him for 70 years. At that moment he started thinking about what he calls 'profuse connection', the interconnections that permeate life and thought. How can one manage all the changing relationships? How can one represent profuse connection? Xanadu was meant to channel this temporal flow, to represent complexity, at the same time preserving the interconnections that held it together. The issue was always about structure; build it right and small, and it will become vast ('or even build it WRONG and small, like the World Wide Web', Nelson quips (2012)). Current tools cannot represent the tangle of the real world and its burgeoning mass of information; we need an alternative paradigm. The computer world could be so much better.

Like Vannevar Bush and Douglas Engelbart (a close friend), Nelson also has a theory about the inheritance and transmission of human knowledge. The knowledge that we pass on to each other is itself a vast, intertwingled (a term Nelson coined) network, an accumulation of different disciplines and fields of knowledge, 'a corpus of all fields' (Nelson 1965, 145). This corpus is constantly shifting and changing; like biological life, it is evolving. It is a 'bundle of relationships subject to all kinds of twists, inversions, involutions and rearrangement: these changes are frequent but unpredictable' (Nelson 1965, 145). If we wish to preserve human knowledge, then we need to understand how it works and preserve its structure. We need to maintain the interconnections, the original paths or trails through ideas, because:

> Thoughts and minds themselves, of course, do not last [...] 'Knowledge', then – and indeed most of our civilization and what remains of those previous – is a

vasty [*sic*] cross-tangle of ideas and evidential materials, not a pyramid of truth. So that preserving its structure, and improving its accessibility, is important to us all. (Nelson 1987, 157)

Xanadu was proposed as a vast digital network to house this corpus of ideas and evidential materials, facilitated by a special linking system. The linking system would be based on 'the fluidity of thought – not just its crystallized and static form, which, like water's, is hard and cold and goes nowhere' (Nelson 1993, 1/13).[2] He wanted this system to stretch around the planet, embracing all our stray works of literature and scholarship, all the information that would otherwise be lost to us. He saw this as the 'manifest destiny of literature' (Nelson 2010c, 111). Xanadu is a case study in Derrida's will to totality. It would be a mini-universe of words that remember where they have been and where they might yet be: the 'Pleasure Dome of the creative writer' (Nelson 1987, 141).

The story of Xanadu is the greatest image of potentiality in the evolution of hypertext. Nelson invented a new vocabulary to describe his vision, much of which has become integrated into contemporary hypermedia theory and practice – for instance, the words 'hypertext' and 'hypermedia'. As he told me in 1999, 'I think I've put more words in the dictionary than Lewis Carroll. Every significant change in an idea means a new term.' Nelson came up with many significant changes, and consequently many new terms, some of which I discuss below. He also recruited or inspired some of the most visionary programmers and developers in the history of computing, many of whom went on to develop the first hypertext products (although this doesn't impress him: 'the problem with inspiring people is that they then try to credit you with things you don't like' (Nelson 2011)). His writings and presentations concerning the 'digital repository scheme for worldwide electronic publishing' (Nelson 1993, 3/2) have been plundered by theorists and practitioners the world over. Media opinion, however, is divided: 'Boon or boondoggle, nobody is quite sure', as the *Economist* put it (cited in Nelson 1993, preface).

I explore in more depth in this chapter the evolution of the Xanadu design and the ideas behind it. For now, I wish to emphasize this mythical dimension to Xanadu. Though Nelson does not like the word 'mythical' as it implies the project is imaginary, it must be said that Project Xanadu has been under development for 50 years and has never been completed. Nelson has, however, released numerous products along the way – including the multidimensional organizing system ZigZag (1996), and more recently XanaduSpace (2007), a system for working with parallel documents (both are available for download on the Web). Neither of these applications are globe-spanning archives or publishing systems, however.

Like Bush's Memex, Xanadu has become the stuff of legend within the hypertext community, largely due to the inspired writings of its creator and the lack of a complete prototype. But unlike Bush's Memex, which existed entirely on paper, there have been numerous attempts to create the design as Nelson described it, none of which have realized this colossal vision. Like a spectre of the future, all we have of Xanadu is its simulacrum, its ideals, its ideas – and some tantalizing shells of code. To Nelson's dismay, Xanadu has (unfairly) been hailed as 'the longest-running vaporware project in the history of computing' (Wolf 1995, 1).[3] This is unfair because Nelson has actually produced a number of deliverables along the way, if not Xanadu itself. This will be explained in more detail later.

To complicate matters, the code behind Xanadu has been in a state of perpetual rewrite for decades.[4] This technical evanescence makes it a difficult subject to write about. I have chosen to divide this chapter into two main parts. The first is the evolution of the vision, which is not at all straightforward; the second is an explanation of the Xanadu system itself – its technical design, the criticism of this design and the attempts to build it. A simple explanation of the Xanadu system is long overdue, as anyone who has tried to navigate the developer forums (or Nelson's prescient but stubbornly nonlinear books) can attest. I wrote this chapter after interviewing Nelson in Japan over a two-day period in 1999 and again in Melbourne in 2011. The interesting part of the explanatory section is how far it departs from the first. The issue is not that Xanadu has failed as vision (it captured the imagination of a whole generation of developers), but that the vision has failed to realize itself qua technical artefact.

Much has been written about Project Xanadu over the years. Nelson himself doesn't have the time to keep up with it all – and even when he does, as he put it to me in 2010, 'anything people write about me will be insufficiently praising, and so it's very hard to read it' (his comments on this current chapter were prolific). This chapter is not an attempt to write a linear, causally linked history; interested readers can find that story elsewhere.[5] It is also not the story of Ted Nelson's life. He published his autobiography, *Possiplex*, in 2010. I am interested in Nelson's vision and the impact of that vision. The remarkable thing about Xanadu is that, despite countless setbacks, it refuses to die. Its logo is, appropriately enough, the Eternal Flaming X. Paisley and Butler (cited in Smith 1991, 262) have noted that 'scientists and technologists are guided by "images of potentiality" – the untested theories, unanswered questions and unbuilt devices that they view as their agenda for five years, ten years, and longer.' Nelson is often accused of hand waving and lucid dreaming, but Xanadu has nonetheless become the most important vision in the history of computing.

Ted Nelson at Keio University, Japan 1999. Photo © Belinda Barnet.

Ideas and Their Interconnections: The Evolution of the Idea

People ask me why I carry a stapler. The answer is to attach pieces of paper to each other. Such an archaic concept. Photographers carry cameras, gunfighters carry guns: I CONNECT THINGS! [...] The problem with paper is that every sentence wants to break out and slither in some other direction, but the confines of the page forbid us to. So that if the page could sprout wings, or sprout tunnels off to the side, the parenthesis, instead of having to stop after some point, could go on forever. (Nelson 1999a)

Nelson wears a lanyard across his neck and shoulder with three pens attached to it (when I first met him in 1999 it had sticky notes, at another point a stapler – the 'system is evolving' as he put it in a personal communication, 2012). He has been wearing it since 1997. The belt is filled with tools to connect things with, tools to deal with a world of paper. Like Bush, Nelson is painfully aware that ideas are easily lost in conventional indexing systems, that they are disconnected from each other and that 'serious writing or research' demands connecting ideas together. Frustrated by the lack of a global, real-world system that might do this for him, and 'outraged' by the confines of paper (Nelson 1999b, 1–2), he feels the need to do this manually.

As Nelson talks, he frequently stops to note ideas down in a Filofax-compatible notebook.[6] Later he will clean up these notes and transfer them to storage. His personal archive is legendary; it constitutes several massive storage containers that house notes and items dating right back to the origins of personal computing. He is correct that this collection will one day prove useful for scholars (I would love to get my hands on it), but at the moment it is impenetrable. His records have been accumulating, without any indexing system, since 1951.[7] He is waiting for Xanadu.

Nelson uses several different filing formats, and changes between them depending on the situation.[8] 'Loose sheets, large spiral-bound notebooks, bound notebooks sold at stationery stores […] Filofax is a lot of trouble but then so is everything else', as he put it to me in 2012. He has been experimenting with different formats for many years:

> I was continually trying different systems for organizing ideas. File cards […] were clearly hopeless. I tried index tabbing, needlesort cards, making multiple carbons and cutting them up. None of these solved the basic problem: an idea needed to be in several places at once […] But then, in graduate school, I took a computer course. (Nelson 1993, 1/24)

Nelson's struggle against the paradigm of paper led him to design an alternative. In 1960, at Harvard University, he took a computer course for the humanities, 'and my world exploded' (Nelson 2010c, 99). He understood immediately that computers were all-purpose machines that could be put in the service of information handling. Like Engelbart, he did not believe that computers were mathematical tools for engineers. He saw a solution to his problem of information handling, and he also saw a future where paper might be eliminated. 'The prison of paper, enforcing sequence and rectangularity, had been the enemy of authors and editors for thousands of years; now at last we could break free' (Nelson 2010c, 120). In his autobiography, he details the cavalcade of ideas that came to him at this point.

One of the first ideas was based on his own 'terrible problem' keeping notes on file cards.[9] The problem was that his cards really needed to be in several different places at once; new projects were built on earlier ideas, new documents were built on earlier ideas, so these items should be reusable by reference. As Nelson puts it, the ideas and insights 'came out of my life and I wanted them linked back to those original contexts' (2012). Perhaps the computer might solve that problem; it could link them together. This idea would later prove important in the design of Xanadu:

> Many of my file cards belonged in several places at once – several different sequences or projects. Each card – call it now an entry or an item – should be stored only once. Then each project or sequence would be a list of those items. (Nelson 2010c, 103)

Imagine if the same item could appear in multiple places. You could connect each item to its original by an addressing method and retrieve them on a computer screen. Because this would be reuse by reference rather than by copying, you could trace each item back to its original source. This idea – that you should be able to see all the contexts of reuse, and that you should be able to trace items back to their original source – would 'drive my work to the edge of madness' (Nelson 2010c, 104). It would later become the kernel of Nelson's most innovative idea: transclusion.[10] Transclusion, and also the ability to visually compare prior or alternative versions of the same document on screen ('intercomparison') were integral to the design of Xanadu. Over the next 40 years, Nelson would hone these ideas and experiment with them in various incarnations.

In 1960 Nelson announced his term project: a writing system for the IBM 7090, the only computer at Harvard at the time, stored in a big, air-conditioned room at the Smithsonian Observatory. In the 1960s computers were 'possessed only by huge organizations to be used for corporate tasks or intricate scientific calculations' (Nelson 1965, 135). The idea that expensive processing time might be wasted on writing, of all things, was deemed crazy by the engineering community. Nelson ignored this. He proposed a machine-language program to store documents in the computer, change them on-screen with various editorial operations, and print them out. But this was no mere word processor (which in any case didn't exist at the time); Nelson envisioned the user would be able to compare alternative and prior versions of the same document on-screen. Computers should be able to support the history of our ideas, and comparison between them. A writer should be able to cast her eye back over previous versions of the same document, discern the evolution of her ideas and recover old sections and paragraphs if necessary. This is why computers were better than typewriters, better than paper; they had an unlimited memory.

The second part of Nelson's idea took shape in the early 1960s, when there was 'a lot of talk around Cambridge [Massachusetts, where Harvard is located] about Computer-Assisted Instruction, for which there was a lot of money' (Nelson 1993, 1/26). It was not so much a design at this point, Nelson stressed in response to my request for documents from the time, 'it was an idea that may have been on only one file card' (Nelson 2012). At this time he conceived of what he called 'the thousand theories program', an explorable computer-assisted instruction program that would allow the user to study different theories and subjects by taking different trajectories through a network of information. 'This idea rather quickly became what I would eventually call hypertext' (1993, 1/26) – although the term was not actually published until 1965. He thought of this system as incorporating many separate, modularized paragraphs, each with branching choices: writing as a tree diagram, not a single line or sequence. Ideas, Nelson maintained, are inherently diagrammatic, not syllogistic. We think in terms of objects, and the connections between them (Nelson 1999a). Nelson believed that computers should be able to support human thought in this way.

This belief led to another idea, which Nelson drafted as an academic paper while teaching sociology at Vassar College in 1965. He wants to stress at this point that there was no single eureka moment as 'the ever-changing designs had been swirling in my head for five years' (Nelson 2012). The concept was clear enough, however, to put it down on paper and publish it for the first time. This revised design combined two key ideas: side-by-side intercomparison and the reuse of elements (transclusion). He thought about the architecture of the system and decided to have sequences of information that could be linked sideways. As with his first design, this would all occur on a computer screen, visually, in real time. He called this system 'zippered lists'.

Zippered lists permitted linking between documents: like the teeth in a zipper, items in one sequence could become part of another ('EXCEPT', Nelson wrote in response to this chapter in 2012, 'the two sides of the zipper don't have to be in the same order'). Versions of a document could be intercompared; an item could be an important heading in one sequence and a trivial point in another, and all items could be written or retrieved in a nonsequential fashion. Links could be made between large sections, small sections or single paragraphs. Links could be made between different versions of the same thing. Most important, however, chronological stages and sections in a document could be retrieved and compared. Writers could trace the evolution of an idea.

Again, the important thing about this design was that it exploited the storage and display facilities of a computer. This kind of writing simply could not be done on paper, which is so clumsy by comparison, and so limited in its storage capacity (Nelson 1965, 98). This system was called the Evolutionary List File (ELF). In his autobiography, Nelson reflects that the ELF design was 'strange and hard to understand. In fact, it was quite bad' (Nelson 2010c, 151). It did, however, include facilities to compare versions of a document and reuse elements from these versions. Both of these ideas would make their way into Xanadu in some form, but the zippered list in particular would eventuate in a 'deliverable' 30 years later ZigZag.

> The zippered list essentially became ZigZag, and the transclusion relationship
> which comes up as an equals sign [in the diagram in that paper] is essentially the
> xanological transclusion. (Nelson 2010c)

VASSAR COLLEGE

January 5, 1965

TO: Members of the College Community
FROM: Faculty Science Club
SUBJECT: Lecture on Computers by Theodor Nelson,
           Instructor in Sociology
           8:00 p.m. Wednesday, January 27 - The Aula

The Faculty Science Club is pleased to sponsor the talk described
below for the benefit of all members of the College community
interested in learning more about uses of the computer in the
academic environment.

COMPUTERS, CREATIVITY, AND THE NATURE OF THE WRITTEN WORD

No special background is necessary to understand this; indeed,
"special" background may well be detrimental.

Everybody's misimpression of electronic computers -- a misimpression peculiarly acute among "computer people" -- continues
to restrict the general use of computers to essentially
numerical tasks. Inherently these machines have far broader
capacities; the limits are not of technology, but of imagination.

This talk will first describe the structure and generality of
the stored-program digital computer. The computer is NOT
mathematical: if it is the most perfect adding machine, it is
also the most perfect typewriter, electric train control,
filing cabinet, movie projector, and musical instrument. But
whole new attitudes will be needed, and liberal-arts personages
will have to learn to program, before computers can make their
real contribution to civilization.

The speaker will describe his own experiments in this direction --
trying to build "systems" for the handling of creative (and
academic) materials -- ideas, words, and other things. A
succession of approaches, and their increasing generality, will
be explained.

The philosophic consequences of all this are very grave. Our
concepts of "reading", "writing", and "book" fall apart, and
we are challenged to design "hyperfiles" and write "hypertexts"
that may have more teaching power than anything that could
ever be printed on paper.

Please feel free to invite any interested students.

                            Sue Lumb, President
                   Robert Rehwold, Vice-President
                        Stanley Novak, Secretary

Vassar College Lecture Invitation, 1965. This was the first time Nelson's word hypertext (or 'hypertexts') appeared in public. Thanks to Ted Nelson for permission to republish.

Crucially, the design also got him published. The word 'hypertext' appeared in print for the first time in 1965 after Nelson presented the concept at two conferences. Early in the year he gave a paper at the World Documentation Federation Conference (abbreviated as FID) called 'The Hypertext', but Nelson recalls the crowd was small and it didn't have much of an impact. He gave another one at the ACM 20th National Conference in August of 1965, this time to a larger crowd.[11] He recalls that FID proceedings came out a few weeks before the ACM presentation, so that was the first time the word 'hypertext' appeared in print.

It was not the first time that the word 'hypertext' had appeared in public, though. That was in an invitation to a talk Nelson gave at Vassar College, 'Computers, Creativity and the Nature of the Written Word', on 5th of January 1965 (actually it's the word 'hypertexts'). This was only a mimeograph, though, not a publication – as Nelson pointed out to the author (2012).

The ACM paper was his first paper explaining the term, however, and he thinks most of the computer scientists in the world at that time were in the audience (Nelson 2010c, 153). This paper, entitled 'A File Structure for the Complex, the Changing and the Indeterminate', described a type of computer-supported writing system that would allow for branching, linking and responding text. The system would be composed of either 'written or pictorial material', and its defining feature is that the information would be 'interconnected in such a complex way that it could not be conveniently presented or represented on paper' (Nelson 1965, 96). This idea, that hypertext cannot be printed, would stay with Nelson. Also in the mid-1960s, Nelson coined the terms 'hypermedia' and 'hyperfilm' – terms that employed the same ideas behind hypertext and were meant to encompass image and film. The concept of hypertext was never meant to be restricted to just text.

Contrary to modern use of the word 'hypertext' to refer to networked text (see for example Delaney and Landow 1995, 7; Stefik 1997, 21),

> Nelson always meant 'hypermedia' when he said 'hypertext'. It's one of the things that people get wrong about Nelson. They think that they've invented hypermedia and he only invented hypertext. He meant 'text' in the sense of corpus, not text in the sense of characters. I know this for a fact because we've talked about it many times. (van Dam 1999)

Nelson tends to think in many different media and directions at once. Distinguishing between image, text and sound is pointless in a digital environment. This 'new form of computer-supported writing', Nelson wrote in 1965, will organize and represent 'all our complex informational arrangements' (Nelson 1965, 144). It will contain whatever we want it to contain, stem the loss of great ideas and preserve all the interconnections. But most importantly, it will preserve all the different stages in an idea's evolution. These stages are usually lost or discarded in codex filing systems.

> The physical universe is not all that decays. So do abstractions and categories. Human ideas, science, scholarship and language are constantly collapsing and unfolding [...] I believe that such a system as the ELF ties in better than anything previously used with the actual processes by which thought is progressively organized. (Nelson 1965, 97)

Like Vannevar Bush before him, Nelson seeks a defense against loss – in particular, information loss. We are what we can remember, and we remember best when information is appropriately organized. As Bush wrote in the early 1930s, so Nelson believes that traditional methods of archiving, storage and retrieval are inadequate to deal with complex data. All methods of paper impose connective restrictions that mask the true structure of ideas. The benefit of a global hypertext system would be 'psychological, not technical' (Nelson 1965, 145), and its creation is of the utmost importance. Like Bush and Engelbart,

Nelson feels a great sense of urgency about this. We are 'trapped' in the wrong paradigm – codex culture – which is not the way the mind works (Nelson 1993, 321). We need a new paradigm, and we need it soon. 'We will have to stop reading from paper. We can no longer find what we need in an increasingly fragmented world of information' (Nelson 1967, 23).

Interestingly, a number of hypermedia and web-based systems have appeared in university computer labs over the past twenty years that claim to provide historical backtrack. They also claim that the problem with the computer world is that it doesn't accommodate the dimension of time, because it is caught in the 'paradigm drag' of paper:

> One more operation that isn't possible in the world of paper but might be useful if you could get it is 'time travel' – restoring some particular context from the past [...] Our candidate for replacing the desktop is Lifestreams. In Lifestreams [...] every document you've ever created or received stretches before you in a time-ordered stream, reaching from right now back to the day you were born. You can sit down and watch new documents arrive: they're plunked at the head of the stream. (Gelernter cited in Steinberg 1997)

Oddly, Gelernter contrasts this architecture to Xanadu, which he told *Wired* is just about 'documents organized in relation to other documents by means of links' (ibid.).[12] Contra Gelernter, Xanadu has always been about cycling through time, treating documents as evolving versions. Lifestreams (Yale University), Posterous and Sweetcron (lifestream blogging software), Shipman and Marshall's Visual Knowledge Builder (or VKB, which was influenced by Xanadu) and Linda (Scientific Computing Associates) are all contemporary systems that embody historical backtracking in some form.

As I explain over the next few pages, many of Nelson's early ideas have recently been built, often without recourse or reference to Nelson's work in the area (with the exception of VKB, which does acknowledge Nelson's influence). We might go so far as to say that the dream of a universal digital archive and publishing system originated with Nelson; Bush built analogue machines.[13] Nelson has also managed to articulate this dream in an infectious fashion, tailored to the digital era.

The key ideas that had made their way into Nelson's vision by 1965 (Nelson maintains these were present for him by 1960, and merely published in 1965) were historical backtracking, links and transclusion. He did not use the term 'transclusion' in print, however, until he published *Literary Machines* in 1980 (I refer to a 1993 reprint here, which is not exactly the same as the original).[14] The link, as Nelson saw it, would instantly take the user from one place to another, and that place would contain the excess, the overflow, the past or future of the previous idea. Unlike writing on paper, the link would consequently allow for a natural sequence of ideas, like thought itself. Links as Nelson saw them were deeply tied to sequence: ideas are only meaningful in relation to where they have been and where they might yet be. Navigation is pointless unless we remember where we have been. The link is central to the concept of hypertext, and according to Nelson, this facility makes writing in hypertext different from writing on paper.

Nelson's next job, in 1966, was at a publishing house. Here he chose to rename his design 'Xanadu', for its connotations in literary circles.

> As the mysterious palace in Coleridge's poem 'Kubla Khan' – a great poem which he claimed to have mostly forgotten before he could write it down – Xanadu seemed the perfect name for a magical place of literary memory. (Nelson 1993, 1/30)

Nelson responds angrily to suggestions that Xanadu is an impossible dream, but in selecting this name, he at least admits the irony. 'Kubla Khan' is the Romantic era's most famous unfinished poem; had Coleridge not been disturbed by an anonymous visitor, it would have been an epic masterpiece. Orson Welles (whom Nelson identifies as one of his 'big three' heroes (Nelson 2010c, 360)) used the word 'Xanadu' for *Citizen Kane*'s extravagant, uncompleted mansion. The tantalizing but unrealized potential of this literary work permeates its memory, much like Xanadu's unrealized potential.

It also permeates Nelson's memory. He is filled with a deep regret about his life and the failure of his vision: 'I see today's computer world, and the Web, as resulting from my failure' (Nelson 2011). Although people were and still are inspired by his design, like Coleridge's 'Kubla Khan', it exists *in potentia*. Everyone from Stewart Brand to Alan Kay seems to have been 'inspired' by Nelson, but nobody has built the design exactly as he wants it. 'Nobody is building my/our design! They are building things vaguely like hearsay about the design!' (Nelson 2012).

One of the first people who thought they might try to build *part* of Nelson's design was Andries van Dam (I stress 'part' here because van Dam had ideas of his own that he wanted to explore at the same time, such as print text editing). In 1967 van Dam bumped into Nelson at a conference, and Nelson promptly told him about hypertext. They already knew each other; they had both attended Swarthmore, a private liberal arts college. This encounter inspired van Dam to build the Hypertext Editing System (HES) at Brown University, which was intended to 'explore this hypertext concept' (van Dam 1988). Nelson went to Brown at his own expense to consult in its development, but he found the experience deeply frustrating. He argued for the elaboration of HES's hypertext features, but he believes that HES emphasized paper printout and formatting to the neglect of online reading and writing. Nelson wanted true hypertext, which cannot be printed. As he sees it,

> This very, very clearly led to today's web [...] They left out transclusion, left out multiple windows [...] This trivialization became people's notion of hypertext. (Nelson 1999a)

We explore this issue further in the next chapter. For now, it is enough to note that HES did not fulfil Nelson's vision.

Not to be deterred, he looked around for work in the computer field. He wanted recognition from the computing community (he had already published three papers in the field), but came up against the dominant paradigm at the time: computers are calculating machines. Nelson is a self-described liberal arts type rather than an engineering type – a dichotomy he deplores as it kept him 'away from computing for so long' (Nelson 1987, 25).[15] As Engelbart discovered in the late 1960s, if you tried to talk about interactive computing, the engineering community dismissed it as babble about the human side of things.

Engelbart gives equal credit to Nelson for discovering the link. They were both working on similar ideas at the same time, Engelbart told me in 1999, but he had the facilities and funding to build a machine that demonstrated those ideas (Engelbart 1999). As an engineer Engelbart was more concerned with constructing the tool system than theorizing it, more aware of how ideas will change qua technical artefact. For this reason, Engelbart had more basis for conversation with the computer mainstream than Nelson did. The computing community has always wanted deliverables; writing papers is something humanists do (Nelson notes at this point 'so do computer people. But I learned they just go for check-marks on the road to tenure, but don't get you a job or backing' (Nelson 2012)). At the Fall Joint Computer Conference in

Nelson in Melbourne, 2010. Photo © Belinda Barnet.

1968 Engelbart actually showed the world what text on computers would look like, and how links could facilitate such a system. Due to this work, Engelbart is finally getting the credit he deserves, but discussion of Xanadu still positions it in left field.

Nelson was inspired by Engelbart upon first meeting him, though Nelson did not like the 'hierarchical' structure of Engelbart's system. He dedicated his book on Xanadu, *Literary Machines*, to this 'visionary of The Augmentation of Human Intellect [...] and (what this book is largely about) THE TEXT LINK' (Nelson 1993). In our interview, Nelson singled out Engelbart as an inspiration in the early years. As Nelson sees it, they shared an original vision: to construct a digital network that utilized the computer not as a calculating machine, but as a machine to boost human thought – or as Nelson puts it in *Computer Lib* (1987), a 'thinkertoy'. Nelson had also been thinking about incorporating a pointing device of some kind for several years before he saw NLS, but the 'mouse thing' immediately made sense when he saw it in action:

> I visited Doug in the Spring of 1967 because we talked about my coming out to work for him. Two things on that trip. Well several, one was – I loved the guy of course, everybody does, and I saw the mouse. Up till then I thought it would be light pens, well obviously the mouse thing worked better. (Nelson 1999a, 2)[16]

The mouse was not the only thing that obviously worked. NLS embodied some of the proposed features of Xanadu by 1968. The ability of the user to link, revise and window documents in real time across the screen was a strong similarity, as was the idea that a system might be able to preserve and track changes. As Engelbart wrote in 1963 of the 'hypothetical writing machine' that was to become NLS:

> Trial drafts can rapidly be composed from rearranged excerpts of old drafts, together with new words or passages which you insert by typing. Your first draft may represent a free outpouring of thoughts in any order, with the inspection of foregoing thoughts continuously stimulating new considerations and ideas to be entered. If the tangle of thoughts represented by the draft becomes too complex, you can compile a reordered draft quickly. (Engelbart 1963, 6–7)

With screen-based computing and historical backtrack, this paragraph could have been an excerpt from Nelson's 1965 paper:

> [The idea of links in NLS was] by no means new. To go back only as far as 1945, Vannevar Bush, in his famous article 'As We May Think' describes a system of this type [...] Bush stressed his file's ability to store related materials in associative trails, lists or chains of documents stored together. (Nelson 1965, 135)

By 1970, in both NLS and in the proposed Xanadu system, the user would point a mouse at links in the document and bring the appended reference to the screen. Information was stored and retrieved based on a networked structure (for Engelbart, this structure was a public, hierarchical web; for Nelson it would be more unrestricted and personal). Nelson built this concept around the academic reference and incorporated the mouse from NLS. As explained earlier, Engelbart claims the idea of links and trails came from Memex.

Nelson did not stay to work for Engelbart in 1967, though Engelbart 'half-invited' him. Nelson asked for a job, and 'Doug said, "Well, we need a programmer right now"' (Nelson 2010c). Nelson considered this for a moment and then declined. He didn't think he could teach himself to program quickly enough. Also, at a deeper level he felt that NLS, though brilliant at what it did, was too hierarchical.

> I did not see the opportunity of working with Doug because I thought, no, that's hierarchical, I just – I don't want to do that [...] And obviously if I joined that project I'd be living in that paradigm. (Nelson 2010c)

NLS also had fixed-length character limits on all its statements, which was anathema to Nelson. These differences did, however, have a purpose. NLS was designed to boost work groups and make them smarter; it evolved around the technical activities of a group of engineers. For this reason, NLS emphasized keyboard commands, workflow and journaling. Xanadu was intended, like Bush's Memex, to be a very personalized system – to empower the individual. Xanadu would 'free the individual from group obtuseness and impediment' so that they could 'follow their interests or current line of thought in a way heretofore considered impossible' (Nelson 1993, 0/3). To Nelson, links were not just part of an augmentation toolbox; they were the essence of a revolution – an ideological revolution. Literature need no longer be linear. We don't have to read the same books in the same order. We don't have to learn at someone else's pace and in someone else's direction. Hypertext furnishes the individual with choices: 'YOU GET THE PART YOU WANT WHEN YOU ASK FOR IT' (Nelson 1993, 2/16).

This aspect of Nelson's vision cannot be ignored. Xanadu was (and still is) personal in the most libertarian, 1960s Californian sense. Links, Nelson maintains, furnish the individual with choices, with the right to choose. Nelson engaged in a rhetoric of liberation about hypertext well before George Landow discovered digital media; Nelson pioneered technological utopianism in the digital era. Unfortunately, these inspired presentations, filled with individualistic, egalitarian rhetoric didn't help the engineering world take his design seriously.

This writing system, like the computer itself, is 'FOR PERSONAL FREEDOM, AND AGAINST RESTRICTION AND COERCION' (Nelson 1987, 2). As Nelson sees it, everybody should be able to create what they want and put it on the system, from bad 'zines and pamphlets to great novels, and everybody should be able to quote or cite another document. When someone explores this information, their trails and their personal experiences of it should be preserved in all their uniqueness. Hypertext is more than just a technological shift, claims Nelson. It is an ideological overhaul of the way we read, write and learn literature – the way we think. COMPUTER POWER TO THE PEOPLE! (Nelson has a habit of writing in capitals when he talks about computers and personal freedom.)

A system with links and historical backtrack needs only an economic basis to become a publishing system. Nelson believes that hypertext should not only be an 'archive for the world' but a 'universal instantaneous publishing system' (Nelson 1993, 2/4). Every document should have an author who owns it and is the only one who may change it – though this authorial token may be passed – and anyone may make a transclusive copy or enhance it with links. Materials should be reusable by anyone, with credit and payment going to the original author. In other words, the concept of authorship, ownership and quotation as we know it can and should be scrupulously preserved – and soon.

As Nelson sees it, we are witnessing the 'slow death' of literacy in contemporary multimedia; the institutions that protect it and ensure its integrity are dying (Nelson 1999a). Xanadu is 'an intensive pursuit of "lost" or "forgotten" values' in this regard (Moulthrop 1991, 695), an epic of recovery. And although they failed to 'recover' copyright or ownership from the clutches of contemporary multimedia, Nelson's early writings certainly forecast a problem here. In 'the digital world [...] copyright law is totally out of date. It will probably have to break down completely before it is corrected' (Negroponte 1995, 58).

As a forecaster in the field of computing, Nelson has been remarkably successful (Rheingold 1985, 299). In his 1965 paper, Nelson claimed that computers would eventually 'do the dirty work of personal file and text handling' (Nelson 1965, 85). In 1967, inspired by NLS, he predicted a networked structure of information that would 'be read from an illuminated screen; the cathode-ray display; it will respond or branch upon actions by the user. It will be a succession of displays that come and go according to his actions' (Nelson 1967, 195). Needless to say, interactive multimedia has happened, but not the kind of interactive multimedia Nelson intended.

By the late 1970s, 'having offended anyone in the academy who could help him' (Rheingold 1985, 302), Nelson found a few like-minded friends and programmers and attempted to direct the development of Xanadu himself.[17] One of the most important collaborators was Roger Gregory, then a science fiction fan working in a used-computer store in Ann Arbor, Michigan. Gregory had technical skills that Nelson wanted: training in computer programming and an ability to make computers work. Gregory began to write shells of Xanadu code with Nelson full-time in 1979 (they'd known each other since 1976) and continued for the next decade.

In an interview with the Internet Archive, Gregory says he got a group together at Swarthmore and designed a system that he 'almost had working' by 1988, when he organized funding through Autodesk, an American software corporation (Gregory 2010). He'd been running the group as a volunteer organization for ten years prior to this. Gregory seems to sigh and shake his head a lot in this interview; he clearly has some regrets.

By 1983 Gregory claims that he wanted to 'get some work done' on Xanadu without Nelson interfering ('Ted can be very distracting. [He] is really brilliant but...' (Gregory 2010)). So Gregory set the company up so that 'we had Ted in Sausalito and us in Palo Alto' – a significant car drive away (Gregory 2010). He also signed an agreement with Nelson that gave him the 'technical rights' in 1983 – the right to do the development and find backing (which he did five years later, through Autodesk). This was called the Silver Agreement, and 'we all signed it with silver brush pens, since silver was the color of the future, the color of Xanadu' (Nelson 2010c, 244). It was incorporated into the Autodesk Agreement in 1988.

Nelson, of course, was not happy about losing these rights, but he trusted Gregory to get the job done. Nelson would drive down to Palo Alto for weekly meetings, but he 'felt like an outsider' in his own project. He did not feel welcome at the meetings, and felt 'they resented me' (Nelson 2010c, 264). Interestingly, he had also felt this about the HES team at Brown two decades earlier; he hadn't felt welcome in any project he had inspired.[18] Ultimately, and sadly for both Gregory and Nelson, the Autodesk project fell through.

Nelson is sensitive about this subject, possibly because of the scathing article that Gary Wolf published in *Wired* (1995), which painted the Autodesk project as a tragedy and Nelson as technically ignorant ('only Nelson's ignorance of advanced software permitted him to pursue this fantasy'). The article was wrong on several counts, and Nelson published his own reply to it (Nelson 1995b). One of the more painful things that Wolf – whom Nelson fondly refers to as 'Gory Jackal' – implied in this article was that Nelson 'caused the Xanadu fiasco at Autodesk' (Nelson 2010c, 285).

Nelson has a different version of events. He believes the Autodesk collapse happened because the Xanadu Operating Company (XOC, the company

Gregory was in charge of) tried to 'change horses mid-stream' (Nelson 2010c, 285). Gregory's team rebelled in 1988 and decided they wanted to redesign the system based on completely different principles. From Gregory's perspective this was madness; they almost had the thing working at this stage. Nelson, Gregory and Gregory's team were all at odds with one another. Gregory lost the battle and was demoted to programmer, and the team threw out his code. They set out to create a completely different Xanadu.

As Nelson notes in his autobiography, this decision 'brought disaster' (2010c, 263). Autodesk eventually pulled the plug on XOC in 1992, having spent up to $5 million trying to develop it. Although Wolf claimed that Autodesk had poured 'millions of dollars and years of effort' into Nelson's project (Wolf 1995), Nelson retorts that Autodesk didn't invest in him personally:

> No. Autodesk invested, not in my projects, but in the company founded by Roger Gregory – XOC Inc. – which had a president, a board of directors (on which I did not serve) and many stockholders […] Xanadu was not my project anymore, and I had no say in its development. (Nelson 2010c, 371)

There was, however, an argument in Wolf's article that hit home. It is the computing world's longest running unfinished project. This makes Nelson despondent. He feels like Vice Admiral James Stockdale, 'the American prisoner in Vietnam who endured by his grim optimism for the long term – I am absolutely certain that my work will be proven right eventually, and empower the world at last' (Nelson 2010c, 339).

Although Nelson seems to figure in every major history of computing and multimedia (for example Segaller 1998; Wardrip-Fruin and Montfort 2003; Ceruzzi 1998; Rheingold 2000; Abbate 1999; Shurkin 1996 and Bardini 2000) as the man who dreamed up hypertext, he is not a known quantity outside of the digerati. The people he appears beside in such histories – Doug Engelbart, Bob Metcalfe, Tim Berners-Lee – have attained worldwide recognition (and in the case of Metcalfe, wealth) and have directly influenced the course of computing with their systems. Nelson's influence on computing history is undeniable, but harder to touch; all we have of Xanadu is a tantalizing design, its ideals and its ideas.

> You know, [Nelson] gets his name in the newspapers, but there isn't a company that has him as a serious consultant. He's not going to influence IBM, he's not going to influence Compaq or Intel or any of the people who really could make a difference. [Although] I think his ideas are really being absorbed by the world over time. (van Dam 1999)

One aspect of the design that the Web has vindicated is Nelson's vision for the commercial provision of network access. In 1980 Nelson pitched the idea of 'Xanadu Information Franchises' in his book *Dream Machines*. These franchises would be local computer stations where data shoppers could access material from a global information system, distributed over the telephone. They would be everywhere: the McDonald's stands of cyberspace. He even included a sketch of the interior, complete with a snack bar and jingles. It was a whimsical idea, but it predicted the domestic penetration of ISPs and data portals in what would eventually become the Web. Sceptical readers,

Ted Nelson with the author, 2010. Photo © Belinda Barnet.

Stuart Moulthrop writes, might see in this vision of Xanadu yet another domain of the postmodern theme park. 'Gentle readers, welcome to Literacyland!' (Moulthrop 1991, 695). Xanadu has always been part technical design, part utopian business plan.

Visions take longer to influence the engineering world than prototypes. Nelson's ideas have been absorbed over time, but not always due to his direct advocacy. In the next section, I look more closely at his major project, Xanadu, and at the design of this system – a task more difficult than it seems. Until quite recently the design itself was shrouded in secrecy (Wardrip-Fruin 2003, 441), a fact that certainly did not help its promotion.[19] Nelson is also reluctant to list the technical aspects of Xanadu, as it detracts from explaining the paradigm shift that Xanadu represents ('You see, as soon as you start listing things, you're out of understanding the paradigm and into understanding features' (Nelson 1999a)). It is always difficult to extricate technical design from Nelson's philosophy; the two are mutually constitutive.

The Xanadu System

My principal long-term concern is the exact representation of human thought, especially that thought put into words and writing […] to maintain a continuing evolutionary base of material and to track the changes in it. (Nelson 1997)

Nelson is proposing an entirely new 'computer religion'. This religion attempts to model an information system on the structure of thought and the creative process behind writing, 'if we can figure out what that is' (Nelson 1993, 2/5). One thing that we do know, however, is that the nature of thought is change. Consequently, maintains Nelson, a system that is true to thought should be able to retrieve and track changes regardless of the current state of the document. Like the shifting currents he remembers under his grandfather's boat, connections change over time; Xanadu attempts to represent this complexity.

Historical backtrack and intercomparison imply the ability to transcend change, to recall and control the different stages in the evolution of a document. In addition to transclusion (though he did not use that word back then), these concepts have been integral to Nelson's projects for over forty years. But how does the technical design of Xanadu work as a proposed universal publishing system and archive?

In our 1999 interview Nelson hit upon the sentence he had 'been looking for years' to explain the design in a nutshell:

> Xanadu is a system for registered and owned content with thin document shells, reusable by reference, connectable and intercomparable sideways over a vast address space. (Nelson 1999a)[20]

I will unpack this in three parts. First, there is the principle that documents should be 're-usable by reference': ideas evolve bit by bit, and these bits should not be stored redundantly. For Nelson, the computer offers the opportunity to track these pieces in memory, to track their use or citation. Second, there is the idea that these bits might be identified not by where they are, but by what they are 'over a vast address space' navigable by links. These concepts ground Nelson's more recent idea of transclusion, which is at the heart of Xanadu's most innovative commercial feature: transcopyright, a 'system for registered and owned content'. I will then discuss the relationship between these ideas and the web, and perhaps more deeply, why the web has ignored them.

In most computer applications, it is necessary to make and keep several copies of the same document. This is because we wish to ensure the safety of recent work, or because we wish to keep track of former states of the same work. It is also because we wish to have the same work in different places – hence mirror sites on the web. Nelson believes that these purposes have been mistakenly fused into the single practice of making multiple copies. As he puts it, if you are repeatedly making small changes and then storing the unchanged material, there is redundancy.

He proposes a storage system that takes care of backtrack automatically, filing just the changes chronologically. The part you want is retrieved and integrated on the fly, and the 'document' becomes a series of alternative versions (note that this is how Wikipedia works now, and they have given Nelson credit for it). In this system, a user can scroll through time as well as space in one's work, tracing the evolution of ideas and comparing versions. In essence, the Xanadu system holds modular pieces of a document, not whole documents in multiple places. These parts are reusable in the same document, but most important, they are reusable by reference outside of the document. Interestingly, Nelson points out that Vannevar Bush's Memex actually used transclusions: 'He created a new trail on which you put things that were on old trails' (Nelson 2011).

This approach is more economical than making multiple copies, but it also allows each item to remain connected to its original source. For accuracy, for the availability of context, with micropayment for the quote' (Nelson 2012). The Xanadu system tracks the location of spans of text, in the same document or in other documents. Liberatory rhetoric aside, this fact cannot be ignored: the system would meticulously control and track information. This point shouldn't come across as sinister: it is simply the design for a new digital literature.

The Xanadu system also allows users to create any type of link between anything they want to link. Ideally, links in Xanadu should be bivisible and bifollowable – capable of being seen and followed from the destination document as well as the originating document ('unfortunately, since the collapse of [code versions] xu88 and the nonexistence of xu92, this criterion can no longer be met in the simple Xanadu I'm working on', notes Nelson (2012)). In contrast, links on the Web are univisible and unidirectional, largely due to the fact that they are embedded in the content itself; for a link to be visible and followable from both ends, the author of each page needs to edit the content and insert a link. Nelson calls this 'one-way hypertext', a simplified (and for Xanadu alumni, fundamentally broken) version of hypertext.

Directionality brings us to an important point: document versions in Xanadu are navigable via a parallel – not an embedded – linking structure. The document structure must remain separate from the linking structure. In HTML, users are required to go into the content, edit it and place links inside that content. As a result, the text is festooned with markup, like a tattoo of anchor tags, which obviously interferes with transclusive reuse. It also means that bivisible and bifollowable links outside your own document are impossible; linking to someone else's URL dumps you at the top of the page, not at the particular quote or image you were referring to (unless the destination

document has conveniently included 'anchor' tags in the content for you).
A linking structure should be separated from the document structure, maintains
Nelson. In 1997 he wrote an essay titled 'Embedded Markup Considered
Harmful' where he outlined the reasons that HTML and its parent language,
SGML are just plain wrong.

> There is no one reason this approach is wrong; I believe it is wrong in
> almost every respect. But I must be honest and acknowledge my objection
> as a serious paradigm conflict, or (if you will) religious conflict. In paradigm
> conflict and religious conflict, there can be no hope of doctrinal victory; the
> best we can seek is for both sides to understand each other fully and cordially.
> (Nelson 1997)

The Web is not Xanadu, and embedded markup is one of the reasons. Another
reason is that, in Xanadu, documents must be identified by what they are,
not where they are. On the Web, all we have is the URL – a place on a server
somewhere. Users then face the problem of 'updating' links when the destination
document is moved; if the URL of a document changes, all referring links become
dead ends because the URL points to a single position on a particular computer
(the server), not the information itself. In the Xanadu system, links of any type
would attach themselves not to a positional, geographical address, but to specific
characters – Nelson calls this a 'span': pieces of a document. Hence, because
objects are not identified as a location but by what they are across a vast address
space, links would update automatically as their position changed. No dead
ends. No 404 errors. This is not to say that only one copy of a document may
exist on the Xanadu server; rather, there would be numerous 'instances' (Nelson
1995b) throughout the network and on the user's machine. These disparate bits
or instances would be collected into a single virtual object – a bit like the 'list' of
file cards Nelson envisioned 40 years ago. Every document would be uniquely
identified character for character, wherever it was. Xanadu would be the perfect
archive, the perfect memory machine: its trails would never fade.

   Like all grand visions, Xanadu has its critics. One of the most common
criticisms is that it is a pipe dream – and given that it has been under
development for more than 50 years yet never been completed, this sentiment
is understandable. The most widely read piece on Nelson, Wolf's feature
article in *Wired*, condemned the project outright as technically infeasible.
'[The] colleagues were trying to build a universal library on machines that
could barely manage to edit and search a book's worth of text [...] They
always had too much data to move in and out of memory', he says, referring
to the 128k machines that Nelson's programmers were working with in the
early 1970s (Wolf 1995). Xanadu was, he claims, an impossible dream; 'even

today, the technology to implement a worldwide Xanadu network does not exist' (Wolf 1995). Strong words on Wolf's part – words that can still be found on the worldwide network of the Internet.

Nelson took this criticism quite badly; 'some have said that the purpose of [this article] was to engineer my suicide; if so, they nearly got their trophy' (Nelson 2010c, 285). It's never a good idea to tell someone that their lifelong dream is impossible.

With respect to the technical infeasibility of Xanadu at least, Wolf was wrong. Nelson claims this is because he 'seriously garbled the idea of transclusion' (Nelson 1995b). I contend it is because Wolf thought the Xanadu system required vast quantities of data to be moved in and out of computer memory. As we have explored, the idea behind Xanadu is to point at the data and then re-create pieces of it as a virtual object, rather than storing the 'corpus of all fields' on your hard drive (or for that matter, 'trying to build a universal library' (Wolf 1995) on a single machine). Why store vast tracts of text in memory when the parts you want can be securely identified and retrieved with a link (Nelson 1995a, 2)? Wolf's criticism missed the essence of Xanadu: everything is finely dispersed, tracked and controlled in pieces, and these pieces can exist anywhere, in any number of places. It is the design for a distributed archive.

In Wolf's defence, the article was written in 1995 – and it was not entirely clear in 1995 that the web would scale. As Mark Bernstein points out (2012), transclusion can also be computationally expensive, arguably outstripping the capabilities of machines from 1995 (though not, I would argue, from 2012). Regardless, history has proven Nelson right; the web has scaled, and our networks are now powerful enough to run distributed databases on numerous machines.

Integral to this idea of pointing at bits of a document rather than storing multiple copies of it in memory is the concept of transclusion. An author who wishes to quote uses transclusion to 'virtually include' the passage in the author's own document. As Nelson is fond of saying, all this means is making and maintaining connections between things that are the same (Nelson 1995a), or 'deep connectivity' as the Udanax community term it. Remote instances remain part of the same virtual object, wherever they are. This concept underpins Nelson's most famous commercial feature, transcopyright:

> The on-line copyright problem may be resolvable by a simple, sweeping permission method. This proposed system, which anyone may use, allows broad re-use of materials in exchange for automatic tracking of ownership. Payment goes to the original publisher and credit to the original author. (Nelson 1995a)

In other words, transcopyright reframes the question, 'how do we prevent infringement of copyright?' as 'how can we allow reuse?' As with all copyright, permission is needed to republish. Copyright holders choosing to publish on a system with Xanadu-like transclusion automatically grant permission for others to transclude their material, provided it is purchased by the recipient. Necessarily, a mechanism must be put in place to permit the system to charge for use, a micropayment system that provides a bridge to the original from each instance. Critically, this bridge should never break; links should not be outdated. At the same time, the bridge must leave no trace of who bought the pieces, as this would make reading political. As such, Xanadu would require a micropayment system parallel to the docuverse. This is Nelson's economic infrastructure.

The Web has actually evolved to incorporate numerous micropayment systems, but they neither work according to Nelson's system of transclusion, nor acknowledge Xanadu in any way. W3C even has a markup system for web micropayment on a pay-per-view basis (see W3C 1999).

The dual structure of links and transclusion has not been incorporated into the Web either. As Nelson puts it:

> The web is a universal, world-wide, anarchic publishing system. It completely vindicated my 35 years of saying that a universal, worldwide, anarchic publishing system would be of enormous human benefit. There is no question of whether it is of benefit. It just does it all wrong, that's all. (Nelson 1999a)

Nelson's concept of hypertext influenced Tim Berners-Lee, who appropriated Nelson's term to describe his language (HTML, or Hypertext Markup Language, which describes how graphics and text should be displayed when they are delivered across the Web). But as Nelson stated, 'HTML is like one-tenth of what I could do. It is a parody. I like and respect Tim Berners-Lee [but] he fulfilled his objective. He didn't fulfil mine' (Nelson 1999a). Although I don't have the space here to go into the evolution of HTML, I'll note that Berners-Lee shared Nelson's 'deep connectionist' philosophy, and his desire to organize information associatively.

> A computer typically keeps things in rigid hierarchies [...] whereas the human mind has the ability to link random bits of data. When I smell coffee, strong and stale, I find myself in a small room over a corner coffeehouse in Oxford. My brain makes a link, and instantly transports me there. (Berners-Lee 1999, 3)

From milk to white, from white to air, from air to damp: this is association as Aristotle formulated it 2,000 years ago (*De Memoria et Reminscentia* cited in Yates 1997). Berners-Lee also believed that:

> A piece of information is really defined only by what it is connected to, and how it's related. There really is little else to meaning. The structure is everything [...]

> All that we know, all that we are, comes from the way our neurons are connected [...] My desire [is] to represent the connective aspect of information. (Berners-Lee 1999, 13)

However, while Berners-Lee was met with scepticism and passivity, Nelson – with his energetic and eccentric presentations and business plans – received entirely disparaging responses (Segaller 1998, 288).

But Nelson slogs on, ideals held high above the mud. And he is not alone: the Xanadu vision lives on in the minds (and evolving code) of hundreds of computer professionals around the world. The extended Xanadu community is even wider, and has spawned several organizations devoted to the pursuit of a 'solution' to the 'problem' of contemporary information storage and publishing based on Nelson's vision. In 1999 Udanax (run by Roger Gregory) released pieces of the elusive source code for Xanadu, Udanax Green and Udanax Gold (udanax.com). Xanadu Australia, another offshoot, is run by Andrew Pam, Nelson's longtime friend and collaborator. The vision refuses to die.

> The Xanadu Australia formal problem definition is: We need a way for people to store information not as individual 'files' but as a connected literature. It must be possible to create, access and manipulate this literature of richly formatted and connected information cheaply, reliably and securely from anywhere in the world. Documents must remain accessible indefinitely, safe from any kind of loss, damage, modification, censorship or removal except by the owner. (Xanadu Australia Home Page 2012)

Xanadu is an 'epic of recovery' (Moulthrop 1991, 695) for the digital era, and it has entered into the imagination of a generation of developers. Unlike Bush's Memex, people keep trying to build the thing as it was first designed. This fact alone is evidence of its impact: technical white papers are not known for their shelf life, but Xanadu's have thrived for over 50 years.

Chapter 5

SEEING AND MAKING CONNECTIONS: HES AND FRESS

It is said that the character of Andy in *Toy Story* was inspired by Andries 'Andy' van Dam, professor of computing science at Brown University; several of the Pixar animators were students of van Dam's and wanted to pay tribute to his pioneering work in computer graphics. This piece of trivia has proliferated across the Web in recent years. It started in the IMDB database for the film and now makes an appearance in everything from Webster's online dictionary to Wikipedia. Van Dam thinks it's a cute, little story but probably not true ('I've tried to stamp it out but it won't die' (van Dam 2012)). He is proud, however, that the book he coauthored with James Foley, *Computer Graphics: Principles and Practice*, appears on Andy's bookshelf in the film, and that a number of his old students were, or still are, important contributors at Pixar (including producer Galyn Susman and vice president of software Eben Ostby). For a bespectacled professor in his early 70s, van Dam has attained a fair amount of fame; he's certainly the only hypertext pioneer to have made it into a Hollywood blockbuster, even if he is confined to the bookshelf.

In this chapter I trace the development of two important hypertext systems built at Brown: the Hypertext Editing System (HES), codesigned by Ted Nelson and van Dam and developed by van Dam's students, and the File Retrieval and Editing System (FRESS), designed by van Dam and his students. Brown University has played a major role in the development of hypertext systems and humanities computing since 1967, thanks in no small part to van Dam's work in this area, and the Institute for Research in Information and Scholarship (IRIS) he helped establish there with William Shipp and Norman Meyrowitz in 1983.

As Andreas Kitzmann put it, 'the history of hypertext could not be complete without acknowledging the tremendous amount of work done at Brown University' (Kitzmann 2006, 15). I focus here on van Dam's work, but also briefly explore two other systems developed at Brown: the Electronic Document System (EDS), developed under van Dam's leadership, and Intermedia, developed under Norman Meyrowitz's leadership (Meyrowitz would go on to be president of Macromedia Inc.).

Ted Nelson was codesigner of HES, and his ideas about hypertext inspired the HES project in the first place; van Dam credited Nelson for this contribution both in our interviews (1999, 2011) and in all his public talks and published work. Nelson still feels, however, that he has been 'given no more credit than his [van Dam's] undergraduate students' (Nelson 2012). Unfortunately Nelson fell out with the HES team during its design and implementation in 1967, and he has grown angry over the ensuing years. He is now bitter about the experience, largely because he feels his vision was sidelined in favour of print text editing. HES was 'effectively a word processor with linking facilities' that 'led directly to the modern word processor' (Nelson 2011), which from Nelson's perspective is where it all started to go wrong. This is when the world started to sink 'into the degeneracy of paper simulation' (Nelson 2011). We explore this in more detail shortly.

Along with Engelbart's landmark NLS system, HES and FRESS constitute the first generation of hypertext systems. This is not a chapter about dusty old antiques from the dawn of computing science, however; in many respects, FRESS by 1968 was more interactive than present-day HTML. HES and FRESS had technical chutzpah. HES was the world's first word processor to run on commercial equipment – 'the first "visual word processor"', as Nelson points out in the chapter he omitted from his autobiography, titled 'The Dark Brown Years' (2010b, obtained by permission).[1]

HES was also the first hypertext system that beginners could use, and it pioneered many modern hypertext concepts. As we saw in Chapter 3, Engelbart's NLS predated HES slightly, but NLS ran on proprietary equipment and required significant technical knowledge to use, which was one of the main criticisms of NLS at the time. HES, in contrast, could be used by a novice after ten minutes of instruction. It introduced interactive reading and authoring to the humanities and the text link to lay users; it established a technical precedent for other systems to follow.

FRESS was van Dam's second attempt at a hypertext system and it incorporated some ideas from Engelbart's NLS (van Dam did not see NLS until after HES had been built). Nelson was not involved with FRESS and did not keep abreast of the projects after he left Brown ('I don't know anything about FRESS. I just closed off' (Nelson 2011)). Both of these systems were built at a time when computers, in large part, were still seen as tools for mathematical calculations; there were no word processors. HES was particularly difficult to get off the ground. Van Dam recalls that in the 1960s, 'the whole idea of a user in an interactive computer loop was still foreign to most people' (1999). Like Engelbart, the HES team encountered much resistance to their ideas; the world was not ready for text on a screen.

This explains why van Dam emphasized print text editing from the outset, much to Nelson's dismay: they were trying to sell hypertext to people who used typewriters. From Nelson's perspective, this obsession with paper crippled the hypertext concept. He dubs it 'the great dumb-down of hypertext' (Nelson 2010b). In conjunction with the fact that HES implemented one-way rather than two-way links, Nelson feels it was like 'putting a ball and chain on what the system could become' (Nelson 2010b).

In the material that follows, I rely on technical articles and manuals from the time, but also on oral histories obtained from Nelson and van Dam in 1999 and again in 2011. I use Nelson's omitted autobiography chapter as well, though he was reluctant to let me quote from it as it is still under revision. Nelson has his own version of events around HES, and I tell that story here as he told it to me. Nelson's and van Dam's stories are different. Van Dam does not, however, feel bitter about the experience. He was surprised to hear that Nelson is angry about the project: 'what is he emotional about at this point? I don't get it?' (van Dam 2011). Van Dam can't recall Nelson feeling angry at the time either:

> We demo'd the system together to multiple potential funders (*Time–Life*, *New York Times*, etc.), again with his taking proper pride in it and its potential. We used the database on electroplating patents that he had created for those demos. (van Dam 2011)

But 40 years later Nelson feels that his design was sidelined, and his ideas were 'deeply wronged' (Nelson 2012). That said, he still wants to be recognized for his contributions. Irony is at play here. Nelson believes that he always felt angry, but that 'I held my head up [at the time] and kept my temper through the whole thing. You could say I swallowed my anger, which is why I am vomiting it now' (ibid.). In response to this chapter, he stated that it is 'acceptable' but 'the principal omission, from my point of view, is the dynamic between [van Dam] and myself. You have sanitized it' (ibid.).[2]

In his recent autobiography *Possiplex* Nelson states that he 'wrote to the presidents of Brown University and the Association for Computing Machinery, requesting an ethics hearing for how I was treated at Brown University in the 1960s. Predictably, both parties declined' (Nelson 2010c, 172).[3] The upshot is that HES did not fulfill his vision of Xanadu. To be fair to van Dam and his team, however, their intention was never to build Xanadu in its entirety; HES was simply a rapid prototype, an unfunded bootleg experiment. It has also been, historically, hard to fulfill Nelson's vision.

This personal disagreement should not detract from the pioneering work that the HES and FRESS teams did. There were no word processors at the time, let alone word processors with linking facilities. It may have been tied to the 'ball and chain of paper' as Nelson puts it, but it was a landmark system.

Van Dam's background in computer graphics is significant to this story, so we shall begin there; his experience in the field meant that hypertext, when Nelson shared the idea with him, was 'instantly obvious' (van Dam 1999). As the chapter on Xanadu stated, hypertext was certainly not obvious to anyone else whom Nelson encountered at that time, with the notable exception of Doug Engelbart.

Van Dam's Early Work

Andries van Dam has more than a passing interest in graphics. The Pixar animators put the Foley and van Dam book on the *Toy Story* shelf because he was one of the earliest computer graphics pioneers, forming ACM SICGRAPH, the forerunner of ACM SIGGRAPH, in 1968 with IBM sponsor Sam Matsa.[4] Van Dam is more renowned for his work in this field than he is in hypertext systems. 'My identity is much more tied up with graphics and interaction. Most people don't even know my hypertext background' (van Dam 2011). His students from the 1960s, 1970s and 1980s have gone on to make important contributions of their own; among the more famous are Randy Pausch, professor of computing science at Carnegie Mellon (who lost his battle with pancreatic cancer several years ago), and Andy Hertzfeld, a key member of the original Apple Macintosh development team in the 1980s. One of the seven founders of Microsoft, Bob Wallace, was a lead designer on FRESS as an undergraduate.

Van Dam wrote his PhD thesis in 1966, the second computer science PhD in the world, on the 'digital processing of pictorial data' using a system that simulated associative memory (van Dam 1964). Like Engelbart, van Dam believes that visualization and spatialization are the most efficient ways of representing and navigating complex data: the human eye is a powerful machine. The question is, which model best allows us to represent and interact with complex data? The model necessarily 'forgets' something in translation. It is a simplification, an abstraction from a human process; the question is 'the *level* of abstraction' (Machover 1998, 83).

The data model on which van Dam did his doctoral work was called MULTILIST, developed by Professors Noah Prywes and Josh Gray at the University of Pennsylvania. It simulated a multilinked list system, based on language keywords. As we see in the chapter on Storyspace, linked lists were one of the earliest (and most obvious) ways of implementing hypertext;

this function was possible in many of the early computing languages, including LISP, and later Pascal. Linked lists are a basic way of connecting elements that exhibit a relationship, using pointers to indicate the next element (or 'node') in a list. Items associated in this way can be retrieved together.

MULTILIST organized information as modular nodes accessed via keywords, and the nodes were put on whatever list applied for a given keyword. Van Dam used MULTILANG and MULTILIST to do computer graphics on a line printer. Using this system for graphics was considered heresy by Noah Prywes, who grew quite angry at van Dam at his dissertation defence ('he started screaming at me that I had perverted MULTILIST and MULTILANG' (van Dam 2011)). Van Dam is no stranger to offending people with his technical ideas. 'In any case, that's the system I used, so this idea of nonlinear information structures was completely familiar, and I'd read articles about how human memory apparently works, associative memory' (van Dam 2011).

Many of the hypertext pioneers were exposed to (or in Bush's case, explicitly attempted to build) projects that simulated human associative memory. Several of the pioneers were also involved with early artificial intelligence (AI) projects. Jay Bolter and Michael Joyce, for example, did residencies at the Yale AI lab, as the next chapter describes, and Engelbart was deeply influenced by the early cybernetics community in the 1950s; he modelled the human psyche as a technical system and proposed a fundamentally technical solution to the problem of human knowledge. A continuity in metaphor exists between AI models of associative memory and hypertext, a continuity that is reflected in the title of this book.

In his senior year in college, van Dam worked on early AI projects involving perceptrons; this is a simple type of neural network first invented at Cornell in 1957. These were later 'debunked in a very scathing analysis by Marvin Minsky and Seymour Papert, so they sort of went out of fashion' (van Dam 1999), at least until reincarnated as the more sophisticated neural networks in use today. MULTILIST and MULTILANG were also basic attempts to model associative thought – as van Dam put it:

A very simple simulation of the kind of associative trails you might find in the human brain, where things that are connected together are somehow retrievable, one from the other. Not because they are physically co-located, but because the brain in its wiring apparently links them somehow. And that's what Bush was referring to when he said 'the mind instantly leaps' […] You could say that hypertext is a very crude analogue to what must happen for the storage of facts and information in the human brain, where things that are logically linked are logically retrieved together. (van Dam 1999)

For van Dam, this vision of a human sitting at a computer screen and following linked trails through stored information was obvious once he heard Nelson explain it, because it organized information associatively and promised to make knowledge work more efficient. Van Dam had already seen a multilinked list system in his doctoral work at the University of Pennsylvania, so he was receptive to Ted's suggestion that they should prototype a system on the IBM 2250 display.[5]

Nelson soon discovered, however, that van Dam had no problem modifying his (Nelson's) vision – first by introducing print text editing as a primary task. Second, he wanted one-way links rather than Nelson's concept of two-way links. According to Nelson, who disagreed with this direction, 'these two decisions determined it right there [...] Locking it to paper killed the big vision. The one-way links made it trivial and stupid' (Nelson 2010b).

Van Dam, however, had to find support for the system. From his perspective he had to sell it to a paper-based world, which was one reason he tied it to print text editing: 'there was no way we could implement just an online hypertext system; that was not sensible in our world' (van Dam 2011).

> I [also] wanted a system for writing articles, class notes, syllabi, proposals, etc., and it was obvious to me that online editing was the way to go. But once a document is created, you can't distribute it without going to paper. At the time there was no online community, and most people had no visual displays, certainly no Internet. Thus the print medium was the only way to distribute and share documents. (van Dam 2011)

This 'pissed Ted off [...] because part of his hypertext religion was that intrinsically nonlinear documents can't be printed and they have to be read on a tube' (van Dam 2011). Nelson, of course, thinks the reason is simpler; van Dam 'wanted to do it his way, that's all' (Nelson 2011). Nelson did not respond favourably to having his vision modified.

Van Dam emphasizes from the outset that his model of association was also different from Engelbart's ('I didn't even know Doug and his model at the time' (van Dam 2011)); in NLS, the system imposed a hierarchical tree structure upon all textual contents. NLS evolved around a group of engineers; it was multiuser. When Nelson and van Dam set out to create a hypertext system, they decided that their model of association would be personalized, with fewer restrictions. 'HES was also single-user and personal because there was only one graphics display at Brown – ours [...] Unimaginable today' (van Dam 2011). The Hypertext Editing System was designed for personal text editing, information retrieval and nonsequential writing.

> This is one of the differences between ours and Engelbart's system. That system imposes a hierarchical tree structure upon all textual contents, in contrast to our unstructured 'string' of text approach. While many benefits accrue from this automatic structuring, it does reflect an arguable theory of human thought. (Carmody et al. 1969, 301)

Theories and models of human thought aside, I have been arguing that NLS's hierarchical structure was based as much on the fact that the system itself was multiuser, and that it was the centrepiece of (the first) large-scale software engineering project, as it was on Engelbart's conception of the structure of language and thought. The technical process of tracking code versions and reconciling these with design specifications, bug reports and change requests within a team of engineers does not allow for 'unstructured' or personalized associations.

Nelson and van Dam were both more interested in the personal, scholarly activity of writing; they set out to automate the operations normally performed upon text by writers and editors. These operations are not the result of teamwork, but of personal techniques for operating on the written word. If they agreed on one point in designing HES, it was that it should have a freewheeling character.

The Design of HES

As we saw in the chapter on NLS and Engelbart, a lot was going on in the computing industry in the late 1960s. Timesharing had hit the industry, and the minicomputer had begun to establish its markets. Computing had begun to move into the wider arena of 'data processing'. A computing paradigm shift was occurring. As van Dam notes in *Computer Graphics* (the book he co-authored with Steven Feiner, John Hughes and James Foley that appeared on Andy's shelf in *Toy Story*):

> Another major advance of the late sixties was attaching the display to a minicomputer; with this configuration, the central time-sharing computer was relieved of the heavy demands of refreshed display devices, especially user-interaction handling, and updating the image on the screen. (Foley et al. 1995, 10)

This was the domestication of computing. But although universities and businesses were adopting data processing, processing power was limited, and universities meted it out like gold to the places where it was needed most – in their opinion, physics and engineering departments. 'Text was not "data"; it was something academics and journalists manipulated with pens or typewriters' (van Dam 1999). Computers were 'for scientists and engineers to solve *serious* problems', van Dam remembers his then VP for Finance saying, and he was told, 'If you want to crank out papers you can damn well use a typewriter' (van Dam 1999). This vision of a human sitting at a computer screen and writing or navigating linked text was not an obvious one. As Engelbart observed in an interview with the author, 'the idea was wacky even in the seventies, when we had it working – real hypermedia, real groupware working' (Engelbart 1999).

Technology already existed, however, for editing text on a computer; it was called a 'line' or 'context' editor (van Dam 1999). This system was designed for writing or editing computer programs, but it was often used covertly to create documentation. Like Doug Engelbart, who unbeknownst to van Dam was working on the NLS/Augment system at the same time, van Dam saw the need to tailor computing technology to the humans who used it.

Van Dam stated in an interview with the author that 'one of the things I was always pissed about is that Ted never told me about Engelbart, even though he claimed he knew of his work' (van Dam 1999). In response, Nelson retorts:

> Your quote makes it sound as though he thinks I was deliberately keeping Engelbart a secret from him. No: having seen Engelbart's system at first hand in 1966, I considered its hierarchical structure unacceptable, and therefore irrelevant to what we were doing. (Nelson 2011)

However we slice it, van Dam was not aware of the groundbreaking work that Engelbart was doing in 1966 and 1967. What he was aware of, however, was that an editing system that sufficed for computer programmers would not fulfill the needs of writers and scholars.

Van Dam bumped into Nelson at the 1967 Spring Joint Computer Conference in Atlantic City. They already knew each other, and had been friends at Swarthmore in the late 1950s: 'we played Frisbee with these great beer trays' (Nelson 2011). Nelson also cast van Dam in his first rock musical: 'he and his wife were both – both had parts in my great rock musical which, by the way, was the pivot of my life in a sense' (Nelson 2011). When Nelson was a keynote speaker at the 2001 Digital Arts and Culture conference, van Dam introduced him with the comment that he's 'known [Ted] longer than anyone else in my adult life – literally since my freshman week in 1956 at Swarthmore College' (Lloyd 2001). They had some catching up to do.

Andries van Dam, Wikimedia Commons. Licensed under a Creative Commons License.

Passionate and eloquent, Nelson told van Dam about what he'd been doing since he left Swarthmore: hypertext. 'He had nothing to show for this idea, no prototypes or work in the sense that computer scientists talk about work – i.e. software, algorithms, things that are concrete', recalled van Dam (1999). What Nelson did have was a vision of what hypertext should look like, and an infectious enthusiasm for the idea.

Nelson had in mind an entirely new genre for literature, and he had a new word to describe this vision (which was first published in 1965): hypertext.

> Nelson's vision seduced me. I really loved his way of thinking about writing, editing and annotating as a scholarly activity, and putting tools together to support that [...] I had this wonderful graphics display, and my students and I were working on various graphics applications at the time. He talked me into working on the world's first hypertext system and that sounded cool. (van Dam 1999)

According to Nelson, who refers to van Dam as 'von Drat' in his autobiography (I have been editing this out in quotes here), van Dam invited him 'to come to Brown to "implement some of your crazy ideas"' (Nelson 2010b). Nelson claims in his omitted chapter that this experience cost him both time and money (Nelson 2010b). Van Dam, however, recalls that Nelson entered into this collaboration willingly, that it was an unfunded 'bootleg project' from the beginning (van Dam hadn't even told his sponsors) and that in return he got a team of 'eager beavers' willing to try and implement a small part of his vision.

Van Dam gathered a team and began work. He stressed in his communications to me that the idea was never to 'realize' Xanadu. The intention was much smaller and more circumspect: to 'implement a *part* of his vision. We were not able to implement or even understand the breadth and scope of that [larger] vision' (van Dam 2011). Nelson, however, was under the impression that his designs would be honoured.

Nelson was initially very excited. He went up there 'at his own expense' (van Dam 1988) to consult in the development of HES, but found the experience frustrating. He sent van Dam a memo shortly after the project started at Brown, outlining how he wanted the system to look: 'Naturally, it's on some bloody disk and somewhere – I have all these scrambled disks, like most people, I think, with stuff misarranged [...] But anyway, the first day we met, as soon as I got there, he swept that aside' (Nelson 2011). Nelson also drew up extensive 'Implementation Notes', 24 pages of handwritten instructions and diagrams that can still be found on the Web in the Xuarchives (Nelson 1968).

The cover page is dated 6–10 March 1968 and Nelson states on it that the instructions are 'presented candidly here, in the hope of getting across what has been on my mind so that the appropriate implementation details can be handled by those as may thenceforward understand them best' (Nelson 1968, 1). These notes describe Nelson's vision in detail. They cover the ELF design, Xanadu, StretchText and Nelson's screen-based graph display idea. Nelson didn't want to hover around in the background watching the team build a part of his vision; he wanted the design to be produced as faithfully as possible. 'Let's put it this way: I feel that van Dam should have treated me the way he would have treated Buckminster Fuller if he'd asked Buckminster Fuller to come in' (Nelson 2011). That didn't happen.

As observed previously, van Dam and his team wanted to explore the hypertext concept, but they also had their own plans (which Nelson strenuously opposed). The team set out to design a dual-purpose system for authoring, editing and printing text documents, which could also be used to browse and query written materials nonsequentially. From Nelson's perspective, this was a compromise on his design – 'No', said Nelson after reading this chapter, 'consider using the word "betrayal"' (2012) – it was simulating paper, and hypertext was a mere footnote to the system.

Nelson spent much time at Brown arguing for the elaboration of HES's hypertext facilities, and remembers a constant battle to deepen the model of hypertext the HES team were working with, and a struggle against their 'fixation' with producing printed documents. 'I reduced the design to two windows on the screen, referential editing. He [thought] this was raving, so I dumbed it down to one screen' (Nelson 1999a).

The HES team were trying to convince the world that the whole concept of handling text on computers was not a waste of time and processing power. The world knew text handling as a paper-based thing, so they made it one page, one screen, attached to a printer. 'Not only were we selling hypertext, but at the same time document processing, interaction. Many people were still computing with cards', recalls van Dam (1999).

Doug Engelbart was also having trouble convincing the world that humans and machines might work together interactively. No funding body in the country would support the idea of a completely nonsequential, online web. Perhaps more important, van Dam already had a vision of what his writing system should do, a vision based on improving an existing human activity: creating and editing print documents.

Although Nelson now remembers his time at Brown as a struggle, he certainly made an impression on the students there — and inspired them. Gregory Lloyd was an undergraduate at Brown in 1968. He recalls that 'Andy's main undergraduate course was applied math 101, 102, 103 and 104' (Lloyd 2011); this was a large commitment for students and consisted of two courses in the fall and two in the spring. They were pioneering computer science courses, the only ones offered at Brown at the time; van Dam was trying to build computer science at Brown and to create a tradition of using students to do research work (like programming HES). To do that, he first had to convince students that computing science was a good idea, and then teach them how to program. He wanted at least 30 people 'who were brave or foolish enough to sign up' for this suite of subjects (Lloyd 2011), so he did something very clever. He introduced Ted Nelson at an introductory lecture.

> Ted proceeded to do what I call Ted and Andy's Medicine Show. Very dramatic, so, essentially just spotlights shining down on a lecture table in a darkened auditorium. Ted walks up and does a classic Ted presentation [...] He opened his jacket pocket and pulled out his little custom-sized cards, and described how he not only used the cards to record things he wished to remember, but he had a custom pocket sewn into his jacket [...] [He told us] he had tried many methods of organizing them, [all of which] he said were totally ridiculous and unusable. And then he launched into what he really wanted to do at Brown, which was [...] to use a computer to capture an editable corpus of the world's literature. (Lloyd 2011)

Nelson is a master performer; his presentations are vibrant and theatrical. The undergraduates were bowled over and signed up immediately. Many would go on to have stellar careers in computing. Students who worked on HES or FRESS included John Gannon, former chair of computer science at the University of Maryland; Greg Lloyd, president and cofounder of Traction Software Inc.; John Guttag, former head of the Department of Electrical Engineering and Computer Science at MIT; Frank Tompa, former department chair at University of Waterloo; Ed Lazowska, former department chair at University of Washington and currently, the Bill and Melinda Gates Chair in Computer Science at the University of Washington; and IBM fellow Diane Pozefsky. Van Dam created a tradition with this course of training and then recruiting his own computer science students. One of the principal designers of FRESS was undergraduate Bob Wallace, who would go on to become one of the founders of Microsoft and the inventor of shareware.

The project was exciting. The HES team designed a system for the composition and manipulation of manuscripts, which could also be used as a reading machine to browse and query complex written materials online. They did not wish to inflict line numbers on the user or to 'make him program little changes in his data' (Carmody et al. 1969, 8) as line editors for computer programmes did. Reading, writing and editing documents should be simple, and the tools should be suited to the task. Importantly, there were no concrete distinctions between 'readers' and 'writers' – these activities were both accessible to users.

> One of the canons of Nelson and my shared beliefs (also Doug Engelbart's) was that there should be no artificial distinctions between readers and writers in the user community for our systems – the two activities are totally and intrinsically linked. While it is mandatory for a scholarly community, it clearly was envisioned to be dangerous for a commercial community, hence the clear separation on the Web. (van Dam 2012)

With the exception of wikis, you obviously can't go about editing the pages you visit on the web. HES had a different model. Because they wished to emphasize the place of 'ordinary' text editing as well as the more radical concept of nonsequential, online reading and writing, they called the project the Hypertext Editing System – a name meant to embrace this dual purpose. 'I tried to kill two birds with one stone', recalls van Dam (2011).

Nelson recalls, however, that the system was initially called simply 'hypertext', and that he felt this was inappropriate:

> [Van Dam] said they were going to call the system 'Hypertext'. I protested: hypertext is the kind of writing it will make possible! The system needs a different

name, I insisted. But he laid down the law [...] [The] name was later lengthened
to Hypertext Editing System or HES. (Nelson 2010b)

From van Dam's perspective, even with a name that included 'editing', it was
still a hard sell. He recalls his chairman at the time saying, 'why don't you
stop with all this hypertext nonsense, and do something serious?' to which
van Dam replied, 'Walter, I am doing something serious' (van Dam 1999). At
Brown, van Dam 'had multiple reactions, from "cute" to "I don't get it" to my
being in a pissing contest to be allowed to use the university's only mainframe
computer' (van Dam 1999).

IBM, however, thought the project serious enough to provide funding
through a research contract. This commitment, recalls van Dam, put the
project on much more legitimate ground and ensured that the undergraduates
who had been programming HES as a bootleg graphics project were then
paid for their efforts (van Dam 1988).

HES was set up on an IBM 360/50 with a 2250 display, and ran in a 128k
partition of the operating system that controlled the 512k of main memory
available. The user sat facing a 12-inch-by-12-inch screen, browsing through
portions of texts. Original text was entered directly via a keyboard, and the
system itself was controlled by pressing function keys and by pointing at the text
with a light pen or with the keyboard (Carmody et al. 1969, 4). The activities
of the user corresponded directly to the operations normally performed upon
text by writers and editors. The user was able to manipulate pieces of text as
though they were physical items: correcting, cutting, pasting, copying, moving
and filing drafts. A press release invoked the analogy with scissors and paste
pots (though the press gleefully reported it with the typo 'past posts' (Lloyd
2011)).

> Our philosophical position [was] essentially that the writer is engaged in very
> complicated pursuits, and that this work legitimately has a freewheeling character
> [...] therefore it became our intent to provide the user with unrestricted 'spatial'
> options, and not to bother him with arbitrary concerns that have no meaning in
> terms of the work being performed. (Carmody et al. 1969, 8)

The HES team did not wish to store text in numerical pages or divisions
known to users, except as they might deliberately divide text, create links or
number headings. Rather than filing by page number or formal code name,
HES stored text as arbitrary-length fragments or 'strings' and allowed for edits
with arbitrary-length scope (for example, insert, delete, move, copy). This
approach differed from NLS, which imposed fixed-length lines or statements
upon all content; Engelbart's 4,000-character limits created a tighter, more

controlled environment. These limitations meant that Engelbart could implement his system more efficiently (van Dam 1999). HES was deliberately made to embody a freewheeling character, as nonstructured as possible.

The system itself comprised text 'areas' that were of any length, expanding and contracting automatically to accommodate material. These areas were connected in two ways: by links and by branches. A link went from a point of departure in one area (signified by an asterisk) to an entrance point in another, or the same, area.

The HES team used Ted Nelson's concept of a hypertext link (though from Nelson's perspective they 'flattened' this by making the jumps one-way). Doug Engelbart was incorporating the same idea into NLS independently. 'I hadn't heard of Engelbart. I hadn't heard of Bush and Memex. That came quite a bit later,' van Dam recalls (van Dam 1999). Links were intended to be optional paths within a body of text – from one place to another. They represented a relationship between two ideas or points: an intuitive concept. Branches were inserted at decision points to allow users to choose 'next places' to go.

In his autobiography, *Possiplex*, Nelson claims credit for the back button in HES. As he pointed out in an email to the author, there was no back button in NLS, so this was the first instance in the history of hypertext. In NLS the user could 'return' to the top of the hierarchy, but did not simply page back to the previous screen or point in the text. Nelson remembers it this way:

> What happened was van Dam said, 'Well, if you jump to the next thing, how's the user going to stay oriented?' I said, 'It's very simple. You give them the back button and put the addresses on a stack' […] They [the HES team] argued, maybe it was ten minutes, maybe it was an hour, I have no recollection, but it felt more like an hour that we argued about this and finally they tried it. (Nelson 2011)

Van Dam feels that 'it would be a very natural concomitant to unidirectional links' (van Dam 2011). Either way, the back button was implemented early on.

The HES team employed 'human factors' techniques to design a system that guided and explained the user's every move without loss of effectiveness (Carmody et al. 1969, 14). The system was much easier to use than NLS, perhaps because it was created as much for writers as for engineers. Speaking from the year 2012, the editing features of HES seem almost trivial. At the time, however, it was difficult to convince people in a commercial environment that it was not an excessively complicated typewriter. As van Dam recalled in an interview with the author:

> Remember, we were doing hypertext at a time when there were no word-processing systems either. HES is one of the very first word processors […]

I believe HES was the first document editor, specifically designed for documents, to run on commercial equipment, and NLS was the first document editor to run on a proprietary system, predating HES. (van Dam 1999)

One of van Dam's tasks was to convince humanities scholars and writers that this process was more efficient than using a pen or a typewriter. HES used a standard 32-key IBM function keypad, but when, in the late 1960s, they gave demos to writers whose business was words, not engineering, they would 'freak out' over all the buttons (van Dam 1999). So van Dam learned to use progressive disclosure, not frightening people with too many buttons.

I made a plastic overlay which I essentially used to cover up all but five of the editing buttons: insert, delete, move, copy and jump. Then we would do an entire demo for half an hour or so with that [...] and then we would play peek-a-boo, strip off the first overlay, and lo and behold, there was another row of function keys. (van Dam 1988)

In early 1968 HES did the rounds of a number of large customers for IBM equipment, for example, *Time–Life* and the *New York Times*. All these customers based their business on the printed word, but HES was too far out for them. Writing was not something you did at a computer screen. They had seen programs that set type, and maybe some programs for managing advertisements, but the concept of sitting in front of a computer and writing or navigating text was foreign to them.

The best I ever got was from people like *Time–Life* and the *New York Times* who said this is terrific technology, but we're not going to get journalists typing on computer keyboards for the foreseeable future. (van Dam 1999)

As we now know, however, in less than a decade journalists (and executives) would be typing on computer keyboards.

In late 1968 van Dam finally met Doug Engelbart and attended a demonstration of NLS at the Fall Joint Computer Conference. As we explored in Chapter 4, this was a landmark presentation in the history of computing, and the audience, comprised of several thousand engineers and scientists, witnessed innovations such as the use of hypertext, the computer 'mouse' and screen, and telecollaboration on shared files via video conferencing for the first time. The NLS demo was celebrated in December of 2008 at its 40th anniversary with almost all of the original team led by Doug Engelbart on stage and Andries van Dam as the outsider commentator.

The Hypertext Editing System (HES) IBM 2250 Display console at Brown University. Original photo by Greg Lloyd, 1969. Licensed under a Creative Commons License.

For van Dam this system set another, and entirely different, technical precedent. The line or context editor was old technology. NLS was the prototype for creating, navigating and storing information behind a tube and for having a multiuser, multiterminal, cost-effective system. He went on to design the File Retrieval and Editing System (FRESS) at Brown with his team of star undergraduates and one master's student. As van Dam observed in the Hypertext 1987 conference keynote address:

> [My] design goal was to steal or improve on the best ideas from Doug's NLS and put in some things we really liked from the Hypertext Editing System – a more freeform editing style, no limits to statement size, for example. (van Dam 1988)

The HES project was frozen as the team started work on the next-generation system. Meanwhile, the HES source code was submitted to the IBM SHARE program library. Van Dam proudly recalls that it was used in NASA's Houston Manned Spacecraft Center for documentation on the Apollo space programme (van Dam 1987). For what it was designed to achieve, HES performed perfectly.

Nelson is adamant that the legacy of HES is modern word processing, and that it also led to today's Web browser.

> The design of HES became the design of FRESS [...] then Intermedia, then imitated by Notecards and then by the World Wide Web. (Nelson 2010b)

Van Dam, for his part, thinks this is overreaching. 'I think Nelson, when he feels that the "bad example" that HES set had reverberations in the bad design of the Web or browsers, is giving our humble little effort an order of magnitude more credit than it deserves' (van Dam 2011). He doesn't feel that HES had a long shadow – if only it were that influential.

> I do not believe that if you were to talk to the people who designed the browser, Mark Andreessen, and Tim Berners-Lee, who designed the HTTP protocol, and the early notions of the World Wide Web, that they would say, 'Yeah, we read those early papers and we were deeply influenced by them.' (van Dam 2011)

That HES engendered the Web, or inspired its design, is debatable. For his part, Tim Berners-Lee claims in his autobiography that he had seen Dynatext, a later commercial electronic writing technology that van Dam helped launch after HES (see DeRose 1999), but that he didn't transfer this design to HTML (Berners-Lee 1999, 27).

Nelson, however, believes that HES demonstrated a technical paradigm to the world at a higher level: 'this is what hypertext looks like and what it can do. People [saw] this, and they [thought] oh that's what hypertext is' (Nelson 1999a). Perhaps a future scholar might have time to investigate Nelson's claim more closely; suffice it to say, for our purposes, the migration path is not clear.

HES, as a first prototype, naturally had its shortcomings. Van Dam's next system, FRESS, was designed to improve on them. HES was programmed specifically for the IBM System /360 and the /2250 display; there was no device independence. Van Dam had seen the benefits of device independence in Engelbart's demonstration; in NLS 'the command line [...] worked on basically any device. So they had really engineered in good device independence from the beginning' (van Dam 1999). FRESS was the first hypertext system to run on a readily available operating system and commercial hardware: it was built for the IBM VM/370, an off-the-shelf timesharing system, and could even run on cheap alphanumeric terminals incapable of multiwindow views.

Second, HES wasn't multiuser; it was specifically targeted towards the 2250, a machine for individual use (van Dam 1999). The benefits of having a multiuser system were also obvious from Engelbart's demonstration of

NLS (Ceruzzi 1998). A multiuser system allowed teams of people to work together more easily. In NLS the tendency towards knowledge exchange and collaborative work were more than just system side effects; they were goals. Van Dam decided to make FRESS multiuser. Although FRESS 'didn't have the kinds of chalk-passing protocols that NLS had' (van Dam 1999) – in NLS, for instance, multiple users could work with a shared view of a single document in progress – it was designed from the outset to run on a timesharing system and to accommodate multiple displays of different types and capabilities, from teletypewriters to glass teletypes (simple CRT screens) to multiwindowed powerful displays with pointing devices.

But the most popular development for novice users in FRESS was not its capacity to accommodate multiple displays and users; it was the 'undo' feature – the feature of which van Dam is most proud (van Dam 2011). FRESS pioneered a single-level undo for both word processing and hypertext. Every edit to a file was saved in a shadow version of the data structure, which allowed for both an 'autosave' and an undo. Brown staff and students understood immediately the importance and usefulness of this feature (van Dam 1999).

Had Nelson stuck around long enough, perhaps he would have, too. One of his greatest obsessions, as we have seen, has always been keeping track of the history of documents. Nelson, in response to this chapter, retorts in the margin that he had 'no option of sticking around'; it was 'made clear [van Dam] didn't want to see any more of me' (2012). Nelson also believes:

> I argued for Undo from the beginning, in my designs from 1960. At some point
> […] this became BRANCHING undo. (Nelson 2011)

Nelson's 1965 ACM paper (Nelson 1965) does make mention of historical backtrack. In this article he proposes a hypertext system called Zippered Lists, which 'must not commit the user to a new version until he is ready. Indeed, the system would have to provide spin-off facilities, allowing a draft of a work to be preserved while its successor was created' (85). This is not a clear-cut design for undo, however; FRESS was the first to develop such a function. As Chuk Moran (2012) notes in his PhD thesis on undo, 'FRESS was the first to implement an undo command'.

Importantly, FRESS had no size limitations. According to van Dam, an important philosophical distinction between NLS and FRESS was that 'Doug had these 4,000-character limits on his statements, and that was an anathema to us. It was an anathema to Ted, when he started out, to have limits on anything' (van Dam 1999). The FRESS team believed that the system should not force you into an unnatural usage pattern, so software paging allowed for essentially unlimited document sizes while maintaining performance.

Working in the FRESS environment, the user could not tell the difference between a two-page and a 200-page printed file, and could actually specify how all this would be viewed in the first place. FRESS borrowed many of the viewing specification ideas from NLS.

At the same time, hyperlinks in these files were addressable down to the character. The granularity was as fine as sand. As van Dam put it in our interview, 'I don't want to go to a book, I don't want to go to a chapter, I want to go to the actual quote!' (1999). In NLS, a link took you to a statement. In FRESS it could take you to a character. So in this sense, van Dam points out, 'I think we had a "creamier" hypertext than NLS did' (van Dam 2011).

Another aspect of FRESS that the Web has not implemented is bidirectional linking. HES had unidirectional links, which the FRESS team decided to change. FRESS was the first hypertext system to provide bidirectional linking. It was also groundbreaking in that it provided different options to visualize this field of links and references, to see the global context for work: a map. This feature was probably a result of van Dam's longtime interest in graphics, and Nelson certainly would have demanded it from the very beginning.

The outline functionality in FRESS was inspired by NLS – or as van Dam put it, 'was a straight rip-off' (van Dam 1999). For readers who are not familiar with this terminology, an outline processor is a specialized word processing program for handling and displaying outlines. One of its most powerful features is the ability to suppress lower levels of detail and see the global context for work (Conklin 1987, 25). The user can view just the top n levels of the structure – a map whose level of detail is user-defined – which facilitates rapid movement between sections and makes editing and global navigation easier. But most importantly, in FRESS:

> [we] had an ability to see the structure space, a visualization of all the structure in the text, the outline structure and the cross-referencing structure. You could do structural rearrangements in that structure space in a quick overview mode and you would thereby induce those same edits in the text itself. (van Dam 1988)

In sum, FRESS provided a variety of coordinated views and conditional structure and view-specification mechanisms. The user had final control over how and how much of the document was being displayed, unlike with embedded markup like HTML. FRESS also afforded partial separation of structure from formatting and hypertext semantics. All of these features were designed to be easy to learn, based as they were on a multiwindow function key and light pen interface, in addition to a command-line interface (in contrast to NLS, which had a more complex, and correspondingly more powerful, command language).[6] FRESS actually displayed and handled complex documents better than nonhypertext 'word processing' systems of the time. It was so intuitive and efficient that it 'was used as a publishing system as well as a collaborative hypertext environment for teaching, research and development' (DeRose and van Dam 1999, 7). It was also used at Nijmegen University and Philips Eindhoven in the Netherlands (DeRose and van Dam 1999, 19).

But FRESS was not a runaway success at Brown, and the project received little financial support. As with HES, 'computer scientists didn't think it was computer science, and humanists weren't paying for technologies' (van Dam 1999). The most difficult group to deal with were the staff in charge of computing. In those days, computing time on the university mainframe was allocated via a virtual accounting system. You got n-thousands of dollars in your account (this was called 'virtual money' or 'funny money'), and when you ran out, your time was up. Van Dam and the FRESS team, of course, were always arguing for more.

> Under the Brown system, the computer is just as much a public utility as the library, and you can no more cut off people based on their field from the computer than you can cut them off from the library [...] Only by threatening to go public and let the campus know that the engineers and physicists were treating the computer as their private fiefdom [did I] get the money. (van Dam 1999)

The FRESS team kept going. Engelbart kept going. Ted Nelson kept writing and publishing and inspiring audiences of young hackers and bright-eyed alumni. And slowly, very slowly, the computing community began to realize that text and hyperlinks on a computer might just work.

The university was still using FRESS for creating documents and printing them out into the late 1970s. In 1976 the National Endowment for the Humanities supported a FRESS application for teaching English poetry (Catano 1979). The FRESS team, and particularly van Dam, had wanted to use the system explicitly for teaching since its inception. In the NEH-sponsored course, students did all of their critical course reading and writing in the online FRESS docuverse. An annotated poetry repository was created in FRESS, with a large collection of poems by Spenser, Tennyson, Blake and others (DeRose and van Dam 1999, 19). Students' and teachers' comments were integrated into the web as the course proceeded, prompting further response and debate in the manner of contemporary teaching webs and wikis (the term 'web' was used in accordance with Vannevar Bush's understanding of the term as a cluster of trails (Bush [1945] 1991)). It was the first time hypertext had been used as a central teaching tool in the humanities, and arguably the first online scholarly community.

Hypertext at Brown: The Electronic Document System (EDS) and Intermedia

Van Dam's next project at Brown, his third hypertext system, was called the Electronic Document System (EDS) or the Interactive Graphical Documents system (IGD). This tool was designed for presenting predominantly graphical documents, something that had interested him for over a decade. It had high-resolution colour graphics capabilities and the ability to incorporate simple 2D animation sequences, the first hypertext system to do so. It was a visually rich system. For this reason, EDS 'represents Brown's first hypermedia system' (Yankelovich, Myerowitz and van Dam 1995, 69), and set the system apart from FRESS, which, like HES, was primarily text-oriented. Van Dam built this system at Brown from 1978 to 1982 with his students, among them PhD student Steven Feiner[7] and undergraduates Randy Pausch and David Salesin (currently head of research at Adobe), and a visiting scientist from the Hungarian Academy of Sciences, Sandor Nagy.

Like FRESS, EDS also provided a variety of coordinated views, but it went further by allowing colour graphic representation of the information web. As van Dam put it in his Hypertext '87 keynote address:

> We spent a lot of time figuring out how to elide, that is, hide, information graphically. We had a 'detail button' that let us view things at varying levels of detail. So the author could move these windows around, look at pages and chapters at arbitrary levels of detail, iconically create various kinds of buttons and specify actions to take place when the reader invoked a button. Such actions could include animation and taking a link to another page. (van Dam 1988)

In 1983 Andries van Dam, William S. Shipp and Norman Meyrowitz founded the Institute for Research in Information and Scholarship (IRIS) at Brown. Their most notable project was Intermedia, a networked, shared, multiuser hypermedia system explicitly designed for use within university research and teaching environments. Intermedia was started in 1985 and sponsored by the Annenberg/CPB project and IBM (Meyrowitz 1986, 196). From the outset, it was built to support multiple users on a network of computers accessing the same content – perfect for teaching course material at universities. It supported bidirectional links for both text and graphics, and had three levels of access: read, write and annotate. Intermedia was also the first object-oriented system built at Brown, and had more multimedia functionality than either FRESS or EDS.

Crucially, Intermedia kept the document structure separate from the link structure. FRESS only partially differentiated between content and hypertext structure;[8] the separation between content and structure was far more complete in Intermedia, an innovation that would prove important. One of the main problems with the World Wide Web is that the link structure is embedded in the document structure. The separation between document and link structure in Intermedia meant that:

> [The] English Department might have a web referencing all of the Shakespearean tragedies along with links pertaining to color imagery in those plays, while the Religious Studies Department might have a web referencing those same plays with links pertaining to religious symbolism. (Yankelovich, Meyrowitz and van Dam 1991, 74)

Intermedia was not just an 'experiment' in building a hypertext system, as HES more clearly was; Intermedia's pedagogic and research import was evident from the very beginning. It was used in several undergraduate courses at Brown from 1986, and some of the course material survives to the present day. For example the *Victorian Web*, a resource hypertext originally created by George Landow in Intermedia and later ported to Storyspace and the Web, is still thriving online[9] and is considered an important 'proof of concept' for using hypertext in pedagogic settings. 'The proof of the Intermedia pudding', writes Kitzmann, was always 'in its actual application and use' (Kitzmann 2006, 16).

The Intermedia system integrated some new developments in the computing field in the 1980s. It was originally written for IBM workstations, then ran on A/UX. It incorporated some elements of the Macintosh user interface and the multiuser capabilities of Unix (although Unix was actually developed in 1969, it was not widely adopted in academic circles until the late 1970s and early 1980s). Like many of the hypertext projects from the mid- to late 1980s, it was also programmed in Mac Pascal and made use of the Macintosh Toolbox (though some of these were in emulation mode), which provided the 'best direct manipulation interface' (Meyrowitz 1986, 189). Intermedia was so tied to Apple Computer's implementation of the Unix operating system, A/UX, that changes in this operating system ended the system's considerable reign in pedagogic circles in 1990. Much of the content from the system had to be ported to Storyspace, a system we explore in the next chapter. As George Landow writes:

> In 1990 Apple Computer, Inc. effectively put an end to the Intermedia project, part of which they had funded, by so altering A/UX, their version of UNIX,

that all development of the program ceased, and when Apple made new models of the Macintosh fundamentally incompatible with the earlier version of A/UX, it became clear that no one could use Intermedia even in a research situation. Nonetheless, Intermedia ran at Brown essentially without maintenance for two years – itself an astonishing tribute to software of such complexity – while we sought another system. (Landow 1992)[10]

Shortcomings aside, Intermedia provided a very rich hypermedia environment for scholars for the years it was in use.

Hypertext and the Early Internet

FRESS occurred on the cusp of the network era – 1969. Memex was intended to be a personal machine, for use as an extension of one's own memory. Similarly, HES was neither networked nor multiuser. It was intended to be a personal (and scholarly) device, to produce printed documents for scholars but also to facilitate their individual associations within and between documents. But NLS and FRESS were pioneering networked multiuser hypertext systems. They were shifting across to a different technical phylum – from the personal, idiosyncratic memory aid to the public archive. From 1968 on, research into hypertext systems focused not on the creation of personal devices, but on distributed systems. The technology of networked communication became the early stages of the Internet.

Doug Engelbart's NLS was one of the first nodes in the fabled ARPANET, which eventually spread its wires around the globe to become the Internet. However, as van Dam observed in an interview with the author:

I don't think [...] that any of us truly envisioned that you could have what we have today, because the issues of interoperability just seemed far more insurmountable in those days. We didn't have networks with the kind of bandwidth that you do today. So, I certainly never foresaw the World Wide Web. It surprised me. (van Dam 1999)

Van Dam says he didn't foresee the Web; neither he nor Doug Engelbart could have imagined where their technologies would lead. But it is undeniable HES became the first working example of hypertext on commercial equipment, and in that sense Nelson believes it became an image of potentiality for future hypertext technologies. So although there was much resistance to Nelson and van Dam's original project, it spawned and legitimised a new field of research: hypertext.

There is still much work to be done in this arena, work that van Dam continued to do at Brown, and Engelbart at the Bootstrap Institute (now called The Doug Engelbart Institute) – the organization he founded to continue evolving the relationship between humans and computers. Because 'the things we decide now will continue to haunt us for decades. Decades' (van Dam 1999).

Chapter 6

MACHINE-ENHANCED (RE)MINDING: THE DEVELOPMENT OF STORYSPACE

Re:minding.
*And yet. But still. (*Mais encore*) Still flowing.*

—Michael Joyce, 2011

Michael Joyce has kept a journal for many years. Before he begins to write, he inscribes the first page with an epigram: Still flowing. As anyone who has read Joyce's fictions or critical writing will attest, his work is replete with multiple voices and narrative trajectories, a babbling stream of textual overflow interrupted at regular intervals by playful, descriptive whorls and eddies. If there is a common thread to be drawn between his hyperfictions, his academic writing and his novels, then it is this polyglot dialogue, as Robert Coover terms it, a lyrical stream of consciousness. Joyce can tell a story. And he has told many stories: four books, 40 scholarly essays, and at last count (my count), a dozen fictions.[1] What courses through this work is a gentle concern, or even fixation, with how stories are told – with 'how we make meaning, as if a caress' (Joyce 2004, 45). The metaphor of water is an appropriate one. Like Ted Nelson, who had his first epiphany about the nature of ideas and the connections between them as he trailed his hand in the water under his grandfather's boat, Joyce has long been concerned with how to represent a multiplicity of ideas and their swirling interrelationships, with how stories change over time. In the essay 'What I Really Wanted to Do I Thought', about the early development of Storyspace, Joyce writes:

> What I really wanted to do, I discovered, was not merely to move a paragraph from page 265 to page 7 but to do so almost endlessly. I wanted, quite simply, to write a novel that would change in successive readings and to make those changing versions according to the connections that I had for some time naturally discovered in the process of writing and that I wanted my readers to share. (1998, 31)

That novel would become *afternoon* (Joyce 1987), the world's first hypertext fiction. The development of Storyspace is, at least in part, the story of Joyce's quest to

A NOTE ON SOURCES

Historians attach great importance to primary evidence – source material and documents that were created at the time under study. Matthew Kirschenbaum notes in his recent book, *Mechanisms*, 'The single indispensable source for the early history of Storyspace is Joyce and Bolter's report to the Markle Foundation which funded Storyspace for a crucial development year in 1985' (2008, 172). The copy I use here is held at the Michael Joyce Archives at the Harry Ransom Research Centre, dated 1986 (hereafter 'the Markle Report'). The Markle Foundation is a charitable organization concerned with technology, healthcare and national security. The Markle Report was written during the first development cycle for Storyspace and describes over 60 typed pages both the research process behind the program and the tool itself as it was used at the time; for this reason, I rely on it heavily.

That said, human memory is fallible, but so are paper documents. The Markle Report was written mainly by Joyce, and in the manner of any document assembled in haste and addressed to a funding body, it presents a particular view of the task at hand (and sometimes gets the minor details mixed up). As Joyce put it when I queried his use of some terms in the report, 'I feel like I'm hoisting my own petard, but obviously I wrote the whole Markle Report; my imprecisions of language are coming back to haunt me' (Joyce 2011a). To get a more detailed picture I supplement this source with oral histories obtained in 2011 – most particularly the recollections of Michael Joyce, Jay David Bolter, John B. Smith and also Mark Bernstein, who has maintained the code for the last 20 years. Stuart Moulthrop and Nancy Kaplan have kindly helped with some of the minor details, and Michael Joyce provided me with a copy of his unpublished manuscript 'Re:mindings' (he was reluctant to part with this, but I'm glad that he did; one day it will become a beautiful book). I also rely heavily on Joyce and Bolter's critical work because this theory influenced the development of the system.

find a structure for what did not yet exist, or as he wrote in the Markle Report, to find 'a structure editor [...] for creating "multiple fictions"' (Bolter and Joyce 1986, 12). As we have seen in this book, the early hypertext systems were built to embody particular visions about how the human mind and memory work, to represent the 'complex interconnections' that hold between ideas. Each system (re)presented a different model of these interconnections, and of the perceived complexity underlying a mass of information. As Jay David Bolter put it, 'Electronic symbols [...] seem to be an extension of a network of ideas in the mind itself' (Bolter 1991, 207; see also Joyce 1998, 23). Storyspace is no exception; Joyce intuitively felt that stories disclose themselves in their connectiveness, and that 'we are associative creatures. That's what we do' (Joyce 2011a).

Unlike van Dam, Engelbart or Bush, however, Joyce is first and foremost a writer, and a very different kind of writer; he is both fluent and prolific.

Storyspace was designed for writers, and the image of potentiality that guided Joyce was a literary one; it started with an idea for a novel.

In every interview Joyce has given about *afternoon* or the development of Storyspace, the leitmotif of a 'story that changes each time you read it' returns like a Wagnerian melody. Joyce's writing is filled with such recurrences, with images and phrases that return again and again; 'recurrence is the sounding of memory in air' he writes in *Othermindedness* (Joyce 2004, 97). As Stuart Moulthrop observed in response to this chapter, the name 'Joyce' is of course an echo, 'an echo he won't acknowledge for fear of trading on homonymity'.[2] This particular image, the image of a multiple fiction, is important enough that it appears verbatim or near verbatim in many of his essays on hypertext (for example Joyce 1998, 31; Joyce 2004, 123 as a 'multiple story').

Although he is quick to point out that 'it wasn't a matter of just bringing a set of ideals and aspirations to Bolter', and then building a system to do that (Joyce 2011a), the idea of a novel that changes with each reading was obviously important to him, based on its longevity in his own work. In our interview, he actually corrected my phrasing: 'Forgive this, this is like an English teacher. It's not *every* reading in the sense of every different reader, but I said *each* reading, and I had in mind readers who would go back to a text again and again' (2011a). If Storyspace has an origin legend, then it begins with this multiple fiction; in Vassar College's version of the tale, Joyce 'looked at his little Apple II in the early '80s and said, "I'll bet you could do a story that would change every [*sic*] time you read it". He called around, looking for such software, and it didn't exist' (Vassar College Innovators Web Site 1992). Apocryphal stories aside, what is clear is that as a novelist, Joyce was thinking about the process of writing, and even more importantly, about the internal connections that exist in stories – connections that might, with the aid of a computer, be shaped by potential readers.

In the early '80s, as a classics professor working at the University of North Carolina, Chapel Hill, Jay David Bolter was also thinking about the computer as a writing space, and about the connections that hold between ideas. His department had been pioneering research into the computerization of classical scholarship since 1975, led by David Packard (son of billionaire computing pioneer David Packard Sr, the co-founder of Hewlett Packard). Unlike his contemporaries, and crucially for the future of humanities computing, Bolter had a background in computer engineering; he completed a masters in computer science in 1978 as well as a PhD in classics in 1977, both from UNC, and was a member of the Committee for Computer Applications (APA) from 1981.[3] As a classics student at UNC in the late 1970s, he remembers in our interview, he was the 'only student in the class who had a computer science background' (Bolter 2011). He became Packard's assistant for a couple of years and worked on his pioneering mini-computer system IBYCUS (Bolter 2011).

IBYCUS was the first computer to allow the editing, search and retrieval of classical texts in a fully integrated desktop package.[4] When Packard left UNC, he left his computer there, and Bolter was responsible for running IBYCUS for a few more years.

> This was really my first important humanities application and it was at that time
> that I started thinking about the impact of the computer as a technology, which
> led to my book *Turing's Man*. (Bolter 2011)

Consequently, when he started working with Joyce in 1983, Bolter had been thinking about the relationship between computing and classical scholarship for a few years.[5] Joyce remembers he 'felt drawn to Jay's vision because he was concerned with questions of how the epic narrator, how the Homeric narrator, adjusted stories so they changed' (Joyce 2011a).

As we saw in the chapter on HES, computing science was engaged in a love affair with AI in the '70s and '80s; it was particularly intent on modelling the perceived structure of the human mind and memory, imitating nature and improving on it (a topic that Bolter critiques in the first edition of Writing Space (Bolter 1991, 171–5), unfortunately removed from the second edition published in 2001). Both Joyce and Bolter spent a year as visiting fellows at the Yale AI Project, Bolter from 1982 to 1983, and Joyce from 1984 to 1985. Bolter recalls there was 'a general paradigm of representation that AI was following at the time, which was the concept of basically linked structures, interlinked structures, nets of ideas' (Bolter 2011), a concept that was also central to Storyspace. 'Crucially', he recalls, 'the AI community didn't see this as writing, they saw it as thinking. In other words, they thought they were [actually] modelling the mind' (Bolter 2011).[6]

From 1980 to 1987 there was a second boom in this area, and large amounts of money were available for research.[7] It was a glamorous field, and both Bolter and Joyce felt the gravitational pull of it. In the Markle Report they note that their 'collaboration stems from, and has been energized by, work in artificial intelligence' (Bolter and Joyce 1986, 12). It might be worth reflecting at this point that, whereas the project of hypertext has been all too successful with the proliferation of the Web, AI remains arguably fictional. In the 1980s however, there was a brief resurgence of hope as the new technology of 'expert systems' and artificial neural networks picked up steam.

Given the prominence they ascribe to this research, I will briefly explore here some of the work produced at Yale. Joyce, in particular, was influenced by the ideas of the indomitable Roger Schank, Director of the Yale AI Project and author of a seminal book in AI called *Dynamic Memory*, first published in 1982 (it has subsequently been revised – the 1999 edition is the one I will be referring to here). Joyce picked up the term 'remindings' from Schank's work, probably from this book, noting in *Of Two Minds* that Schank is 'nearly alone in artificial intelligence researchers in using the computer as a test bed for expressing representations of thought' (Joyce 1998, 165).

He also spent a couple of years corresponding with Natalie Dehn, a researcher at Schank's lab, who used the term extensively in her work on story generation programs.[8] When Joyce first began corresponding with Dehn in 1983 she was working on a story generation program called TALE-SPIN that attempted to simulate an author's mind as she makes up a story (Dehn 1981). The ideal structure editor, write Bolter and Joyce in the Markle Report, would facilitate 'machine enhanced reminding' (Bolter and Joyce 1986, 40).

For Dehn, the process of writing is also deeply influenced by the author's own memory. 'This memory needs to contain not only facts about the storyworld thus far constructed, but also prior knowledge of memorable episodes, characters, etc. in the author's life' (Dehn 1981, 18). TALE-SPIN was an 'AI attempt at story generation' by making up Aesop-fable-like stories that were the consequence of a particular storyworld (Dehn 1981, 18). It was a world simulator, and this world included the characters that lived in it and their goals and motivations. TALE-SPIN behaved, in effect, like an author's memory. It had to keep track of these characters and their specific environment, access the material and reformulate the narrative based on these items. To explain and describe this process of reformulation and retrieval she also borrowed the term 'reminding' from Schank.

For Roger Schank, 'reminding' describes the association of episodes in human memory, and the remodelling that takes place upon recall (hence the title of his 1999 book, *Dynamic Memory*). A library does not have a dynamic memory; it changes with great difficulty. Human memory, on the other hand, is constantly rewriting the connections between episodes and changing the categorizations and associative trails of information. It does not recall information so much as reconstruct it (hence 're-mindings'; not just bringing episodes to mind again and again, but building them afresh each time).

> When we process events as they happen, we need to find particular events in memory that are closely related to the current input we are processing. But how do we define relatedness? What does it mean for one experience to be like another? Under what labels, using what indices, do we look for related episodes? (Schank 1999, 21)

These are questions about the relationship between ideas, and how the mind snaps instantly from one item to another, to paraphrase Bush. They were also questions, Joyce recalls, that made sense to him during his fellowship.

He would sit with Dehn and members of Schank's group, and 'once they got over the initial hump of my being the story-generation person, there was this wonderful sense that they were concerned with questions that I could recognize as a writer' (Joyce 2011a).

From early on in the piece, due to the high profile of this field and their involvement within it, Bolter and Joyce evidently felt the need to stress that Storyspace was not AI. 'We hasten to note', they wrote in 1986, 'that STORYSPACE in [no] way embodies what could legitimately be called AI' (Bolter and Joyce 1986, 33). Such an observation would be entirely unnecessary for a hypertext system now, but in 1986, by contrast, most 'computer people' who were tinkering with networks were doing AI.[9] They go on to note with no small sense of irony that 'we may be among a very small number of current software developers who do not claim to be doing AI' (Bolter and Joyce 1986, 34).

Bolter published a book shortly after his fellowship at Yale that would become a classic in computing studies, *Turing's Man: Western Culture in the Computer Age* (1984). In *Turing's Man*, he sets out to 'foster a process of cross-fertilization' between computing science and the humanities and to explore the cultural impact of computing (Bolter 1984, xii).[10] He also introduces some ideas around 'spatial' writing that would recur and grow in importance in his later work: in particular, the relationship between early Greek systems of place memory loci (the art of memory) and electronic writing.

The seeds behind Bolter's oft-cited and influential observation from *Writing Space* that hypertext 'is not the writing of a place, but rather a writing with places, spatially realized topics' (Bolter 1991, 25) germinated here, in the early 1980s, in his reflections on computers and the classical arts. The classical art of memory represented information by attributing to it spatial characteristics, and similarly, 'the computer makes a geometer out of anyone with a computational problem to solve' (Bolter 1984, 99). In the chapter in *Turing's Man* titled 'Electronic Memory', Bolter writes,

> The computer [...] offers us a 'new dimension' in the representation of information. In building such structures, computer memory is associative rather than linear. It allows us to follow networks of association in our data, as indeed human memory does. This fact was particularly appreciated in the oral culture of Greece and Rome. (Bolter 1984, 163)

Bolter's ideas around 'topographic writing' were nascent when he started collaborating with Joyce in September 1983 (Bolter and Joyce 1986, 10). They would later have a profound influence over hypertext theory and criticism, and also the Storyspace system. From the outset, the nodes in Storyspace were called 'writing spaces', and it worked explicitly with topographic metaphors, incorporating a graphic 'map view' of the link data structure from the first version, along with a tree and an outline view (which are also visual representations of the data). 'The tree', Bolter tells us in *Turing's Man*, 'is a remarkably useful way of representing logical relations in spatial terms' (Bolter 1984, 86). Also in line with the topographic metaphor, writing spaces in Storyspace acted (and still act) as containers for other writing spaces; an author literally 'builds' the space as she traverses it, zooming in and out to view details of the work, the map making the territory. This is an important point. 'The whole thing about Storyspace was – the big thing about Storyspace [was] – you could write hypertext hyper-textually' as Adrian Miles put it in an interview with the author (Miles 2011).

In his 1991 book *Writing Space*, Bolter uses the term 'topography' to incorporate both its original use as a description of a place and its later use as the act of 'mapping or charting' (Bolter 1991, 25). Topographic writing is 'both a visual and a verbal description', and the design of Storyspace reflected this; 'the line, the tree and the network all become visible structures at the writer's and reader's disposal' (Bolter 1991, 114).

Many of the early pre-Web hypertext fictions were written in Storyspace. Some were not – including Judy Malloy's beautiful 'narrabase' programs that generated stories that changed each time you read them, by randomizing retrieval from a database (the most famous of these is *Uncle Roger* (1986), available on the Web).[11] We might also include here John McDaid's *Uncle Buddy's Phantom Funhouse*, which was produced in Hypercard (1992). This also makes use of a navigational 'map' and topographic metaphor. Both Malloy's and McDaid's work remarkably prefigure the movement in contemporary e-literature toward what Victoria Vesna, following Lev Manovich, calls 'database aesthetics' (Vesna 2007, 234).[12]

Those hypertexts that were written in Storyspace had a strange 'preoccupation with the "topography" of hypertext' (Ciccoricco 2007, 197). The metaphor also seemed to stick in hypertext theory for many years; Joyce (1998), Dickey (1995), Landow (1992), Nunes (1999) and Johnson-Eilola (1994), to name but a few of the 'first wave' theorists, explicitly conjure images of exploration and mapmaking to describe the aesthetics of hypertext, due in no small part to Storyspace and to Bolter's book *Writing Space*. Some ideas, as Howard Rheingold wrote in *Tools for Thought* more than 20 years ago, are like viruses: if they are released at the right moment, they can infect an entire culture (Rheingold 1985, 128).

At the time he started working with Bolter, Joyce had ambitions of his own: he wanted to write a book that changed with each reading, as we have seen. According to the Markle Report (and Joyce's own memory)[13] he was also 'insistent on the non-hierarchical and associative working habits' of writers

(Bolter and Joyce 1986, 24). After they were introduced by Natalie Dehn in 1983, they quickly began 'a deeply engaged discussion about storytelling and what kind of associative thinking we each understood' (Joyce 2011a). They didn't have a formal model at the time – 'not like a formal AI-like model or psychological model' – just some concepts that they were working through in their own writing. Joyce recalls that they would talk every day on the telephone – 'this was well before we were habituaries of email' – and that these discussions were thrilling for both of them; 'it was the most profound intellectual period of my life' (Joyce 2011a). In the manner of all great partnerships, the collaboration would change the arc of their creative vectors far into the future: Joyce would later have 'trouble distinguishing where Bolter's thought leaves off and mine begins' (Joyce 1998, Acknowledgements).

Joyce is still playing with the idea of memory and 're:mindings' in his work, 'in the same way that narrative reforms our understandings of our world and ourselves'; his unpublished manuscript is called 'Re:mindings: Essays after: -net, -narrative, -media' (Joyce 2011b). Bolter would go on to write *Remediation: Understanding New Media* with his colleague Richard Grusin (Bolter and Grusin 2000), which developed a model for reminding in the digital era; in this book, Grusin and Bolter argue that visual media achieve their cultural significance by remodelling or reworking earlier media (hence '*re*mediation'). There is a double logic to remediation, a contradictory impulse towards both immediacy and hypermediacy. 'Our culture wants both to multiply its media and to erase all traces of mediation: ideally it wants to erase its media in the very process of multiplying them' (Bolter and Grusin 2000, 5). To put it crudely, we would like to have the most all-encompassing, richest sensory experience possible, while 'forgetting' that this experience has been shaped in advance by the media that enable it.

When I put it to Bolter that the concept of remindings may have been influential for him personally, he replied that he would 'put that back on Michael':

> I think that Michael was always very interested in the notion of memory and its relationship to storytelling. And I think he always [had this] vision of a technological medium that would somehow capture or do justice to the complex process of memory and reminding. (Bolter 2011)

We might call this a tool for machine-enhanced reminding, a machine for memory – or the 'mind as a writing space', to paraphrase Bolter's chapter title from *Writing Space* (Bolter 1991; removed from the second edition in 2001). Bolter wanted to emphasize in our interview that he never believed hypertext to be any more than a metaphor for how the human mind or memory works (Bolter 2011).

The thing about technological visions is that they change; in particular, they change as they are being built into artefacts. Computer languages and hardware have their own limits and capacities, and these impact on the direction of development projects. Andrew Pickering calls this dance, this mutually constitutive dance between vision and artefact, the 'mangle of practice'. When Bolter and Joyce first started tinkering with an early software experiment for the IBM PC to try out some of these ideas, this was precisely what happened: their ideas evolved in tandem with the software experiments.

In the Markle Report, Joyce refers to an early program Bolter brought to their discussions called TEXT (Bolter and Joyce 1986, 12). According to Joyce, this 'was a kind of offering', something to 'try out the ideas we were having about what we understood narrative and thinking to be' (2011a). Bolter believes this program was called GLOSSA: 'TEXT or GLOSSA, the names were changing rather casually at that point' (Bolter, 2011) – but either way the name is not important.[14] Joyce was primarily using an Apple II at this stage; he soon acquired a Macintosh ('not, however, before he purchased an Apple Lisa [using grant money] for something like $11,000, or $9.8 billion in today's money', adds Stuart Moulthrop in the margin of this chapter).[15] GLOSSA was written for the IBM PC in Pascal, one of the high-level development languages in use at the time.[16] The precursors of Storyspace, TALETELLER, TALETELLER 2, and also the original Storyspace, were all written in Pascal – and by 1985, when both Joyce and Bolter were using Macs, Apple had its own Mac Pascal.[17] Once converted to Mac, Bolter and Joyce were committed. 'Once we went to the Mac we never went back' (Bolter 2011).

One of the most basic and enduring tools in Pascal is linked lists, which is a simple way to store and present 'elements' using pointers to indicate the next element (or 'node') in a list. In our interview Bolter pointed out that he had taken a lot of computer science courses, and 'linked lists obviously are the key to thinking about hypertext, if you want to implement it in the most obvious way' (Bolter 2011). GLOSSA was a basic implementation in this sense, based on Bolter's experience with classical texts. 'You'd tab a text and then you'd be able to associate notes with any particular word or phrase in the text [...] an automated version of classical texts with notes' (Bolter 2011). It wasn't clickable because the IBM PC wasn't clickable at the time; the user would move the cursor over the word and select it. This link data structure formed the basis for their future experiments 'only in the sense that it had this quality of one text leading to another' (Bolter 2011).

In his well-researched chapter on *afternoon*, Matthew Kirschenbaum suggests that Storyspace has 'significant grounding in a hierarchical data model' (Kirschenbaum 2008, 173) that has its origins in the tree structures of 'interactive fictions of the Adventure type' (Kirschenbaum 2008, 175). This is an interesting

Joyce in the computer lab he ran in Jackson, Michigan, when he was working on Storyspace.
Photo courtesy Michael Joyce.

observation, and Joyce mentions adventure-type fictions as an influence in the
Markle Report (Bolter and Joyce 1986, 19).[18] When questioned, however, neither
Bolter nor Joyce believe that they were influenced by adventure-type games,
except in the sense that they were 'a kind of zeitgeist at the time' (Bolter 2011).
Joyce in fact recalls they were trying very hard to avoid hierarchical structures
(2011a). Human memory is fallible though, and data models are very hard to
trace at any rate. They always reflect something else, popping up everywhere –
like the grin of the Cheshire cat, as McAleese points out (1999, v).

For my part, I'd like to suggest that if there is a technical 'origin' to the
tree-like data structure in Storyspace, it is more likely to have come from
the functions at hand in the computer language Bolter was using, namely
linked lists, than from adventure-type games. Linked lists were pervasive in
computer science and software design at the time. In other words, the tree-like
structures were just part of the forest of software design.[19] In my investigations
into hypertext history, one surprising find is that this very basic programming
function has been quite influential. This is a far more pedestrian explanation,
almost trivially true, but sometimes programming is about implementing the
most obvious sequence of instructions.

The first product of Joyce's and Bolter's conversation around the original program, GLOSSA, was called TALETELLER – a name that stuck until 1985 (Kirschenbaum 2008, 174). Bolter had GLOSSA in hand when they first started collaborating, but its successor, TALETELLER, was a product of tinkering together. As Joyce recalls:

> We would have these conversations, we'd talk about things, and [Bolter] would say, 'Let me try this in code', and then shoot back something and say, 'Well, is this going to work?' [...] TALETELLER was an attempt to hack together, and without any visual structure, the kind of associative program that would work for what we wanted to do. (Joyce 2011a)

Around this time, Joyce started preparing what he called 'pseudocode' to explain his ideas, a delightful mash of poetic handwritten text, symbols and logical notations. Given the lyrical, polyglot style of his fictions and critical work, we would expect no less in his technical project; Joyce has always written to his own loony-tune music, to paraphrase him in *Of Two Minds* (Joyce 1998, 181).

In his book *Mechanisms*, Kirschenbaum explains how this pseudocode was eventually used to plan and write Joyce's fiction *afternoon* (Kirschenbaum 2008, 182–3). 'Joyce generally uses an arrow → to indicate a link, and symbols for various operators', for example an ampersand to indicate an AND condition (Kirschenbaum 2008, 182). Joyce thinks the process may have been a little more complicated than that, however, and that the pseudocode was more like a lyrical 'mnemonic' than a draft or plan. The trope of memory returns:

> There exist only scraps of notes from writing [*afternoon*] in the Harry Ransom Centre archive and they are (and were) mnemonics for some fairly complex sequences of the fiction, which otherwise I wrote totally 'in' the system of Storyspace, reading and re-reading sequences, and experiencing guard field permutations, from the first. Indeed this was why, in your wonderful phrase in the next paragraph, I was 'hyperconscious' of where the narrative has already been. (2012)

Joyce's 'urge toward a novel that changes each time it is read' (Joyce 1998, 181) inspired the most distinctive feature of Storyspace: guard fields. As we have seen, one of Joyce's key rhetorical strategies is recurrence (the 'sounding of memory in air'), phrases that appear again and again as the writing progresses, relying heavily on the reader's own memory of previous instances of the same phrase or node to alter their present experience. He is hyperconscious of where the narrative has already been. Guard fields control a reader's experience of the text based on where they have been. This is done by placing conditions on the activation of links, so that certain paths can't be taken until the reader has visited a specific node. The reader's experience is thus literally as well as metaphorically shaped by the path already taken, enabling Joyce to repeat terms and nodes throughout the work and have them reappear in new contexts. Conversely, they enable Joyce to ensure that readers don't access key nodes until they have seen or visited others; although the narrative seems to be following a path that may have been followed before, it changes slightly at the next turn.

The most famous example of the use of guard fields is the 'white afternoon' node in *afternoon*; the node that reveals that Peter may have inadvertently killed his own son. Hypertext critic Jane Yellowlees Douglas (Joyce's favourite reader, whose dissertation was on *afternoon*) argues this node 'completes' the work for her, but it is accessible only after the reader has seen a certain sequence of other nodes; 'a succession of guard fields ensures that it is reached only after a lengthy visitation of fifty-seven narrative places' (Yellowlees Douglas 2004, 106). Guard fields are a powerful device, and one that Joyce deploys to full effect in *afternoon*. According to the Markle Report, Joyce 'agitated' for them to be included in the design of Storyspace from the outset, and Bolter quickly obliged in their fledgling program:

> It was just a matter of putting a field into the link data structure that would contain the guard, and then just checking that field […] against what the user did before they were allowed to follow the link […] It was [that] idea you know and it was Michael's. (Bolter 2011)

Guard fields, along with the topographic 'spatial' writing style, have remained integral to the Storyspace program for 30 years hence.

In 1985 Bolter became involved with an interdisciplinary research group at UNC directed by a colleague from computer science, John B. Smith. Smith formed this research group when he returned to UNC as a faculty member in 1984 (Smith 2011). Bolter and Joyce have always credited Smith as a coauthor of Storyspace, but Smith wanted to clarify in our interview that he wasn't involved in the development of either TALETELLER or Storyspace – he feels he made more of an intellectual contribution insofar as 'there was a sort of cloud of ideas that we were all drawing on in the discussions we'd have in this research entity at UNC, Textlab' (Smith 2011).

Textlab was comprised of three people from computer science including Smith, a cognitive scientist called Marcy Lansman and Bolter from classics. The group would have weekly meetings at Chapel Hill, and 'would debate and discuss' problems and issues around hypermedia, data structures and the visual representation of writing and thinking (Smith 2011). Textlab was a very productive group, and they developed a number of hypertext systems between

1984 and 1989. Primary among them was the Writing Environment (WE), the system with which Smith was most closely associated. This expository writing system was contemporaneous with Storyspace.

The development of the Writing Environment was Textlab's major project. WE was a hypertext system explicitly designed in accord with a 'cognitive model of the writing process' (Smith et al. 1986). Unlike Bolter and Joyce, Smith and the rest of the WE team were 'not interested in prose, in fiction' (Smith 2011); WE was designed to produce paper documents for professionals. Users could represent their ideas as nodes, move them into 'spatial' clusters and link them into an associative network. Crucially, this network was not intended to be read at a screen like Storyspace fictions are. WE would assemble the nodes in sequence and print a linear document. If the user edited this tree structure, then the structure of the corresponding printed document would change. The model was derived from a review of the literature in cognitive psychology, composition theory and the nascent field of human computer studies (which would later become Human Computer Interaction (HCI)). Bolter coauthored a seminal paper on WE in 1986 with Smith, Lansman, Stephen Weiss, David Beard and Gordon Ferguson, and contributed to its development.

From the outset in the discussions this group were having, however, it became apparent to Smith that:

> Jay was more interested in the Macintosh hardware, and he was also interested in applying these ideas to literature and a literary context. So Jay at some point said 'Okay, I think I'm going to set off and do an alternate system', probably incorporating a lot of the ideas that were floating around in this group, and also, of course, creating new ideas of his own. (Smith 2011)

The Markle Report refers to a system that 'strongly influenced Storyspace' at this time called PROSE, credited to John B. Smith (Bolter and Joyce 1986, 13). Smith does not recall making a system called PROSE, however, and believes the report is referring to an early version of WE (Smith 2011).[20] Although there was actually a program around at the time called PROSE (Prompted Revision of Student Essays, built by Nancy Kaplan, Stuart Davis and Joe Martin),[21] both Joyce and Bolter believe that WE was far more influential.[22] Either way, the discussions that this interdisciplinary research entity were having, and the 'cloud of ideas' surrounding the development of what would become WE in Textlab, influenced the development of Storyspace.[23]

Joyce and Bolter's next implementation, again in Pascal, was called TALETELLER 2. They both emphasized the influence of the Macintosh user interface on their thinking at this time, particularly the idea of representing the working space as a series of nested levels or spaces, inspired by the 'idea of containing documents inside folders' (Bolter 2011). The way the Mac did this was too cumbersome and hierarchical, however; on a Mac the user retrieved a piece of text only by 'going into the document folder to open the document' (Bolter 2011). This file structure was not designed to be redrawn at will; the assumption was that users were concerned with editing documents, not their *connections* to other documents. Bolter and Joyce wanted it to be more 'fluid, so basically documents and folders are the same thing, you can open any particular cell and it can be either a document or it can be a container [for another document]' (Bolter 2011). Again, the metaphor Joyce and Bolter had in mind was the writer as cartographer – not the writer as Apple filing clerk.

The Markle Report refers to a meeting at this time with Dr Kristine Hooper from the Apple Educational Division, who presented the Aspen Movie Project at MIT, an early hypermedia system that allowed the user to take a virtual tour of surrogate travel through the city of Aspen, Colorado.[24] This system had a navigation map overlaid above the horizon that allowed the user to jump to a two-dimensional city map.

> This reinforced a decision, prompted by both Bolter's initial working paper and the limitations of the Macintosh screen, to present users with a small (but enlargeable) depiction of the hierarchical tree which would largely serve as a mapping space and for manipulation of large-scale structures, i.e. deleting and moving sub-trees. (Bolter and Joyce 1986, 20)

As noted earlier in this chapter, the topographic metaphor has always been integral to this hypertext system – both in the interface design and in the development of technical functionalities. 'From the beginning', remembers Joyce, 'we tried to find the consonant, physical, visual structures that would suit associative [writing]' (Joyce 2011a). In 1985 the team dubbed the program Storyspace, a name chosen to reflect this metaphor. Also in 1985, they received a grant from the Markle Foundation 'to study methods for creating and presenting interactive compositions [...] by developing a microcomputer-based "structure editor"' (Bolter and Joyce 1986, cover). Aside from providing a much-needed injection of funds at the time, this resulted in the Markle Report, which has proved most useful historically.

Although this report covers dozens of influences and design decisions over almost 60 pages, there is no reference to Joyce's fiction *afternoon*, only to his 'ambitious but somewhat unformed' desire to create a multiple fiction (Bolter and Joyce 1986, 12). Joyce did, however, have a copy of *afternoon* to present and distribute one year later at the Hypertext '87 conference at UNC Chapel Hill, November 13–15. If hypertext had a coming-out party, then it was this first ACM hypertext conference.

Many of the systems we have explored in this book were presented at Hypertext '87, and many of the personalities behind them were walking the halls. It was an exciting time, recalls John Smith; it was the first large international conference devoted to hypertext, and 'the hypertext community discovered that it was bigger than anyone realized' (Smith 2011). Joyce and Bolter were there, at their 'famous, but not mythological rickety table, where we sat outside the plenary sessions' (Joyce 2011a), and Smith was there with his Textlab colleagues presenting the Writing Environment (Smith actually co-chaired the conference with Frank Halasz). Andy van Dam gave his legendary keynote presentation, as we saw in the chapter on HES.

Apple presented HyperCard with much pomp and ceremony, but it was met with an undertone of disdain (as Joyce recalls it); the feeling was 'we all knew systems that had a good deal more functionality, like FRESS, and we sort of resented being told, "here's hypertext"' (Joyce 2011a). Ted Nelson also presented a paper on Xanadu ('All for One and One for All') and Janet Walker presented a paper on the Document Examiner. 'It was fabulous,' recalls Joyce, 'the whole hypertext world discovered one another' (Joyce 2011a).

> The demos at Hypertext '87 were literally at the center of the conference. One big room, lots of big systems, systems we'd been reading about for years but that you'd never actually seen before. There in one room: Ted Nelson's Xanadu, Engelbart's NLS/Augment, Walker's Symbolics Document Explorer, Joyce and Bolter with Storyspace, [Bernstein's] Hypergate, Meyrowitz and Landow and Yankelovich and van Dam with Intermedia. (Bernstein 2008)

In the midst of this party, Joyce and Bolter presented their paper on Storyspace (Bolter and Joyce 1987). There is a brief note towards the end of that paper, enclosed in parentheses, that a copy of *afternoon* is 'available to interested readers' (ibid., 49). Joyce recalls that he worked hard to get the first version of *afternoon* done by that meeting so he could distribute it on diskette as an example of what could be done in Storyspace. 'Absolutely. It was written for that meeting, I mean not written about that meeting', but distributed as an example (Joyce 2011a). This is a modest estimation of the work, however (Joyce is characteristically modest); *afternoon* was no mere footnote to hypertext history, a little 'example' of the kind of thing you could do in Storyspace.

Along with Stuart Moulthrop's *Victory Garden* and Shelley Jackson's *Patchwork Girl*, *afternoon* is arguably the most important hypertext fiction in the history of computing. Citations of it are too numerous to include here because 'it appears in virtually every scholarly publication on literary hypertext' (Ensslin 2007, 71). If there is a hypertext

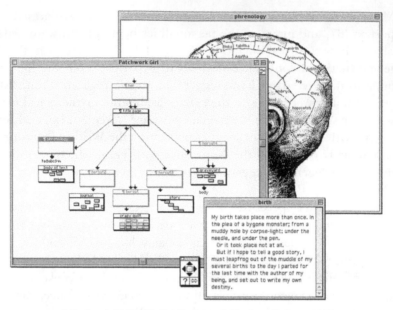

Storyspace map of *Patchwork Girl* by Shelley Jackson. © Eastgate Systems 1995.

'canon', then *afternoon* belongs there: it appears in 'every hypertext seminar in the Western hemisphere' (ibid.).

It also continues to influence Storyspace. Bernstein, who has maintained the code for the last 20 years, pointed out in our interview that his design goal is fairly simple: 'always be able to run *afternoon* and *Victory Garden* and *Patchwork Girl* [...] the agenda related to the writing process is less prominent in my mind than perhaps it used to be in Michael's' (Bernstein 2011). That said, more has been written about *afternoon* than any other work of digital literature. As Bernstein put it, 'If you don't know *afternoon*, you don't know hypertext' (Bernstein 2011). The closest reader of Joyce's fictions has always been Jane Yellowlees Douglas (particularly in her book *The End of Books, or Books Without End?* (2004)), and several new interpretations of *afternoon* have been published in recent years by young scholars – most notably literary critic Alice Bell (2010) and Bangor University's Astrid Ensslin (2007).

For this reason, I won't take the reader through yet another interpretation of *afternoon*; this has already been done elsewhere, and brilliantly. I will simply note that the fiction Joyce distributed on diskette at Hypertext '87 did more than just demonstrate Storyspace; it demonstrated what network literature could be, and arguably opened a space for that genre to evolve. *[A]fternoon* was the realization of Joyce's long-held dream: it is a book that changes with each reading.

As Matthew Kirschenbaum observes in his own chapter on *afternoon*, there is a journal entry in the Joyce Archives, dated 4 June 1988, that notes;

> What is not recorded here, but exists in a series of papers, letters and what-have-you is the experience of succeeding at what I set out to do before Jay and I first contacted each other: 'to write a novel that changes each time you read it' came to be the story, afternoon, which will likely be the centerpiece of S[tuart] Moulthrop's first disk magazine. (Joyce 1988, also cited by Kirschenbaum)

In 1988 Joyce, Bolter and Smith formed a startup they called Riverrun Ltd (a return to Joyce's favourite metaphor, and an evocation of the famous first word of James Joyce's *Finnegans Wake*; the official letterhead from 1990 has running water as its logo).[25] Together they approached Brøderbund Software, Inc., an American software and game manufacturer best known for the *Carmen Sandiego* and *Galactic Empire* games. According to Kirschenbaum, who went through the correspondence between Joyce and Brøderbund, it was eventually dropped in 1989 because of 'what was perceived to be a weakening in the software market, as well as lingering confusion over what the tool did and who its potential audience was' (Kirschenbaum 2008, 176). After Brøderbund, Joyce entered into conversation with Mark Bernstein, the founder of Eastgate Systems. Eastgate signed a contract licensing Storyspace in December 1990 and has distributed it since that time.

Pieces of editing software are not known for their shelf life. None of the first-generation hypertext systems from the 1960s and 1970s have survived into the modern era. Even what we have dubbed the 'second generation' of hypertext systems from the late 1970s and early 1980s, the contemporaries of Storyspace – FRESS, Intermedia, Smith's WE, Apple's Hypercard – are no longer in use. Storyspace, however, has survived for almost 30 years; content is still being written for it, it still being bought and sold, and it is still being used in pedagogic environments, although the user base is probably fairly small (a couple of hundred users). This is virtually unheard of in the history of computing software; packages just don't last that long. The reason Storyspace has survived so long is fairly simple: Eastgate Systems has been maintaining it.

It would be remiss to write a history of hypertext without devoting time to Eastgate and to its founder, Mark Bernstein. In addition to the development of early hypertext systems, 'the history of hypertext was also driven by efforts to create hypertext content for the wider public' (Kitzmann 2006, 8). Eastgate Systems has been the major publisher of hypertext fiction for over twenty years, and published the majority of what is now considered 'serious literary hypertext' (this is also Eastgate's tagline), including Joyce's *afternoon*, Stuart Moulthrop's *Victory Garden* and Shelley Jackson's *Patchwork Girl*.

In addition, Bernstein has maintained and extended the Storyspace code since 1990 (it has been entirely rewritten in C, and doesn't share a single line of code with the original Pascal version, which presents its own conundrum: where is the Storyspace in Storyspace?). He has also made significant contributions to hypertext as a critical discourse.[26] As John Vincler put it on his blog:

> Who has made a more substantial contribution to the field of electronic literature than Mark Bernstein? This makes for a fun parlor game if you know anything about the field. You could name individual authors whose works helped to legitimize the field of born-digital literature. If you go with this approach, you may suggest Michael Joyce, Shelley Jackson, or Stuart Moulthrop, yet all these authors were published on Bernstein's Eastgate Systems. (Vincler 2010)

Eastgate pioneered hypertext publishing in the late 1980s and arguably legitimized hypertext as a creative endeavor. As Australian hypertext theorist and author Adrian Miles remembers it, by 1990:

> They were shrink-wrapping stuff and putting it in envelopes and mailing it out [before the Web]. You've got a physical thing with a cover and a floppy disk or a CD, originally [they were] floppy disks, that you load onto your computer. So from the get go it was sort of stamping itself as 'This is a literary enterprise, it's not experimental', and it's not 'Here are some hypertext experiments.' (Miles 2011)

Eastgate has also been criticized for the dominance of its titles in the hypertext canon, and the fact that the company sells these titles for a profit.[27] It is not universally celebrated in the historical literature. Most notably, Matthew Kirschenbaum managed to write an otherwise brilliantly researched chapter on the evolution of *afternoon* and Storyspace while devoting but a sentence to Eastgate's role in this story ('a small company specializing in hypertext systems research' (Kirschenbaum 2008, 177)) and to Bernstein's role personally (he 'maintains the code' (Kirschenbaum 2008, 162)). Admittedly Kirschenbaum and Bernstein have their own history, and it is best for readers to interpret this themselves rather than have me recount it (Kirschenbaum maintains this is not the reason he didn't include Bernstein: he covered an earlier period in the software's development).[28] It must be said, however, that it was Eastgate's business model that garnered a profile for its authors in the United States and internationally before the Web, a direct 'result of their marketing and distribution by Eastgate systems' (Ciccoricco 2007, 2).

If we have now come to the point where we might talk about a hypertext 'canon', and indeed Astrid Ensslin has published a book arguing we should do just that (Ensslin 2007), this is due in no small part to the publishing and

for directions click yes (y)-- to start press Return

©1987 Michael Joyce
The Eastgate Press Edition 1990
PO Box 1307
Cambridge, MA 02238

Screenshot of *afternoon*, © Eastgate 1990.

marketing of titles by Eastgate. From early on, Bernstein sought to find and publish hypertexts because he felt the literary world needed some real examples; it was all hypertext theory, no 'serious hypertext' (this is also Eastgate's company tagline). As Stuart Moulthrop observes, in 1990 Bernstein stood before the European Conference on Hypertext and uttered the famous first words, 'Where are the hypertexts?' – a question that is arguably still just as urgent. Eastgate was set up to provide an answer to that question.

Bernstein also developed his own hypertext system, which was operational by 1988: Hypergate. Hypergate is noteworthy because it introduced the concept of 'breadcrumbs' – showing whether a link takes you back to a place you've already seen. Bernstein invented this concept, and it eventually made its way into the Mosaic browser (Eastgate never implemented breadcrumbs in Storyspace).

Possibly for this reason, Bernstein was initially more interested in signing Joyce's hypertext fiction, *afternoon*, than he was in Storyspace. As Joyce recalls it, '*afternoon* was my bargaining chip in many ways. That's how I remember things. I made the publishing of *afternoon* contingent on [Eastgate signing Storyspace]' (Joyce 2011a). Bernstein thinks this is overstating the situation. He does remember approaching Joyce about *afternoon*, because it seemed a natural fit, but he 'didn't expect Storyspace to be on offer. I might have seemed more reluctant than I was' (Bernstein 2011).

These discussions went on for some time, starting in 1989, at the Hypertext '89 meeting.

> At Hypertext '89, I had discussions with Michael Joyce where we basically agreed that we were going to do this, and Brøderbund had returned the right to Storyspace to Michael and Jay. So from that time for the next several months we proceeded under the assumption that it would be. (Bernstein 2011)

The contract with Eastgate licensing the development and maintenance of Storyspace is dated 17 December 1990. Over the next five years, a number of hypertext fictions were written in Storyspace and marketed by Eastgate that have since attained (or should attain, according to Ensslin's *Canonizing Hypertext* (2007) 'canonical' status. These include Moulthrop's *Victory Garden* (1991), Carolyn Guyer's *Quibbling* (1993), Jane Yellowlees Douglas's *I Have Said Nothing* (1994) and Shelley Jackson's *Patchwork Girl* (1995). So important was Storyspace (and Eastgate) to the early development of the field, argues Katherine Hayles, that works created within Storyspace have come to be known as the Storyspace School (Hayles 2008, 6). Alice Bell's recent book on hypertext fiction similarly argues for the creation of a hypertext canon, and analyses four hypertext fictions that were created in Storyspace, providing 'a critical theory for the analysis of Storyspace fictions' (Bell 2010, 7).

For my own part, I find it strange that recent theorists are arguing for a formal canon. It is almost as though we have forgotten the lessons of poststructuralism. What, exactly, is wrong with margins and interstices? Isn't that where all the interesting stuff happens? Why canonize it? Stuart Moulthrop wrote a response to Alice Bell's book on Storyspace fiction in the *Electronic Book Review*:

> For Dr. Bell, the adjectival *niche* is a term of suspicion. I disagree, having learned to think of literary or cultural niches not as traps, but as necessary predicaments or premises. As I see it, if dwellers in these dens need to escape anything, it is the niche distinction itself, the overriding concern with separation of specialist and popular markets. (Moulthrop 2011a)

This is the legacy of Storyspace. Whichever side you fall on in this debate, the fact is that Storyspace fictions predominate in what arguably already is (or should be) a hypertext canon.

The arrival of the Web and HTML changed the landscape for hypertext and for Storyspace. Storyspace was originally built (as were all the early hypertext systems) as a standalone system – in this case running under the Macintosh OS. It was not intended to create networked hypermedia like the texts found on the Web. Arguably, it still belongs to the pre-Web era (and by including it in this story, I have contributed to that perception).

Bernstein extended the program in 1995 to enable users to export HTML templates, but as Katherine Hayles points out, 'the limitations of Storyspace as a web authoring program are significant (for example, it has a very limited palette of colors and cannot handle sound files that will play on the web)' (Hayles 2008, 6).[29] Guard fields are also very difficult to implement on the Web, and the HTML link model, as we have looked at in this book, simply cannot support some of the more complicated link models of the earlier hypertext systems.

> The relationship between Storyspace and the Web has never been entirely easy, in part because the Storyspace link model is richer than the Web's and it turns out that for the sorts of things people want to do in Storyspace the richness matters a lot [...] Guard fields are invaluable for large-scale narrative, and we have not come up with an alternative [on the Web]. (Bernstein 2011)

Authors also started turning to Flash and, to some extent, Javascript around the turn of the century. We now have a generation of writers who are willing to script within Application Programming Interfaces (APIs) – or as Stuart Moulthrop puts it, 'a wave of Jay Bolters'.[30] For these reasons, although Storyspace continues to be used to produce standalone works, 'it has been eclipsed as the primary web authoring tool for electronic literature' (Hayles 2008, 6). Like all the first- and second-generation hypertext systems we have explored in this book, the Web presented a completely different model for building hypertexts. Storyspace was never about engaging a crowd, and it has never really entered the Web era.

Bolter has a rather pessimistic view of the Web's impact on networked literature, and on the legacy of Storyspace. 'The Web compromised on the vision of hypertext', he observes. It compromised on the 'literary, political, social vision of the original hypertext movement' (Bolter 2011), and it allowed work to be commercialized quickly and easily. This has its benefits, of course; the Web provides a massive new audience and a quick (and free) way of distributing products to that audience, but the Web obliterated Bernstein's original business model. The whole concept of selling hypertext is made immensely more difficult when everywhere literature is given away for free. As Bolter points out, the literary community 'often revolted against this, because it was so easily commercialized' (Bolter 2011).

The most famous example of this rebellion against the Web is Robert Coover's 'Literary Hypertext: The Passing of the Golden Age' (1999). In this keynote address to the second Digital Arts and Culture Conference (DAC), Coover laments the passing of a specific body of digital literature – what we would now classify as the Storyspace School – and the rise of the 'noisy, restless, opportunistic, superficial, e-commerce driven' Web texts, that 'are about as appealing as a scatter of old magazines on a table in the dentist's lounge' (Coover 1999). The Golden Age of hypertext has passed, the visual usurping the verbal. The margins, in fact, used to be the site for revolutions; perhaps this is why Moulthrop is reluctant to leave them.

Looking back on its history, one of the most interesting aspects of Storyspace is the fact that it bridged the gap between humanities and computing science so early, and that it was taken seriously by both fields. This was largely due to the fact that Bolter 'had a seat in both worlds', as Joyce points out (Joyce 2011a), and collaborated with his engineering colleagues from the outset. Unlike Nelson and Engelbart, Bolter and Joyce were not ridiculed; on the contrary, they both felt embraced by computing science, which set a precedent for future work in the area. In fact, according to Joyce, 'What has gone unremarked is Storyspace's contribution to a dialogue, if not across the two cultures then at least across the engineering and literary communities' (Joyce 2011a).

CONCLUSION

Everything is deeply intertwingled. I have always loved that particular Nelsonism (and there are many to choose from); it has stuck with me for twenty years. In this book we have looked at several early, pre-Web attempts to represent intertwingularity, to represent the deep connections that criss-cross and interpenetrate human knowledge. They were built at different times and from different technical components; two of them (Memex and Xanadu) were never built at all. As a series of machines, they are a motley crew. With the exception of Storyspace, they are also obsolete – had Bruce Sterling continued his Dead Media Project beyond 2001, they would belong properly to that collection.

There are, however, hypertexts created in the '80s that are still read and edited today. George Landow's *Victorian Web*, originally created in Intermedia, then ported to Storyspace and the Web, is one of the oldest scholarly hypertexts. It is still used as course material in Victorian literary studies. Numerous hypertexts created in Storyspace, among them *afternoon* and *Victory Garden*, are still read, studied and argued about in critical literature. We have inherited more than just technical designs from the history of hypertext – we have inherited works of literature.

The '80s was also a period of great critical foment for hypertext theory. Theorists began enthusiastically exploring hypertext from a literary perspective in the late '80s, claiming that the interactive nature of hypertext invites us to reconfigure our conceptions of 'text', 'narrative' and 'author' in a fashion more suited to the nature of the medium (Landow 1992, also Landow and Delaney 1995). Hypertext heralds a new form of writing: instead of the linear, passive narrative of the book and Codex Culture, we have the multilinear universe of the networked system. Poststructuralists, it seems, have been going on about this for decades, confined to the world of print. For Derrida, Foucalt and Barthes, what was 'only figuratively true in print becomes literally true in the electronic medium' (Bolter 1991, 158). The similarities between poststructuralist theory and hypertext were eagerly unpacked by Landow, Joyce, Lanham, Johnson-Eilola, Moulthrop and Bolter among others; the party went on for more than a decade.[1]

The claims made during this period of discovery – when literary theorists 'discovered' hypertext – seem utopian now. But like pieces of literature or bits of pottery from any historical epoch, they should be approached with an historical awareness. The technology was new and exciting (and in some cases, frightening) for humanities theorists in the 1980s, just as French poststructuralist theory was new and exciting for humanities theorists in the 1970s. In many ways poststructuralism saw a renaissance in digital media studies via hypertext theory. It will also be clear by now that many of the inventors we have surveyed here had utopian dreams and visions; they were drinking the same Kool-Aid. Sometimes visions can drive invention.

One dream in particular has recurred throughout this book: a device that 'enables associative connections that attempt to partially reflect the 'intricate web of trails carried by the cells of the brain' (Wardrip-Fruin 2003, 35). More precisely, a tool for thought – a tool that might organize the mass of deeply tangled data that surrounds us. For the world grows more and more complex every day, and the information we are expected to keep track of proliferates at every click. How are we to keep track of the mess?

The problem that Bush identified in 1945 is just as urgent today. The Web has not solved this problem for us – arguably it has highlighted it, in razor sharp text and 16.7 million colours. The Web is without doubt a world-changing and world-opening technology; as Andy van Dam put it to me in 1999, 'the fact that I can reach out and touch stuff in Ethiopia, as it were, is still a surprise to me' (van Dam 1999). Unlike any of the hypertext systems we have looked at here, the Web stretches between countries and engages literally billions of people. But it is not a perfect archive: information gets lost, items are daily replaced or removed, content is duplicated all over the shop. There is no guarantee that the article you visited last week will still be there today. The Web does short-term memory, period. But the Web is not the only way of doing hypertext.

In this book, I have presented some earlier models of the hypertext concept, and in the process, demonstrated that every model has its benefits and its shortcomings. We began with Vannevar Bush's memory extender, or Memex. Memex was an analogue machine that would store information associatively, keep a record of all the interconnections between ideas, but never forget things. The Memex user could join different items together into 'trails', and could re-use the same item in different trails. Although the Memex design changed slightly over decades, what is most interesting is what remained the same: it was a direct analogy to the workings of human associative memory, an alignment between human and machine.

Douglas Engelbart picked up Bush's vision of a symbiosis between man and machine and brought it to computing science. Engelbart also borrowed the idea of associative trails and interactivity from Bush and Memex, but I have argued that the underlying idea of an active partnership between human and device was just as important. Engelbart's guiding 'vision', the vision of person sitting in front of a computer screen engaged in Memex-like activities, became NLS – and NLS became the modern computing environment.

NLS was the first 'built' hypertext system, the first prototype. And aside from the impressive Journal feature, Engelbart's system was hierarchical to its core. NLS imposed a general hierarchical structure on all content. Every item had to have a section header, and underneath that would be some text, and underneath that some subtext. This imposed structure would repel Ted Nelson, who declined an offer from Engelbart to work on the project. It also distinguishes the system from Xanadu, which is opposed to such structures. But in NLS the user could always link from any point in the hierarchy to any other point – the linking could bypass the hierarchy.

The NLS system offered many benefits to users. But NLS operated in its own unique environment, on the machines that Engelbart built to house it. It was also difficult to use. NLS was never intended to connect literally billions of people together like the Web. At around the same time Engelbart was building NLS, however, Ted Nelson was designing a system that was intended to do just that. It was worldwide hypertext, like the Web. It was called Xanadu.

Xanadu would be the perfect archive; it would capture the deeply interconnected structure of human knowledge and make it available to everyone. Content would always be connected to its original source, and copyright and ownership would be scrupulously preserved. It would allow users to compare document versions side-by-side, with 'visible beams' between them. Links would not be one-way like on the Web; they could be two-way. Xanadu would reach into every house and every business, storing and displaying all the world's literature. Unlike the Web, nothing would ever be lost or broken.

One of the reasons that Xanadu could achieve this is that it would separate content from the linking structure. The content would always stay where it is, uniquely identified and unadulterated, and links or citations would simply point back to this content. On the Web, links are 'embedded' in the content – text must be festooned with tags to display correctly. This means that when the content needs to be re-used somewhere else, it has tags all through it. Xanadu would use 'parallel' rather than embedded markup; content would be given a permanent address ('stabilized' in Xanadu lingo) and the links and structure would be an overlay. Most importantly, this original content could be 'transcluded' into other documents by reference. All the while, the original work would remain safe, the connections preserved forever.

But Xanadu, like Memex, has never been built. It is one of the computing world's most enduring dreams. Thinking about this makes Nelson despondent. No amount of reassurance that his vision has influenced people will console him.

One of the people Nelson influenced was Andries van Dam. Van Dam went on to build the Hypertext Editing System (HES) at Brown University with Nelson's help, though Nelson now feels bitter about the experience. This personal issue is a shame, because the HES was revolutionary – it was the first 'visual' word processor, and the first hypertext system beginners could use. It had technical chutzpah.

HES could be used to compose and manipulate manuscripts, but it could also be used to browse and read material. There were no distinctions between 'readers' and 'writers'. As I explained in the chapter on HES, this is no longer the case in commercial hypertext systems; the closest approximation we have are wikis. HES also implemented Nelson's concept of the text link – but they made the links one way (which from Nelson's perspective was heresy). It was also a prototype, and in that sense it actually showed people how hypertext might work. This is an important point. As we explored in the chapter on HES, van Dam spent a lot of time convincing humanities people that writing at a computer screen was not a stupid idea.

HES also led to more hypertext systems at Brown, starting with the File Retrieval and Editing System (FRESS). Unlike HES, FRESS had no size limitations. Van Dam had also seen Engelbart's landmark 1968 presentation by that stage, and decided to make the system multiuser. FRESS was quite powerful for its time, and handled large or complicated documents well – the user had control over how and how much of the document they saw (unlike with typical HTML pages, for example). It did have its limitations, however – limitations van Dam and the team at Brown tried to improve on with subsequent systems.

One of the limitations with HES and FRESS was that the content was not separate from the link structure. As Nelson is fond of pointing out, this is also a problem with the Web. Intermedia kept the content separated and allowed multiple different uses for the same content. At Brown this meant that particular items (for example Shakespeare's plays) could be referenced in multiple different contexts by different departments. FRESS didn't go so far as to 'transclude' the content though (to my knowledge no large scale hypertext system has done that yet). Still, the idea that markup might be held separately from the content is a seductive one. We may wish to keep it in mind for future hypertext systems.

Unlike FRESS or Intermedia, Storyspace was designed specifically for writers. Like the other hypertext systems we have surveyed here, however, it was primarily concerned with representing intertwingularity. The connections between ideas are important, and from Joyce and Bolter's perspective, we should be able to write with them. I have argued in this book that the program was inspired by work in AI and its model of human associative memory, a machine for (re)minding. This emphasis on the relationship between ideas is important: although Storyspace is arguably still caught in a pre-Web era, it enables forms of linking and connectivity that are simply not possible on the Web.

One of the examples we have looked at here is guard fields. Guard fields prevent users from activating links until certain conditions have been fulfilled (for example, you have visited pages A, B and also F). They enable authors to work with large-scale narratives, but they also allow the story to change each time you read it. Storyspace allows writers to make 'multiple' fictions – fictions that literally change based on where you have been.[2]

I am not suggesting that we implement guard fields or transclusion on the Web, or that two-way links will solve your research problems. I am not suggesting we turn everything into a wiki. I want to say that hypertext is not the Web; the Web is but one particular implementation of hypertext. It's the best we've come up with insofar as it actually works, most of the time – and it has stayed the course for 22 years. It is not, however, the only way hypertext can be done.

Imagine a system whose trails do not fade. Imagine if documents and objects could be stored permanently, with their own unique address that never vanished, and retrieved at will. Imagine if any version of these documents could be visually intercompared side-by-side, like the teeth in a zipper – and the quotes or ideas in those documents could be traced back to their original source with a click. Imagine if we could separate the linking structure from the content, and that content could consequently be reused in a million different contexts. Imagine if there were no artificial distinctions between readers and writers. Imagine if we could capture the deeply tangled structure of knowledge itself, but make it better, make it permanent.

'EVERYTHING IS DEEPLY INTERTWINGLED. In an important sense there are no 'subjects' at all; there is only all knowledge, since the cross-connections among the myriad topics of this world simply cannot be divided up neatly' (Nelson 1987).

NOTES

Preface

1 Although Nelson believes one of the Xanadu prototypes breaks this rule: 'The tumbler-addressing system of xu88 was *precisely* for accommodating billions of users' (Nelson 2012).

Chapter 1. Technical Evolution

1 Barnet 2004.
2 A debate, I might add, that I do not intend to contribute to here!
3 Nelson is infamous for his hatred of paper and its limitations, as the reader will discover in Chapter 3, and these limitations inspired him to seek an alternative.
4 Mark Bernstein disagrees with this last point; the people who have written important papers on stretch-text are the same authors and inventors who pioneered chunk-style hypertext. The lineage would 'not be so [different], I think' (2012).
5 Interested readers can find my article on the history of association in Aristotle's work (Barnet 2000).

Chapter 2. Memex as an Image of Potentiality

1 Personal communication, Paul Kahn 2012.
2 Thanks to Paul Kahn for this observation (2012).
3 Though arguably, as Mark Bernstein points out, this was not so important to him: 'he was a scientist and administrator; for Bush, writing was not an end in itself' (Bernstein 2012).
4 Although Bernstein points out that the navy had a few distractions at this time (2012).
5 Nelson writes in response: 'as a self-publisher working on my kitchen table (*Computer Lib*, *Literary Machines*) I couldn't afford it. I hear Microsoft Word does it automatically, but I had no time for that in *Possiplex*, even though I used that benighted software.'
6 This term was omitted from the *Life* reprint of 'Memex II'.
7 Bush was not, however, a neuroscientist; nor was Engelbart. As Paul Kahn stressed in an email to the author, Bush and Engelbart are expressing their feelings and intuition, not their knowledge.

Chapter 3. Augmenting the Intellect: NLS

1 Interestingly, so was Ted Nelson, who said in one of our interviews that he only recently found out that Engelbart was also deeply inspired by Whorf. Bardini, however, recalls that Nelson knew about this as early as 1993 'March 17, to be precise', when Bardini interviewed him in Sausalito. Email to the author.

2 Similarly in the 1980s with the design community.

3 Like Engelbart, Wiener is concerned that humans 'must not let machines become their masters' (Hayles 1999, 85), yet he explicitly promotes computers as 'thinking machines capable of taking over many human decision-making processes' (Hayles 1999, 85). The line blurs at the boundary between thought and technics – a boundary that also concerns Engelbart.

4 Bardini, in response to this chapter, disagrees that the structure was treelike: 'You are right that NLS was highly hierarchical but strangely enough (in my view at least) unlike a tree: what was hierarchical was the instruction/comment structure and the overall modal nature of the interface' (Bardini 2011).

5 'When I asked Doug whether NLS had separable overlay links, he said "You bet!" So that may be an Engelbart first' (Nelson 2011).

6 Bardini, in response to this, says, 'I understand the point that "you could link from anywhere to anywhere" in NLS: that was the beauty of it, and that is exactly why its structure was rhizomatic rather than tree-like. But I do not understand "the mode of transport" metaphor you deploy here. Nor the connection that you make between the freedom to link any two items (hierarchically organized) and an associative logic at work. NLS hypertextual structure was both hierarchical and open, but its overall logic was still connective (in Whorf's sense of the word) rather than associative: you could link freely, sure, but in a "disciplined way", inside a given lexicon and, moreover inside a given hierarchy of statements.' (Bardini, personal communication).

7 Although Engelbart recalls it was *Life* magazine not the *Atlantic Monthly*, Mark Bernstein points out it probably wasn't *Life* – the issue was dated September 10; how much precious airlift capacity would have been allocated to flying magazines to the Philippines for the amusement of enlisted men? (Bernstein 2012).

8 'The problem is to write deeply, with as many ideas as possible, and yet not get caught up in twisty contortions of expression' (Nelson 2012).

9 An anchor tag is not an intrinsic address.

10 A video of the presentation is available at http://www.dougengelbart.org/history/pix.html.

11 Xerox Palo Alto Research Center.

Chapter 4.   The Magical Place of Literary Memory: Xanadu

1 While working at Harcourt.

2 Note that Nelson has his own unique numbering system for pages and chapters in this book.

3 Wolf is Nelson's bête noire.

4 Though as Bernstein (2012) points out in Nelson's defence, all living code is in a state of rewrite.

5 In particular, Pam 1994; Rheingold 2000; and also Nelson's own accounts, 1993, 1995a, and 2010c.

6 'In addition to my notebook, I have a backup system of using sticky notes, which is faster, especially for evanescent notes. Often I write several notes on one sticky [...] Sometimes they go onto pages in the book, if I want to permanize them' (Nelson 2012).

7 'There are many lists, which indeed constitute an indexing system. Compare this to the messy ways other people keep their archives! I believe the index-to-content ratio is high' (Nelson 2012).

8 'No! All have the same purpose, changing for attempted convenience – Sequential capture, rearrangeability, interconnection among parallel timelines' (Nelson, 2012).

9 Nelson believed they would all one day be input to a computer – 'if I become very rich it could still happen' (2012).

10 'Actually', Nelson wrote in 2012 in response to this chapter, 'it WAS the transclusion idea, right then in 1960.'

11 I believe this appeared a few weeks before the ACM conference, but it had much less impact – smaller conference. And people were less interested. So I emphasize the ACM presentation.

12 Admittedly, though, *Wired* doesn't have a good track record understanding Nelson's designs.

13 As were Paul Otlet's and H. G. Wells's imaginings.

14 'The 1980 classic version is entirely different from the entangled technical versions since 1987, and I hope to make them separately available real soon now' (Nelson 2012).

15 With characteristic wit, he calls the two sides the 'fluffies' and the 'technoids', respectively.

16 Nelson now believes the visit was in 1966, according to notes he found while writing *Possiplex* – notes that have since been lost.

17 Only later did I learn that Steve Jobs and Bill Gates also took a directorial role in software development, but they had the power to hire and fire, thus much more leverage (Nelson 2012).

18 As we will see in the chapter on HES, Nelson still feels angry about this experience; 'they could at least have treated me like a guest' (Nelson 2011).

19 Nelson asserts in response, 'The principles of xu88 and the Ent were secret until 1999 – is that Quite Recent? Since then the problem has been getting anyone to understand them!' (Nelson 2012).

20 On reading that sentence again, Nelson wrote, 'GOD that is awful. Nobody in the world would understand that except a project member' (2012).

Chapter 5.   Seeing and Making Connections: HES and FRESS

1 In this chapter Nelson puts 'word processor' in quotes, and notes that the 'sneer quotes are intentional' (2010b).

2 So why did he not express his anger at the time? According to Nelson, 'I wanted to see the project to the end. I am very sorry I didn't leave the first day' (Nelson 2011).

3 I have since seen a copy of this email, addressed to Wendy Hall, president of the ACM, and Ruth Simmons, president of Brown University, dated 26 February 2010 (Nelson 2010a). Van Dam was not a recipient, and was surprised to hear about this request: 'I have no knowledge of an ethics hearing. I've never heard of it' (van Dam 2011). I suspect this is because Nelson has not spoken to van Dam directly about the subject ('Of course I haven't been exposed to van Dam. I don't want to be exposed to van Dam' (Nelson 2011)). Van Dam, for his part, does not feel that Nelson made his feelings clear to him in these intervening years.

4 ACM SICGRAPH stands for Association for Computing Machinery's Special Interest Group on Computer Graphics and Interactive Techniques; ACM SIGGRAPH stands for Association for Computing Machinery's Special Interest Group on Graphics and Interactive Techniques.

5 Nelson, in response to this chapter, said, 'I am surprised he says that doing a system on
   the 2250 was my idea. I have no such recollection. I want credit for a lot of things but
   that's a head-scratcher' (2012).
6 'NLS did one thing better than we did in FRESS – their links were displayed as editable
   text. Ours were hidden, though there was an external view of a link, called an explainer'
   (van Dam 2011).
7 See Feiner, Nagy and van Dam 1982 and Feiner 1990.
8 FRESS's data structure clearly differentiated between raw content on the one hand
   and hypertext and outline structure on the other, but they were intermingled in
   the data structure – the organization of software 'pages' (as in virtual memory
   pages, unrelated to print pages) in a file with embedded structural and format
   information. The structure space was a derivative of the central data structure (van
   Dam 2011).
9 See http://www.victorianweb.org/. Pieces of the *Victorian Web* in Storyspace are available
   from Eastgate Systems.
10 Quoted text not in print version; found only online.

Chapter 6. Machine-Enhanced (Re)minding: The Development of Storyspace

1 In many cases the 'critical' works are also fiction, and the books' are also critical
   works.
2 Joyce, keen as always to create a self-reflexive eddy, has a response to this response.
   He writes, 'Joyce (the living one) is here to prove that Joyce (the dead and everlasting
   one) gave us with *Finnegans Wake* a good example of hypertextual experience. A textual
   hypertext is finite and limited, even though open to innumerable and original inquiries.
   Then there is the possibility outlined by Michael Joyce, hypertexts which are unlimited
   and infinite, a sort of jazz-like unending story' (Eco 1996).
3 See Bolter's CV at http://www.jdbolter.net/bio-and-cv.html [accessed March 2012].
4 See http://www.tlg.uci.edu/about/history.php [accessed March 2012].
5 He had also done some work on interactive text, and gave Joyce a copy of his article
   'The Idea of Literature and the Electronic Medium' in 1983. This was later published
   in *Topic* in 1985. Joyce refers to it in the Markle Report as 'some thoughts on literature
   in an electronic medium' (Bolter and Joyce 1986, 12); see also Bolter 1985.
6 The research led by Brooks at UNC, however, was really more in line with Engelbart's
   way of thinking – 'the computer as intelligence amplification rather than artificial
   intelligence' (Bolter 2011).
7 In the 1980s a form of AI program called 'expert systems' was adopted by corporations
   around the world and knowledge became the focus of mainstream AI research.
   Traditional AI took a backseat to research in this area and in neural networks. In those
   same years the Japanese government aggressively funded AI with its Fifth Generation
   Computer Project. Another encouraging event in the early 1980s was the revival of
   connectionism in the work of John Hopfield and David Rumelhart. Once again, AI
   had achieved success.
8 Matt Kirschenbaum details this correspondence well in his chapter on *afternoon* and
   Storyspace; I do not cover it again here.

9 Indeed, as Stuart Moulthrop observed in response to this chapter, hypertext turns AI inside out.

10 Again, the influence of AI is clear in this book; the *New York Times* went so far as to call it 'the most illuminating book that has yet come [our] way on the topic of artificial intelligence' (Ayer 1984).

11 http://www.well.com/user/jmalloy/uncleroger/unclerog.html [accessed March 2012].

12 Thanks to Michael Joyce for this reference.

13 One of the most frequent conversations they had was 'how to avoid the inherent hierarchy that underlies graph theory' (Joyce 2011a).

14 'I think I probably did call it TEXT at one point, but that was such a boring name compared to GLOSSA' (Bolter 2011).

15 Stuart Moulthrop, personal communication.

16 Along with FORTRAN and BASIC. Pascal is obviously still in use, but is no longer the primary development language for Apple machines.

17 'When we called it TALETELLER 2, we were already working on Mac by that time' (Bolter 2011).

18 Although he also mentions numerous cultural and literary influences – the novels of Sterne and Joyce, Cortazar's *Hopscotch*, even jazz music.

19 Stuart Moulthrop, in a prepublication review of this chapter.

20 Joyce and Bolter later confirmed this suspicion.

21 Developed 1985–7 with funding from Cornell University and Apple.

22 Joyce wrote in an email to the author: 'the "strongly influenced" makes me think I mixed up the names of Nancy's program which I knew about but hadn't used, and John's, which Jay indeed felt we had to acknowledge given his work with John's group'.

23 We do not have space to go into more detail about WE here, but it was an important system in the history of expository or 'professional' writing systems; it was presented at Hypertext '87 alongside Intermedia, HyperCard, Storyspace and NLS.

24 Joyce now believes it wasn't a meeting but a conference; 'If I wrote that in the Markle Report, it is incorrect. We didn't have a meeting with Hooper but rather I attended a conference where I heard her speak about, and demo, the *Aspen Movie Project*' (2012).

25 Letter to Barton Thurber from Riverrun, 2 February 1990, Joyce Archives.

26 Bernstein's paper 'Patterns of Hypertext' (1998) is widely cited in the field.

27 For example, Ensslin seeks to redefine 'producer-defined, commercially ideologized' terminology that has come into widespread us as a result of 'specified hypertext software, mostly traded by Eastgate Systems' (Ensslin 2007, 7).

28 Bernstein and Kirschenbaum had a falling-out over the Electronic Literature Organization, and Bernstein resigned. Here is a link to Bernstein's post: http://www.markbernstein.org/ELO.html and here is a link to Kirschenbaum's response: http://otal.umd.edu/~mgk/blog/archives/000087.html. Kirschenbaum believes this didn't influence his scholarship. This is his reply to me in full: 'My "history" with Mark Bernstein (such as it is) was no kind of factor in my not writing about Eastgate Systems at length in *Mechanisms*. Eastgate's role in stewarding Storyspace is well-known, and has been documented by scholars as far back as Thom Swiss's 1996 essay in *Postmodern Culture*: http://pmc.iath.virginia.edu/text-only/issue.996/review-4.996. My chapter, however, concerned an even earlier period in the software's development, based largely on the archival materials housed at the Ransom Center. Whatever our disagreements,

I have, and have always had, much respect for Mark Bernstein's contributions to
hypertext and his role in that community' (Kirschenbaum, personal communication,
2012).

29 Hayles doesn't seem to realize that these limitations also apply to HTML.
30 Comment to the author.

Conclusion

1 Interested readers can see my article on the topic – 'Reconfiguring Hypertext as a
Machine: Capitalism, Periodic Tables and a Mad Optometrist' (1998).
2 That is closer to our experience of human memory than any system we've looked at so far.

BIBLIOGRAPHY

Interviews and Personal Communication

Bardini, Thierry. 2011. Email to the author and comments on the manuscript.
Bernstein, Mark. 2011. Interview with the author.
———. 2012. Comments on the manuscript.
Bolter, Jay David. 2011. Interview with the author.
Duvall, Bill. 2011. Interview with the author.
Engelbart, Douglas. 1999. Interview with the author.
English, Bill. 2011. Interview with the author.
Hall, Wendy. 2012. Email to the author.
Joyce, Michael. 2011a. Interview with the author.
———. 2012. Comments on the manuscript.
Kahn, Paul. 2012. Email to the author and comments on the manuscript.
Kirschenbaum, Matthew G. 2012. Email to the author.
Lloyd, Gregory. 2011. Interview with the author.
Miles, Adrian. 2011. Interview with the author.
Moran, Chuk. 2012. Personal communication.
Moulthrop, Stuart. 2011b. Interview with the author.
Nelson, Theodor Holm. 1999a. Interview with the author.
———. 2010a. Email to Wendy Hall and Ruth Simmons from Ted Nelson, 26 February 2010, obtained by permission.
———. 2011. Interview with the author.
———. 2012. Comments on the manuscript.
Smith, John B. 2011. Interview with the author.
Simpson, Rosemary M. 2012. Personal communication and comments on a chapter.
van Dam, Andries. 1999. Interview with the author.
———. 2011. Interview with the author.
———. 2012. Personal communication and comments on a chapter.

Works Cited

Abbate, Janet. 1999. *Inventing the Internet*. Cambridge, MA: MIT Press.
Ayer, Alfred. 1984. 'Let Us Calculate'. *New York Review of Books*, 1 March. Online: http://www.nybooks.com/articles/archives/1984/mar/01/let-us-calculate/?pagination=false (accessed September 2012).
Bardini, Thierry. 2000. *Bootstrapping: Douglas Engelbart, Coevolution, and the Origins of Personal Computing*. Palo Alto: Stanford University Press.

Barnet, Belinda. 1998. 'Reconfiguring Hypertext as a Machine'. *FrAme: the Online Journal of Culture and Technology*. Online: http://tracearchive.ntu.ac.uk/frame2/articles/barnet. htm (accessed 17 April 2013).

———. 2000. 'Hypertext and Association: Space, Time and Hypomnesis'. *Convergence: The Journal of Research into New Media Technologies* 6, no. 3: 76–100.

———. 2004. 'Technical Machines and Evolution'. *CTHEORY*, 16 March. Online: http://www.ctheory.net/articles.aspx?id=414 (accessed March 2012).

Bell, Alice. 2010. *The Possible Worlds of Hypertext Fiction*. New York: Palgrave Macmillan.

Beniger, James R. 1986. *The Control Revolution: Technological and Economic Origins of the Information Society*. Cambridge, MA: Harvard University Press.

Berners-Lee, Tim. 1999. *Weaving the Web: The Original Design and Ultimate Destiny of the World Wide Web by Its Inventor*. New York: HarperCollins.

Bernstein, Mark. 1998. 'Patterns of Hypertext'. In *Proceedings of Hypertext '98*, Pittsburgh, PA, 21–9 June 1998.

Bernstein, Mark. 1999. 'Where are the Hypertexts?' *10th ACM Conference on Hypertext, Keynote Address, Darmstadt, Germany*. Online: http://www.eastgate.com/ht99/slides/Welcome. htm (accessed 17 April 2013).

———. 2008. 'Interview with Claus Atzenback'. *SIGWEB Newsletter*, Summer. Online: http://www.markbernstein.org/elements/atzenbeck.pdf (accessed March 2012).

Bernstein, Mark, Jay David Bolter, Michael Joyce and Elli Mylonas. 1991. 'Architectures for Volatile Hypertexts'. In *Hypertext '91 Proceedings*, edited by John J. Leggett, 243–60. San Antonio: ACM.

Bogost, Ian. 2010. 'Cow Clicker: The Making of an Obsession'. *Ian Bogost Blog*, 21 July. Online: http://www.bogost.com/blog/cow_clicker_1.shtml (accessed March 2012).

Bolter, Jay David. 1984. *Turing's Man: Western Culture in the Computer Age*. Chapel Hill: University of North Carolina Press.

———. 1985. 'The Idea of Literature in the Electronic Medium'. *Topic* 39: 23–34.

———. 1991. *Writing Space: The Computer, Hypertext and the History of Writing*. Hillsdale: Lawrence Erlbaum Associates.

Bolter, Jay David and Richard Grusin. 2000. *Remediation: Understanding New Media*. Cambridge, MA: MIT Press.

Bolter, Jay David and Michael Joyce. 1986. *STORYSPACE: A Tool for Interaction, Report to the Markle Foundation Regarding G85105*.

———. 1987. 'Hypertext and Creative Writing'. In *HYPERTEXT '87: Proceedings of the ACM Conference on Hypertext*, edited by John B. Smith and Frank Halasz, 41–50. New York: ACM.

Boon, Marcus. 2011. *In Praise of Copying*. Cambridge, MA: Harvard University Press.

Burke, Colin. 1991. 'A Practical View of the Memex: The Career of the Rapid Selector'. In *From Memex to Hypertext: Vannevar Bush and the Mind's Machine*, edited by James Nyce and Paul Kahn, 135–64. London: Academic Press.

Bush, Vannevar. (1933) 1991. 'The Inscrutable "Thirties"'. In *From Memex to Hypertext: Vannevar Bush and the Mind's Machine*, edited by James Nyce and Paul Kahn, 67–79. London: Academic Press.

———. 1939. 'Mechanization and the Record'. *Vannevar Bush Papers*. Library of Congress, Box 138, Speech Article Book File.

———. (1945) 1991. 'As We May Think'. In *From Memex to Hypertext: Vannevar Bush and the Mind's Machine*, edited by James Nyce and Paul Kahn, 85–112. London: Academic Press.

_____. (1959) 1991. 'Memex II'. In *From Memex to Hypertext: Vannevar Bush and the Mind's Machine*, edited by James Nyce and Paul Kahn, 165–84. London: Academic Press.

_____. (1965) 1991. 'Science Pauses'. In *From Memex to Hypertext: Vannevar Bush and the Mind's Machine*, edited by James Nyce and Paul Kahn, 185–96. London: Academic Press.

_____. (1967) 1991. 'Memex Revisited'. In *From Memex to Hypertext: Vannevar Bush and the Mind's Machine*, edited by James Nyce and Paul Kahn, 197–216. London: Academic Press.

_____. 1970. *Pieces of the Action*. New York: William Morrow.

Carmody, Steven, Walter Gross, Theodor H. Nelson, David Rice and Andries van Dam. 1969. 'A Hypertext Editing System for the /360'. In *Pertinent Concepts in Computer Graphics: Proceedings*, edited by Michael Faiman and Jurg Nievergelt, 291–330. Urbana: University of Illinois Press.

Catano, James V. 1979. 'Poetry and Computers: Experimenting with the Communal Text'. *Computers and the Humanities* 13, no. 9: 269–75.

Ceruzzi, Paul E. 1998. *A History of Modern Computing*. Cambridge, MA: MIT Press.

_____. 2003. *A History of Modern Computing* (2nd ed). Cambridge, MA: MIT Press.

Childress, Vincent. 1998. 'Book Review'. Review of *Engineering Problem Solving for Mathematics, Science, and Technology Education*, by E. Frye. *Journal of Technology Education* 10, no. 1. Online: http://scholar.lib.vt.edu/ejournals/JTE/v10n1/childress.html (accessed March 2012).

Ciccoricco, David. 2007. *Reading Network Fiction*. Tuscaloosa: University of Alabama Press.

Conklin, Jeff. 1987. 'Hypertext: An Introduction and Survey'. *IEEE Computer* 20, no. 9: 17–41.

Coover, Robert. 1999. 'Literary Hypertext: The Passing of the Golden Age'. Keynote address presented at the Digital Arts and Culture Conference, Atlanta, 29 October. Online: http://nickm.com/vox/golden_age.html (accessed March 2012).

De Landa, Manuel. 1994. *War in the Age of Intelligent Machines*. New York: Zone Books.

Dehn, Natalie. 1981. 'Story Generation after Tale-Spin'. In *Proceedings of the Seventh International Conference on Artificial Intelligence*, vol. 1, 16–18. Los Altos: William Kaufmann.

Delaney, Paul and George Landow, eds. 1995. *Hypermedia and Literary Studies*. Cambridge, MA: MIT Press.

Dennett, Daniel C. 1993. *Consciousness Explained*. London: Penguin Books.

DeRose, Steven J. 1989. 'Expanding the Notion of Links'. In *HYPERTEXT '89: Proceedings of the Second Annual ACM Conference on Hypertext*, edited by Robert M. Akscyn, 249–57. New York: ACM.

_____. 1999. 'XML linking'. *ACM Computer Surveys* 31, no. 4, article 21.

DeRose, Steven and Andries van Dam. 1999. 'Document Structure and Markup in the FRESS Hypertext System'. *Markup Languages: Theory and Practice* 1, no. 1: 7–32.

Dickey, William. 1995. 'Poem Descending a Staircase: Hypertext and the Simultaneity of Experience'. In *Hypermedia and Literary Studies*, edited by Paul Delaney and George Landow, 143–152. Cambridge, MA: MIT Press.

Dutta, Anindita. 1995. 'The Paradox of Truth, the Truth of Entropy'. Online: http://www.pynchon.pomona.edu/entropy/paradox.html (accessed March 2012).

Umberto Eco. 1996. 'The Future of the Book'. *The Modern Word*. Online: http://www.themodernword.com/eco/eco_future_of_book.html (accessed April 2013).

Edwards, Paul N. 1997. *The Closed World: Computers and the Politics of Discourse in Cold War America*. Cambridge, MA: MIT Press.

Eldredge, Niles. 1996. 'A Battle of Words'. In *The Third Culture*, edited by John Brockman, 119–28. New York: Simon and Schuster.

_____. 2006. 'Intelligently Designed: More on the Lateral Spread of Information'. *The Darwin Blogs*, 22 May. Online: http://www.nileseldredge.com/darwin_blogs_019.htm (accessed March 2012).

_____. 2011. 'Material Cultural Macroevolution'. In *Macroevolution in Human Prehistory: Evolutionary Theory and Processual Archaeology*, edited by Anna Prentiss, Ian Kuijt and James C. Chatters, 297–316. New York: Springer.

Eldredge, Niles and Belinda Barnet. 2004. 'Material Cultural Evolution: An Interview with Niles Eldredge'. *Fibreculture Journal* 3. Online: http://www.fibreculture.org/journal/issue3/issue3_barnet.html (accessed March 2012).

Eldredge, Niles and S. J. Gould. 1972. 'Punctuated Equilibria: An Alternative to Phyletic Gradualism'. In *Time Frames*, edited by N. Eldredge, 193–223. Princeton: Princeton University Press.

Engelbart, Douglas. 1962a. 'Letter to Vannevar Bush and Program on Human Effectiveness'. In *From Memex to Hypertext: Vannevar Bush and the Mind's Machine*, edited by James Nyce and Paul Kahn, 235–44. London: Academic Press.

_____. 1962b. 'Augmenting Human Intellect: A Conceptual Framework'. Report to the Director of Information Sciences, Air Force Office of Scientific Research, Menlo Park, CA, Stanford Research Institute. Online: http://www.invisiblerevolution.net/engelbart/full_62_paper_augm_hum_int.html (accessed April 2013).

_____. 1963. 'A Conceptual Framework for the Augmentation of Man's Intellect'. In *Vistas in Information Handling, Volume 1: The Augmentation of Man's Intellect By Machine*, edited by Paul W. Howerton and David C. Weeks, 1–29. Washington: Spartan Books.

_____. 1986. 'Interview with Henry Lowood', Stanford University. Online: http://www-sul.stanford.edu/depts/hasrg/histsci/ssvoral/engelbart/engfmst1-ntb.html (accessed April 2013).

_____. 1988. 'The Augmented Knowledge Workshop'. In *A History of Personal Workstations*, edited by Adele Goldberg, 185–249. New York: ACM Press.

_____. 1997. 'Doug Engelbart: The Interview' with David Bennehum. *Meme* 3, no. 1. Online: http://memex.org/meme3-01.html (accessed April 2013).

_____. 1998. 'The Strategic Pursuit of Collective IQ'. Paper presented at The Brown/MIT Vannevar Bush Symposium, 12 October. Online: http://www.cs.brown.edu/memex/Bush_Symposium.html (accessed March 2012).

_____. 2002. *Doug Engelbart Institute*. Online: http://www.dougengelbart.org/history/pix.html (accessed April 2013).

Engelbart, Douglas and William English. 1968. 'A Research Center for Augmenting Human Intellect'. In *Proceedings of the AFIPS 1968 Fall Joint Computer Conference 33*, 395–410. Washington: Spartan Books.

Ensslin, Astrid. 2007. *Canonizing Hypertext: Explorations and Constructions*. New York: Continuum.

Feiner, Steven. 1990. 'Authoring Large Hypermedia Documents with IGD'. *Electronic Publishing* 3, no. 1: 29–46.

Feiner, Steven, S. Nagy and Andries van Dam. 1982. 'An Experimental System for Creating and Presenting Interactive Graphical Documents'. *ACM Transactions on Graphics* 1, no. 1: 59–77.

Foley, James, Andries van Dam, Steven Feiner and John Hughes. 1995. *Computer Graphics: Principles and Practice in C* (2nd ed). Boston: Addison-Wesley.

Fracchia, Joseph and Richard C. Lewontin. 2002. 'Does Culture Evolve?' *History and Theory: Studies in the Philosophy of History* 38, no. 4: 52–78.

Galloway, Alexander. 2004. *Protocol: How Control Exists after Decentralization*. Cambridge, MA: MIT Press.

Gibson, W. and B. Sterling. 1991. *The Difference Engine*. New York: Bantam Spectra.

Gleick, James. 2011. *The Information: A History, a Theory, a Flood*. New York: Pantheon.

Greco, Diane. 1996. 'Hypertext with Consequences: Recovering a Politics of Hypertext'. In *Hypertext '96 – Proceedings of the Seventh ACM Conference on Hypertext March 16–20, 1996, Washington, DC*, edited by David Stotts, 85–92. New York: ACM.

Gregory, Roger. 2010. 'Interviewed by Dave Marvit at Ted Nelson Book Launch, 8 October'. Online: http://www.archive.org/details/possiplexrogergregoryinterview (accessed March 2012).

Guattari, Félix. 1995. *Chaosmosis: An Ethico-Aesthetic Paradigm*. Sydney: Power Publications.

Hall, Wendy, Hugh Davis and Gerard Hutchings. 1996. *Rethinking Hypermedia: The Microcosm Approach*. Norwell: Kluwer Academic Publishers.

Hartree, Douglas. 2000. 'Differential Analyzer'. Online: http://cs.union.edu/~hemmendd/Encyc/Articles/Difanal/difanal.html (accessed April 2013).

Hatt, Harold. 1968. *Cybernetics and the Image of Man*. Nashville: Abingdon Press.

Hayles, Katherine. 1999. *How We Became Posthuman: Virtual Bodies in Cybernetics, Literature and Informatics*. Chicago: University of Chicago Press.

_____. 2003. *Writing Machines*. Cambridge, MA: MIT Press.

_____. 2008. *New Horizons for the Literary*. Notre Dame: University of Notre Dame.

Irby, Charles. 1974. 'Display Techniques for Interactive Text Manipulation'. In *1974 National Computer Conference and Proceedings*, 247–55. New Jersey: AFIPS Press.

Johnson-Eilola, Johndan. 1994. 'Reading and Writing in Hypertext: Vertigo and Euphoria'. In *Literacy and Computers: The Complications of Teaching and Learning with Technology*, edited by Cynthia Selfe and Susan Hilligloss, 195–219. New York: Modern Language Association of America.

Joyce, Michael. 1986. 'Draft of Pseudocode for Text Processor'. Folder of files held at the University of Texas at Austin, Harry Ransom Center (PDFs accessed July 2011).

_____. 1987. *afternoon: a story*. Current version sold at Eastgate: http://www.eastgate.com/catalog/Afternoon.html (accessed March 2012).

_____. 1988. Journal entry, 4 June. Held at the University of Texas at Austin, Harry Ransom Center (PDF accessed July 2011).

_____. 1998. *Of Two Minds: Hypertext, Pedagogy and Poetics*. Ann Arbor: University of Michigan Press.

_____. 2004. *Othermindedness: The Emergence of Network Culture*. Ann Arbor: University of Michigan Press.

_____. 2011b. 'Re:mindings: Essays after: -net, -narrative, -media'. Unpublished manuscript, obtained by permission.

Kirschenbaum, Matthew G. 2008. *Mechanisms: New Media and the Forensic Imagination*. Cambridge, MA: MIT Press.

Kitzmann, Andreas. 2006. *Hypertext Handbook*. New York: Peter Lang Publishing.

Knight, Helen. 2012. 'Tech before Its Time: The Missing Hyperink'. *New Scientist* 213: 45.

Landow, George P. 1992. *Hypertext: The Convergence of Contemporary Critical Theory and Technology*. Online: http://www.cyberartsweb.org/cpace/ht/jhup/int2.html (accessed April 2013).

_____. 2006. *Hypertext 3.0: Critical Theory and New Media in an Era of Globalization*. Baltimore: Johns Hopkins University Press.

Lessig, Lawrence. 2008. *Remix: Making Art and Commerce Thrive in the Hybrid Economy*. New York: Penguin.

Licklider, J. C. R. 1988. 'Man-Computer Symbioses'. In *A History of Personal Workstations*, edited by Adele Goldberg, 131–40. New York: ACM Press.

Little, Daniel. 2011. 'What is History?' *UnderstandingSociety Blog*. Online: http://understandingsocietyglobaledition.wordpress.com/2011/10/03/what-is-history/ (accessed March 2012).

Lloyd, Gregory. 2001. 'Digital Arts and Culture'. Unpublished personal conference notes, obtained by permission.

Machover, Carl. 1998. 'An Interview with Andries van Dam'. *IEEE Annals of the History of Computing* 20, no. 2: 81–4.

Manovich, Lev. 2001. *The Language of New Media*. Cambridge, MA: MIT Press.

Markoff, John. 2005. *What the Dormouse Said*. New York: Penguin.

McAleese, Ray. 1999. *Hypertext: Theory into Practice*. Exeter: Intellect Books.

Meyrowitz, Norman. 1986. 'Intermedia: The Architecture and Construction of an Object-Oriented Hypermedia System and Applications Framework'. *ACM SIGPLAN Notices* 21, no. 11: 106–201.

_____. 1991. 'Hypertext: Does It Reduce Cholesterol, Too?' In *From Memex to Hypertext: Vannevar Bush and the Mind's Machine*, edited by James Nyce and Paul Kahn, 287–318. London: Academic Press.

Mindell, David A. 2000. 'MIT Differential Analyzer'. Online: http://web.mit.edu/mindell/www/analyzer.htm (accessed April 2013).

Moulthrop, Stuart. 1991. 'You Say You Want a Revolution? Hypertext and the Laws of Media'. In *The New Media Reader*, edited by Noah Wardrip-Fruin and Nick Montfort, 692–704. Cambridge, MA: MIT Press.

_____. 1997. *Hegirascope*. Online: http://iat.ubalt.edu/moulthrop/hypertexts/hgs/ (accessed March 2012).

_____. 2011a. 'For Thee: A Response to Alice Bell'. *Electronic Book Review*, 21 January. Online: http://www.electronicbookreview.com/thread/electropoetics/networked (accessed March 2012).

Negroponte, Nicholas. 1995. *Being Digital*. Rydalmere: Hodder and Stoughton.

Nelson, Theodor Holm. 1965. 'A File Structure for the Complex, the Changing and the Indeterminate'. In *Proceedings of the ACM 20th National Conference*, 84–100. New York: ACM Press.

_____. 1968. 'Hypertext Implementation Notes, 6–10 March 1968'. *Xuarchives*. Online: http://xanadu.com/REF%20XUarchive%20SET%2003.11.06/hin68.tif (accessed June 2012).

_____. 1987. *Computer Lib/Dream Machines*. Redmond: Microsoft Press.

_____. 1991. 'As We Will Think'. In *From Memex to Hypertext: Vannevar Bush and the Mind's Machine*, edited by James Nyce and Paul Kahn, 245—60. London: Academic Press.

_____. 1993. *Literary Machines*. Sausalito: Mindful Press.

_____. 1995a. 'Transcopyright: Pre-permission for Virtual Publishing'. *Xanadu Australia*. Online: http://xanadu.com.au/ted/transcopyright/transcopy.html (accessed April 2013).

_____. 1995b. 'Errors in "The Curse of Xanadu" by Gary Wolf'. *Xanadu Australia*. Online: http://www.xanadu.com.au/ararat (accessed March 2012).

_____. 1997. 'Embedded Markup Considered Harmful'. *XML.com: XML from the Inside Out*. Online: http://www.xml.com/pub/a/w3j/s3.nelson.html (accessed April 2013).

_____. 1999b. 'The Unfinished Revolution and Xanadu'. *ACM Computing Surveys* 31 (4). Online: http://cs.brown.edu/memex/ACM_HypertextTestbed/papers/64.html (accessed May 2013).

_____. 2010b. 'The Dark Brown Years'. Unpublished chapter omitted from Nelson's autobiography, obtained by permission.

_____. 2010c. *Possiplex: Movies, Intellect, Creative Control, My Computer Life and the Fight for Civilization*. Online: http://www.lulu.com/spotlight/tandm (accessed March 2012).

Nielsen, Jakob. 1995. *Multimedia and Hypertext: The Internet and Beyond*. London: Academic Press.

Nunes, Mark. 1999. 'Virtual Topographies: Smooth and Striated Cyberspace'. In *Cyberspace Textuality: Computer Technology and Literary Theory*, edited by Marie-Laure Ryan, 61–77. Bloomington: Indiana University Press.

Nyce, James and Paul Kahn, eds. 1991. *From Memex to Hypertext: Vannevar Bush and the Mind's Machine*. London: Academic Press.

Oren, Tim. 1991. 'Memex: Getting Back on the Trail'. In *From Memex to Hypertext: Vannevar Bush and the Mind's Machine*, edited by James Nyce and Paul Kahn, 319–38. London: Academic Press.

Owens, Larry. 1991. 'Vannevar Bush and the Differential Analyzer: The Text and Context of an Early Computer' In *From Memex to Hypertext: Vannevar Bush and the Mind's Machine*, edited by James Nyce and Paul Kahn, 3–38. London: Academic Press.

Pam, Andrew. 1994. 'Where World Wide Web Went Wrong'. *Xanadu Australia*. Online: http://www.xanadu.com.au/xanadu/6w-paper.html (accessed March 2012).

Pickering, Andrew. 1995. *The Mangle of Practice*. Chicago: University of Chicago Press.

Rheingold, Howard. 1985. *Tools for Thought: The History and Future of Mind-Expanding Technology*. New York: Simon and Schuster.

_____. 2000. *Tools for Thought: The History and Future of Mind-Expanding Technology* (2nd ed.). Cambridge, MA: MIT Press.

Ryan, Marie-Laure. 1994. 'Immersion vs. Interactivity: Virtual Reality and Literary Theory'. *Postmodern Culture* 5, no. 1. Online: http://www.humanities.uci.edu/mposter/syllabi/readings/ryan.html (accessed March 2012).

_____. 1999. 'Cyberspace, Virtuality and the Text'. In *Cyberspace Textuality: Computer Technology and Literary Theory*, edited by Marie-Laure Ryan, 78–107. Bloomington: Indiana University Press.

Schank, Roger. 1999. *Dynamic Memory Revisited*. New York: Cambridge University Press.

Segaller, Stephen. 1998. *Nerds 2.0.1: A Brief History of the Internet*. New York: TV Books.

Shurkin, Joel. 1996. *Engines of the Mind: The Evolution of the Computer from Mainframes to Microprocessors*. New York: W. W. Norton and Company.

Simpson, Rosemary M., Allen Renear, Elli Mylonas and Andries van Dam. 1998. '50 Years After "As We May Think"'. Paper presented at the Brown/MIT Vannevar Bush Symposium, October 12. Online: http://www.cs.brown.edu/memex/Bush_Symposium.html (accessed March 2012).

Smith, John B., Stephen F. Weiss, Gordon J. Ferguson, Jay David Bolter, Marcy Lansman and David V. Beard. 1986. 'WE: A Writing Environment for Professionals'. Technical Report 86-025, August. Department of Computer Science, University of North Carolina, Chapel Hill.

Smith, Linda C. 1991. 'Memex as an Image of Potentiality Revisited'. In *From Memex to Hypertext: Vannevar Bush and the Mind's Machine*, edited by James Nyce and Paul Kahn, 261–86. London: Academic Press.

Spa, Deborah L. 2001. *Ruling the Waves: Cycles of Discovery, Chaos, and Wealth from the Compass to the Internet*. New York: Harcourt.

Stefik, Marc. 1997. *Internet Dreams: Archetypes, Myths and Metaphors*. Cambridge, MA: MIT Press.

Steinberg, Steve S. 1997. 'Lifestreams'. *Wired* 5, no. 2. Online: http://www.wired.com/wired/archive/5.02/fflifestreams_pr.html (accessed April 2013).

Stiegler, Bernard. 1998. *Technics and Time, 1: The Fault of Epimetheus*. Palo Alto: Stanford University Press.

Tofts, Darren and Murray McKeich. 1998. *Memory Trade: A Prehistory of Cyberculture*. North Ryde: Interface Press.

van Dam, Andries. 1988. 'Hypertext '87 Keynote Address'. *Memex and Beyond*. Online: http://cs.brown.edu/memex/HT_87_Keynote_Address.html (accessed April 2013).

———. 1997. 'Post-WIMP User Interfaces'. *Communications of the ACM* 40, no. 2: 63–7.

———. 1998. Introduction to Session 3B of 'Engelbart's Unfinished Revolution' conference, Stanford University, 9 December. Online: http://www.archive.org/details/XD1903_2EngelbartsUnfinishedRev30AnnSes3B (accessed March 2012).

van Dam, Andries and David Evans. 1964. 'SHIRTDIF – A System for the Storage Handling and Retrieval of Technical Data in Image Format'. *Proceedings of American Documentation Institute* (later ASIS), 323–9.

Vassar College Innovators Web Site. 1992. 'The Never-Ending Story'. Online: http://innovators.vassar.edu/innovator.html?id=12 (accessed April 2013)

Vesna, Victoria. 2007. *Database Aesthetics: Art in the Age of Information Overflow*. Minneapolis: University of Minnesota Press.

Vincler, John. *Deviant Forms Blog*. Online: http://deviantforms.wordpress.com/2010/07/13/elo_ai-rbms10-part-2-mark-bernsteineastgate-the-eld/ (accessed March 2012).

W3C Working Draft. 1999. 15 March. Online: http://www.w3.org/TR/ (accessed April 2013).

Walker, G. 2003. 'The Collector'. *New Scientist* 179: 38–41.

Wardrip-Fruin, Noah. 2003. 'Introduction: As We May Think'. In *The New Media Reader*, edited by Noah Wardrip-Fruin and Nick Montfort, 35. Cambridge, MA: MIT Press.

———. 2004. 'What Hypertext Is'. In *HYPERTEXT '04 Proceedings of the Fifteenth ACM Conference on Hypertext and Hypermedia August 9–13, 2004, Santa Cruz, California, USA*, edited by Jim Whitehead and David De Roure, 126–7. New York: ACM Press.

———. 2011. 'Digital Media Archeology'. In *Media Archeology*, edited by Erkki Huhtamo and Jussi Parikka, 302–22. Berkeley: University of California Press.

Wardrip-Fruin, Noah and Nick Montfort, eds. 2003. *The New Media Reader*. Cambridge, MA: MIT Press.

Wolf, Gary. 1995. 'The Curse of Xanadu'. *Wired* 3, no. 6. Online: http://www.wired.com/wired/archive/3.06/xanadu.html (accessed March 2012).

Xanadu Australia Home Page. 2012. Online: http://xanadu.com.au (accessed March 2012).

Yankelovich, Nicole, Norman Meyrowitz and Andries van Dam. 1995. 'Reading and Writing the Electronic Book'. In *Hypermedia and Literary Studies*, edited by Paul Delaney and George Landow, 53–80. Cambridge, MA: MIT Press.

Yates, Frances A. 1997. *The Art of Memory*. London: Pimlico.

Yellowlees Douglas, Jane. 2004. *The End of Books—or Books without End*. Ann Arbor: University of Michigan Press.

INDEX